Palgrave Studies in Education and Transculturalism

Series Editor
Ranjan Ghosh
Department of English
University of North Bengal
Siliguri, West Bengal
India

This book series is devoted to the exploration of new "transcultural" directions in the philosophy and praxis of educational studies. After the linguistic turn, the cultural turn and the historical turn, this series argues that we are now confronting a transcultural turn and the books in this series will explore, identify and articulate the burgeoning transcultural aspect of education studies, philosophy, theory and pragmatics.

More information about this series at
http://www.springer.com/series/15459

Ranjan Ghosh

Aesthetics, Politics, Pedagogy and Tagore

A Transcultural Philosophy of Education

palgrave
macmillan

Ranjan Ghosh
Department of English
University of North Bengal
Siliguri, West Bengal, India

Palgrave Studies in Education and Transculturalism
ISBN 978-1-137-48025-5 ISBN 978-1-137-48026-2 (eBook)
DOI 10.1057/978-1-137-48026-2

Library of Congress Control Number: 2016955699

Cover design by Samantha Johnson

Printed on acid-free paper

This Palgrave Macmillan imprint is published by Springer Nature
The registered company is Macmillan Publishers Ltd.
The registered company address is: The Campus, 4 Crinan Street, London, N1 9XW, United Kingdom

To Akshaai, my nephew, who has re-educated me

Preface

The book got its trigger from a public lecture on Tagore's educational thought that I was invited to deliver at Wadham College, Oxford University, in 2011. Professor Elleke Boehmer's invitation and the discussion that followed this well-attended event made me wonder if this was the beginning of something that I could configure about Tagore as an educationist. Sumana, my intellectual conscience keeper and a very sensitive reader of Tagore herself, added the inspirational momentum to a possible book-length study. A multilateral reading of Tagore made me wake up to the hard and yet disturbing fact that almost nothing had been written on Tagore's educational thought from the standpoint of transcultural educational philosophy and theory. But this book turned out to be more difficult to write than I had thought. Four years of writing and rediscovering Tagore through an intense engagement with Western and Eastern thought and philosophy were demanding and daunting. My parallel writing projects on theories and the experience of literature and comparative poetics contributed to the framing of my transcultural position within which this book has finally come to rest.

Meanwhile, thought experiments on Tagore resulted in published essays: 'Caught in the Cross Traffic: Rabindranath Tagore and the Trials of Child Education', *Comparative Education Review*, 59, no. 3 (August 2015): 399–419; 'Rabindranath and Rabindranath Tagore: Home, History, World', *History and Theory,* 54, Issue 4 (December 2015): 125–148; 'A Poet's School: Rabindranath Tagore and the politics of Aesthetic Education', *South Asia: Journal of South Asian Studies*, 35, Issue 1, (2012): 13–32. Also, the transcultural and transpoetical Tagore surge gave life to a book series which I now edit: *Palgrave Studies in Education and Transculturalism.*

The overwhelming intellectual and 'resourceful' support from colleagues across the academy nourished and nurtured my writing: Elleke Boehmer, Ankhi Mukherjee, Peter McDonald, Amrit Sen, Ashish Ghosh, K. Daniel Cho, Andrea Bramberger, David Kennedy, Dan Moulin, Walter Kohan, Michael A Peters, Lorraine Kasprisin, Mark Faust, David Carr, J. Mark Halstead, Mark A. Pike, Klas Roth, Pradeep Dhillon, Fazal Rizvi, Marianna Papastephanou, Henry A. Giroux, Melanie Walker, Dennis Hayes, Brahm Norwich, Byron Kaldis, Andrew Stables, Ulla Thøgersen, Sune Lægaard and others. I might have missed out on naming many other people who contributed differently to the completion of the book. The list then, by all means, is 'potentially' incomplete, as any record of intellectual debt inevitably is.

If my 5-year old nephew, to whom this book is dedicated with thoughtful amusement, picks this up to read as an adult some day and reads it to the full to comment and animadvert, I shall be happy to know that his education has remained incomplete. Education is thinking how differently we could be taught and made to learn. Professional degrees withhold us; education is about withdrawal, learning how voids are essential and replenishments are relentless.

Contents

CHAPTER 1

In and Out of Time: The Hungry Artist

In the operative ways of the world, Rabindranath Tagore sees a continuous inhaling and exhaling, a state of sleep and waking, a rhythm of acclivity and declivity and a halting and a restart.[1] In absence and presence, in darkness and light, in concealment and manifestation is such a rhythm maintained. This speaks of a continuity – the yes and the no, the positive and the negative, the attraction and repulsion which become a part of the creative rhythm essential to our understanding of historical situatedness, our ever rhythmic connections with past and present. Tagore observes that 'perfect balance in these opposing forces would lead to deadlock in creation. Life moves in the cadence of constant adjustment of opposites; it is a perpetual process of reconciliation of contradictions'.[2] Historical consciousness builds on the rhythm of opposition, in adjustments between polarities, not through a linear onrush of energy but a circularity which keeps the rhythm of life going. Linearity is not the character of life, writes Tagore.[3] Energy and force built in singular unifocal velocity are destined to create division; it becomes bare, barren and banal with no music, creativity and play. However, when opposite forces meet and multiple forces come together the rhythm of creation constructs its own steps and stages.

India's *itihasa*,[4] Tagore implies, is built in opposition and agonism in which her consciousness has learnt to accept and find a settlement – a poise in conflict, in turmoil, in exchanges that are not always non-aggressive.

R. Ghosh, *Aesthetics, Politics, Pedagogy and Tagore*,
Palgrave Studies in Education and Transculturalism,
DOI 10.1057/978-1-137-48026-2_1

This is the rhythm of *itihasa*. Tagore knows that finding this rhythm is difficult because man is born not to balance but flourish in the extremes. The history of the West, he notes, has not appreciated this balance because imperialism is a unidirectional force – belligerent and pugnacious – which overpowers all that comes in its way to establish sovereignty. But *itihasa* is about learning the dynamics of this rhythm and not merely about recording the tumult of times and documenting the din of events; it is, as Tagore notes, about finding the energy, the power that lies within. Configuring *itihasa* is *tapasya*.[5] Tagore observes:

> It would be wrong for us, when we judge the historical career of India, to put all the stress upon the accumulated heap of refuse, gross, and grotesque, that has not yet been assimilated in one consistent cultural body. Our great hope lies there, where we realize that something positively previous in our achievements still persists in spite of circumstances that are inclement. The best of us still have our aspiration for the supreme end of life, which is so often mocked at by the prosperous people who hold their sway over the present-day world. We still believe that the world has a deeper meaning than what is apparent, and that therein the human soul finds its ultimate harmony and peace. We still know that only in this spiritual wealth and welfare does civilisation attain its end, and not in a prolific production of materials, not in the competition of intemperate power with power.[6]

A tryst with *itihasa* finds a life in investigating the innermost truth and intention of India's consciousness, of human consciousness, building on a philosophy of history where truth and intention (will) are never sundered categories. Tagore was interested in repremising historical experiences or experiences in history in ways that are both peculiar to his sensibility, his own culture and times, and the conditions of the present. His views on historicality and historical experience mediate between the pulls of a strong non-Western sensibility and an informed access to certain paradigms of Western models of historical thinking resulting in what I argue as Tagore's individual way of according a 'global accent' to his vision of history.

Unlike a Hegelian historical consciousness which reads surprisingly anachronic,[7] Tagore is for an inclusivist notion of history where the rhythm of life and values in *itihasa* are found to be immanent and imminent. Constructing a historical consciousness that is 'curatorial'[8] and not exoticist and magisterial, Tagore's sense of *itihasa* dialecticizes identity, differentiality and discrimination that enables better appropriation of tradition and his habitations in modernity. When people get thwarted by the deficit and scarcity of departmental and classified documents that would have lent political, military, and socio-economic information about a country's past they, in haste and despondence, jump to the conclusion that the country has no history, the common understanding being that without politics there cannot be history.[9] But such investigation, Tagore argues, is tantamount to looking for brinjals in a paddy field; the consequent frustration makes one deny paddy as a part of agricultural crop production. Hunting for brinjals and shutting one's eyes to the rest do not speak of wise ways of thinking. History is both brinjals, paddy and the rest.

Learning and knowing one's history is a process that continues to influence us from our childhood – a consciousness that is very difficult to express and an emotion whose trajectory is, most often, impossible to predict and chart. The essence of a nation enters into our consciousness since our childhood, enjoying its near unhindered seepage through our affection, imagination and other imperceptible sources.[10] It is a strange power – a decisive impact, potent and profound, that generates substantial contact between the past and the present. What kind of historical sense does this power with its rare energy, possibility and immanence, produce? India, notes Tagore, has always tried to find a synthesis in pluralism, a solidarity in networks of diversity. Not that it sought to negate and deliquesce the differences that history imprints and makes us inherit; it manifests as a realization that tries to settle on the 'deepest connect'[11] that every kind of difference, dialecticism and divergence possesses. The politics of such historical consciousness is an opening to the negotiations of the other (*sambandhas*) and the self (*swadharma* which is not nativist totalitarianism) through a 'political unity' (rarely effected under a hegemonic dispensation) that honours the capacious character of *itihasa*. His sense of *itihasa* finds a life in dialecticism – the cooptative and collateral character of historical thought which is not a Hegelian sublation or conciliation – with the spirit of acceptance, acknowledgement and approval. Tagore considers this as the 'talent' of *itihasa*: the latency of an energy to create *sambandhas*. This is a continuum, as it were, an envelope holding our belief, intelligence, life, ways, manners and even the afterlife. Just like the life of the hands, legs, head, stomach are not different from each other, rather, cannot be indifferent to each other's existence and functions, this form of *itihasa* does not ignore the 'politics' of pluralist solidarity. Tagore observes that the dharma of India's *itihasa* is a continuity, a non-sectarian way of seeing and believing, the life spirit that knows where its roots are and the head is. Tagore's *aitihāsik* (historian) then makes us believe in the formation of history that has its ownness, a deposition and reserve that is potential enough to communicate even with colonial historiographical ways and certain modules of Western historical thinking. He demonstrates the dignity of native historical consciousness – the *itihasa* of our own living – and builds a historical consciousness that is global not in its overcoming of the local but in a cohabitation that is collaborative and conversational. He teaches us the consciousness of *itihasa* which finds its life in 'listening' – the *swadeshi* reserves of learning and wisdom opening up with dignity and depth the lines of communication with the *videshi* ways of historical thinking and knowledge formation. Dialectical *itihasa* thrives in composure and not compulsive syncretism where release is richness, confinement is credence, liberty is love and self-consciousness is often wisdom. This is the creativity that *itihasa* produces: being born in history needs to complement being born into history.

Historical knowledge, Tagore argues, is not merely a documentary knowledge of the past: it is a realization, a consciousness, an understanding about community, man and his world, his works and means, his dreams and ruin, his survival and flourish.[12] Tagore believes that *jatra* and *kothokatha* are alternate means to give history lessons, and helpful to validate the currency of history in the non-trained public sphere.[13] He implicates 'entertainment' that history can provide, the fun that our different means of unspooling the past can generate. It is not public history but about trying to find the 'public', the 'man', in our historical experiences – less book bound and more life bound. R. Radhakrishnan is right to note that Tagore's poetic vision is a deconstruction of the binary between the 'alien' (British imperialist historiography) and the 'indigenous' (nationalist and nativist historiography and historical consciousness): 'thinking the unthought would have to be both against the local and against the general economy of historical meaning, against a specific history and against history as such'.[14] Tagore's reading of historical figures like Laxmi Bai, Guru Govind Singh, Vir Guru, Shivaji, Siraj ud-Daulah among others is performed through an intersection of two voices – the voice of emotion and everyday existence and the voice of epistemology. This discloses a different historicality not available to historiography and 'under the auspices of such a historicality', as Radhakrishnan argues, 'the worldling of the world is simultaneously ontological and epistemological'. It takes place in a time alien to historiography: a time that is neither stranded in immanence nor interpellated by any regime of transcendence'.[15] *Itihasa* promotes a wordling of these historical figures who are 'poetized into their authentic historicality'[16]; here we have a historical poesis which mediates between the poet and the historian to create a lifeworld.

On similar lines, Tagore sees the truth of the *pratyohik* (regular, everyday) and the vital unfolding of life and emotions in Shakespeare's *Anthony and Cleopatra*. Substantialization of *itihasa* owes as much to the revolutions in the arena of politics, in the domains of love, in the momentous trials of separation and destiny as to the emotional unrest and intensity of the human heart played out in the epic theatre of history.[17] It is here, Tagore notes, that the intermixture of *rasas* come into potent play – *aadi* and *karuna rasa* flowing into historical *rasa* – generating a heart-wrenching immensity and distance. Theodor Mommsen, Tagore observes, would see factual inaccuracy and historical blindness in such writing and depiction.[18] But Shakespeare, the poet-historian that he was, successfully evoked an enigmatic sense of admiration in the minds of the readers and a flush of historical *rasa* which data analysis and verificatory reading cannot destroy. There is no reason to believe that Shakespeare was not conscious of the distinction between poetry and history.[19] Armed with a similar sense of a divide between the two, Tagore is admitting of the pure unchangeability of certain sets of data. Tagore believed that Shakespeare got the rhythm of history and poetry going where the commitment was not to resolve the quarrel between the two but fructify the tension emerging thereof. Shakespeare, as David Quint rightly argues, chose to inhabit the middle ground between historicism and humanism and in many of his plays be it *Macbeth*, *Henry V* or *Julius Caesar* demonstrated Hans-Georg Gadamer's 'effective historical consciousness' where the past and the present put their affect and inputs in collaborative consolidation within a continuum of historical tradition.[20] The intrusion – compulsive and fractious – of 'literary' into history is what problematizes the predicament of the poet-historian and Tagore's essays on historical figures vindicate his position.

Can the philosophy of *itihasa* be both allegorical and verificatory? Can it be 'literary analogs'[21] of our deepest emotional, social and civilizational truths? In the workshop of the poet-historian *itihasa* unveils through these epics in a deeply entangled and diffracted configuration of myth and literary affect. The *kavi-aitihāsik* (poet-historian) constructs his *viraha* (longing) with history[22] not in the sense of *viccheda* (sunderance) but as yearning, a desire to know and experience the emotion that *viraha* generates in its unfulfilment: the enticement, allure and intangibilities of the past disabling the complete domination of the historian. Simon Schama finds a different kind of charm in the kind of history that Herodotus practices or offers in contrast to Thucydides who is fiercely obligated to verificatory and fact-based history – Herodotus's 'relish for gossip, his intuitive understanding of the idiosyncrasies of climate and geography, his primitive ethnography, his unabashed subjectivities, the winning mishmash of hearsay and record, real and fantastic'.[23] Not that one is wrong and the other is more right than the other. Historical narration has its settlement with fabula, tropology, emplotting, encodation, rigour, acts of recounting, well-grounded evidential discourses and, perhaps, some romance. *Itihasa* for Tagore is poiesis having at once the ability to legitimize and 'move' its readers which is not just about 'feigning' or counterfeit. The *kavi-aitihāsik* (poet-historian) has his own fresh critique of epic history – being, at once, a humanist, experimenter, teleologist and narratologist.

Elaborating Herder's *Ideen zur Philosophie der Menschengeschichte* (1784–1791) as a notable expression of the modem historical attitude towards the past, W. Von Leyden writes that Herder recognized 'the variations of human nature within one and the same period and from one age to another' calling for 'separate investigations of each stage in history. He had in mind here what to us has become an obvious truth, namely, that just as two moments may be said to differ, so too neither the ancient Egyptians nor the Greeks were at all times the same; and that, for instance, the art of ancient Egypt should not be judged, as in the hands of Winckelmann, by criteria derived from the consideration of art in ancient Greece'.[24] History is not predominantly about imposing absolutes or universals or a general idea to explain life, events and times. Every kind of history, historical thought, historicality will have a separate measure of time rather 'the measure of its own time'. Tagore's sense and understanding of history has its own measure and metier and is not essentially a linear variable of time, not an Euclidian perspective that pins down historical understanding to fixed coordinates of time progression. He did not choose to emphasize a strong non-Western bias and an entrenched opposition to models of Western time. He was not Michea Eliade's history-fleeing archaic man either. *Itihasa* as a narration or tale of human progress has its own world views (encompassive of both the non-teleological and the domain of political action), intelligible understanding of situations, events, emotions and development without a kind of inscrutable mystique that prejudicially come to get attached with the word. Absolutes cohabit the synchronic; the defined and directed are simultaneous with the unpredictable and serendipitous – *itihasa* creates a delicate interpenetration. Kenneth Inada explains:

> that for the most part, we uncritically accept the condition that the mind, the conscious mind, can only function from the standpoint of temporal parallelism, that is, a parallelism that exists between a mental phenomenon and a perceptual phenomenon. An extension of this is, perhaps, the isomorphic theory of perception. When we become conscious of an object we tend to conclude that perception had been a simple and singular event. We normally do not consider the nature of continuity of the experiential process in ways which do justice to the manifold of overt as well as covert factors in function. The life process, after all, goes on incessantly whether or not we are conscious of an object. The process never takes a holiday, although consciousness does.[25]

Tagore sees life as something perceptible and comprehensible and also a process, interminable and immanent. Tagore, like the Buddhists, does not have any problem dividing time into its past, present and future segments (*atita, paccuppanna, anagata*). But *itihasa* is not always clock time but a construction of the mind, the sense of the mind of space, time and situations; hence, *itihasa* is destined to build its own abstractive attributes. *Itihasa* is not mere understanding of strict forms and lines of interaction and engagements ranging across society, politics and nation; it is making sense of the splits and disruptions of our existence (*khana-vada*). However, Tagore, in line with Buddhist speculations on time, does not believe in time which is exclusively relational, relative, unpredictable and completely non-objectifiable. His philosophy of *itihasa* is not predominantly transitive and relative. 'To use an old metaphor', as Inada writes, 'events are taking place like waves in the vast ocean. In mid-ocean the myriad waves are appearing and disappearing as if each is independent of each other but in truth there are many factors and conditions at play which make it possible for each wave to appear and disappear thus and so. Such is also the nature of the rise and subsidence of consciousness. All this goes to show that relational-origination is a conditioning or compounding phenomenon; it is exhibiting the complex but unique way in which an experiential event transpires'.[26] Tagore knew this compoundness well enough and realized *itihasa* as conditioned on such relational origination. *Itihasa* takes its own *samay* (time) or has its *kaal* (time, also greater time) to come to fruition: its emergence is a process involving at once a rational analytic and a 'play'. So it is hard to accept that time is without any ultimate ontological status. Tagore is not looking into a *nirvana* through *itihasa*. Temporality chains but historicality has its own ways of release. So the truth of Tagore's philosophy of *itihasa* is not illusory and unreal. It has its operative connection with *anubhava* (experience) which stands distinguished from what we understand simply as experience. It is not about directing one's life through the agency of history but agentializing the historicality of our existence – living and doing history together through *aparoksha* (direct experience), *anubhava, dhristi* (vision) and *kalpana* (imagination).

Tagore observes:

> Viewed from the standpoint of intervening space, the distance between the earth and the moon may loom large, and tend to obscure the fact of their relationship. There are many double stars in the firmament of history, whose distance from each other does not affect the truth of their brotherhood. We know, from the suggestion thrown out by the poet of Ramayana, that Janaka, Visvamitra and Rama, even if actually separated by time, were nevertheless members of such a triple system.[27]

Here, Tagore's philosophy of *itihasa* demands being exegesized through time's vexatious relationship with historical distance. Distance (disjuncture and detachment) from the past is a delicate and complex axis on which 'retrospectiveness' (in the words of Eric Hobsbawn) can be rethought.[28] Commitment to *itihasa* and historical intimacy are not submissions to universals of reading; commitment is better realized through 'distancing', alienation, where the present provides multiple ways of configuring our relations to the past – the vagaries of *viraha*. Tagore saw an opening in historical knowledge through such means of distancing provided by values that one's present culture and tradition generate and alienation that imagination, alterity, affect and sensibilities trigger. *Itihasa* mediates with our cultural past as much as it participates with the world outside our culture and tradition. It comes with its connotation in *yatra*, the journey, produced through *pramanas* (means of knowledge), perception, testimony and inference in both the past and the present. To this *yatra* with its own means of knowledge production, Tagore does not fail to add memory (*smriti*). *Itihasa* is both presentative and representative – a *racanashalay*, the room for creation, where *pramanas* come both veridically and affectively. Distance and desire in *itihasa* build their own creativity (*srishtikartritva*).

Is Tagore's notion of *itihasa* sinusoidal?[29] Is the 'rhythm' that Tagore describes in his 'Bharatvarshar Itihasa' indicative of a new sense of tradition where rise and fall, decline and emergence, disruption and continuity are all part of an oppositional progress, the dialectical *yatra* of *itihasa*?

In 'Sahityer Itihasikatha' (Historicality of Literature) Tagore writes:

> One day I had just come back from school at about four-thirty and found a dark blue cumulus suspended high above the third storey of our house. What a marvelous sight that was. Even now I remember that day. But in the history of that day there was no one other than myself who saw those clouds in quite the same way as I did or was similarly thrilled. *Rabindranath happened to be all by himself in that instance.* Once after school I saw a most amazing spectacle from our western verandah. A donkey—not one of those donkeys manufactured by British imperial policy but the animal that had always belonged to our own society and has not changed in its ways since the beginning of time—one such donkey had come up from the washermen's quarters and was grazing on the grass while a cow fondly licked its body. The attraction of one living being for another that then caught my eye has remained unforgettable for me until today. In the entire history of that day it was *Rabindranath alone* who witnessed the scene with enchanted eyes. This I know for certain. No one else was instructed by the history of that day in the profound significance of the sight as was Rabindranath. In his own field of creativity Rabindranath has been entirely alone and tied to no public by history.[30]

History for Tagore forms around four points of engagement: history of the day, the enchantment and thrill, the *pratyohik* (everyday) and 'Rabindranath' existing in his own independence as a seer and meaning-maker. What value and inevitability do 'being alone' have in the construction of a historical experience? Is not being connected to the 'public' – the public gaze, the public approval of an event – another mode of doing history through a different contact and impact? What is this connect that makes history manifest in a rare vitalism and immanence?

It is a kind of dissociative–associative historical consciousness where 'being alone' is also 'being with', where 'being for' is also about 'being without'. The 'being with' is the power that historical sense generates – the historicality built with a cow, donkey, cumulus and light on the trembling coconut fronds. Rabindranath's 'seeing' and being in history contribute to Rabindranath Tagore's reflections on *itihasa*, constructing a compelling mix of the presentness of the past, past and its pastness, presentness and presentification. The investments of historical consciousness in figurements (not mere constructivism) of life-experiences are sublime. This is close to Michael Oakshott saying that 'experience proper is thought: therefore all experience is a world of ideas, or imaginings'.[31] Tagore would prefer to see 'Rabindranath' as 'consubstantial with history'. 'Rabindranath' who builds his own historical moment removed from the public gaze and herd understanding of historicality knows that history is in us and we are in it. We are a part of a continuum called *itihasa* where collective attestation of events helps in the concretization of history and where history remains as an abstraction of our self too.[32] Tagore's involvement in a consubstantial understanding of history makes him see the poetic moment and the moments of history in a unitive strength which, however, does not blur their distinctions completely within a continuity and synthesis. For Tagore the past does not stay external to him; history is about an intimacy with the past as recreated in the present. This 'intimate' moment in history – like watching the donkey being affectionately licked by the cow – is the disruption that conventional history would find in the continuity between the past and the present. For Tagore, however, it is the poet who produces the modality of experience where continuity comes to be maintained in ruptures and in broken bits of communication.

'Rabindranath' lives his 'own' history away from the history of his situatedness in a particular society and community. He is witness to his own history. This rhythm of *itihasa* is formed through a world that exists outside the world that obligates and obtains to the public (*sadharon*), the collective, the herd. This world – its drama and enactments – is almost always lost to the 'pedantic' historiographical thinking. History demonstrates a desperation to vindicate its alternative existence by living through the 'familiar' (the glitter of the dew drops, the coconut trees, the cow fondly licking the body of the donkey) into a world whose alethic disclosures are not for all: history outside history comes with its own *nirmiti* (creation) and *bhava* (emotion). This history is sublime; it dissolves the conventional formal public ways of vindicating and discoursing our experiences and opens onto a world 'without the protective mediation of the cognitive and psychological apparatus that normally processes our experience'.[33] This mediation of history with poetic re-creativity is much more complex than it seems. Rabindranath has lived in and out of history – by extension in and out of time – and realized both in separate moments and simultaneity.

How do Tagore and 'Rabindranath' interact and negotiate their experience of history? This happens in a moment which in its 'quasi-noumenal nakedness' and 'its unusual directness and immediacy'[34] creates both alienation and wonder, estrangement and uniqueness, perception and prison and dissolution of public history into other forms of experiences. It is through 'Rabindranath' that history reinvents itself, unforms its pedagogical and pedantic character to evolve into finer forms of narration and elaboration – revisionary, rejuvenating and reconstructive. Frank Ankersmit observes that 'history comes to us in wholes, in totalities, and this is how we primarily experience both the past itself and what it has left us – as is the case in the arts and in the aesthetic experience. The explanation is that history does not rise up before our minds from data found in the archives in the way that a detective may infer from the relevant data who committed a murder: It is, instead, a "displacement" of the present as dictated by these data, and, as such, it is experienced as a totality no less than is the case with the present'.[35] 'Rabindranath' is the product of a displacement. Experiencing history here becomes nostalgic, a turning loose of passion and curiosity for a moment; historical distance is built not between what we feel in the present and what happened in the past but between two experiences of history – one about the *sadharon* (ordinary) day when Tagore was getting back from school and the other where 'Rabindranath' was born out of the *pratyohik*. This relates both to the different vein of poeticality and historicality, the languaging of separate modes of realization and divisions enacted and found in the subject and the object.

'Rabindranath' stands for a new aesthetic of *itihasa* where knowing, unlike empirical experiences in natural sciences, is an active projection that makes moments act as reservoirs of experience and *eo ipso* auratic by themselves – a projection that unconceals a latent history of the everyday and unhinges the banality of the habits of historical understanding. Here is 'Rabindranath' who stands as a reminder of the impoverishment of history brought about by the occlusion of the individual and the *kavi-manush* by the surfeit and dominance of the average and the public. Rabindranth is in his *srishtikshetra* (field of creativity) where his self is non-colonial, non-Hegelian, non-finite, non-public and yet not unhistorical or ahistorical. 'Rabindranath' is *osadharon* (outside average) by being tied to himself, his emotions, imagination and aesthetics of understanding. 'Rabindranath' effectuates a homecoming through the greater enclosures of Tagore; here, both Tagore and 'Rabindranath' find their home at the limits of world history. *Itihasa* declares its distinct place through intense moments of worlding and the infinitization of the finite which dismantles the aporetic and transcendent paradigms of historical learning and knowledge formation.

The *srishtikshetra* in which 'Rabindranath' revels is not to be misconstrued as a withdrawal from the chains of proper history that cannot look beyond the perimeters of facts and data. Facts of the everyday are minted in solitude; experiences for 'Rabindranath' do not turn phantasmatic. History is built in the tumult of 'moments of intensity' (in the words of Hans Gumbretch),[36] in one's enclosures of seeing; *itihasa* is the 'presence' that 'can produce effects and radiate energy while escaping efforts to identify and apprehend it'.[37] History tied to the *sadharon* misses this kinesis, this unapprehendable flicker of the excess. Writing or narrating the everyday is not what usually happens in the creative workshop of history. But here through the intervention on the *pratyohik* we find the dissolution of the big-time dimension that we attach to historical events, differentiating what is important from what is not. There is a voice behind the weaving of a historical narrative that determines the gods of big and small things. But such dissolution disrupts the continuity of a settled pattern of argument importing digression and detouring. 'Rabindranath' is a consequence of a historical detour. History for Tagore is not romantic outbounding, not relentless splitting of truth: neither a permanent closure on ideological ossification nor postmodern deferral of signification. We are in the midst of Walter Benjamin's 'chronicler' who 'narrates events without distinguishing between major and minor ones acts in accord with the following truth: nothing that has ever happened should be regarded as lost to history'.[38] The *pratyohik* may be lost to the public but not to the hunger of *itihasa*. Seeing a connect among everyday things builds a design on the mind, wakes up the imagination, and arouses the sensibilities usually deemed dormant in the daily grind of living. *Pratyohik*, then, is not about today but a 'today' infused with the sense of the yesterday (*aaj-kal*), a continuous investment in missed historical encounters. 'Rabindranath', in a monadic intensity, 'touches' history through an event seen today but which has its recurrence from the past, in times when he was not conscious of and, when the outside stayed as outside without its inherent drama, play, imagination, emotion and whatever other that composed and intensified its unrealized historicality. Moments in history can act as 'filters' – creative and epiphanous – generating a capacity in history to foreground its latency. *Itihasa* makes its demands on creativity always and not, as wrongly supposed, in its chosen moments. 'Rabindranath' connected with the 'today' (*aaj*) and relished the history of the present, but in such connections revindicated our interminable, always embodied, ligatures with the past (*kal*) – the *aaj-kal* in duet, in dialogue, preparing the scripts of *itihasa*.[39]

Is all historical thinking regulatively bound to the dictates of discursive representations, images, iconography and material relics? Do the gathered and the aggregated symptomatize history as an idea, a 'manifest' or a documentation in truth and conceptual unity? The problem with our past rolling into the present is not in unity and is not always regulated under a conceptual and representational law; it is not a narrative devoid of discrimination. The constellative past for Tagore is composed in discontinuous configuration – Tagore seeing history through inference and causality and 'Rabindranath' experiencing history outside successivity and objectivity – within a dialectic where history exists as an unfinished project. Historical thinking is both a 'movement' and an 'arrest of thoughts',[40] hustling amidst finitude of thinking, the totality of experience and the fragmentation of image and idea. Benjamin writes that 'in order for a part of the past to be touched by the present instant there must be no continuity between them'.[41] 'Rabindranath' leaps out of the unattainability of historical continuity. Tagore 'reflects' on history and history 'refracts' on 'Rabindranath'. The moment that distinguishes 'Rabindranath' from Tagore is the non-actualized possibility which Benjamin sees as generating 'envy'. In fact, the happiness of 'Rabindranath' results in envy too[42]; he is envious of not being able to seize the moment. The moment that 'Rabindranath' encounters is the happiness of an experience in history and of envy for staying alive as a possibility never to be fully actualized. So Tagore engages with history and 'Rabindranath' with missed history, the possible and deferred history in the irrealis, a cognition that sees history in the present and leaves it open for the future too. 'Rabindranath' relished unfulfilled history.

Both 'Rabindranath' and Tagore saw the 'possible' in history and historical moment formation: 'excess over anything that can become given; excess over that which is; remainder that itself is not'.[43] Perhaps, to see Tagore's faith in the 'divine drive' in history as theological determinism or as strict acts of destiny is not appropriate. I would like to see this 'drive' or intention as recognition of possibility, a continuum of actualized, seized, happy moments in cohabitation with the unhappiness of unseized and uncaptured moments, a continued unfulfilment. The fateful dimension of history integrates with the 'truth of emotion' that Tagore so earnestly argued as a category removed from an inflexible submission to evidential truths. History is not an unimpeachable serialization of the factual, the realized and the 'taken place'; history depotentializes itself to include the fleeting, the non-archivable – an invitation to the 'hidden index'. Werner Hamacher's exegesis on Benjamin is relevant to an understanding of the predicament of 'Rabindranath': 'the present, if it is one, does not make claims on the future, but is present alone as that upon which the past makes demands: present is always present out of the past and present for the past. And second, the past not only has in this present its intentional object but its intention comes in it to a standstill: what-has-been shines in the present, if it is one, and unites with the Now of its cognition'.[44] Tagore believes in the now-ing of history, the interruptions that historical consciousness might produce on the ruins of the past, the hunger and drive of history breaking off at moments of fulfilment to digressively produce an emotion, reflection and romance in historical meaning generation. Theodor Adorno's commentary on Thesis VII of Benjamin's 'Theses on the Philosophy of History' is relevant here:

> If Benjamin said that history had hitherto been written from the standpoint of the victor, and needed to be written from that of the vanquished, we might add that knowledge must indeed present the fatally rectilinear succession of victory and defeat, but should also address itself to those things which were not embraced by this dynamic, which fell by the wayside – what might be called the waste products and blind spots that have escaped the dialectic. It is in the nature of the defeated to appear, in their impotence, irrelevant, eccentric, derisory.[45]

Tagore and 'Rabindranath' play up the limits of historicism, dialecticize our understanding of the vanquished and victorious past, feel the potency of *Jetztzeit* (now-time), and also blast the moment of the homogenous course of history.[46] Beiner helps us to note that 'history is a sky-high pile of debris and the assertion of progress is meant to deflect our gaze from this unredeemed debris (thesis IX). Historical materialism means that the vanquished are not forgotten, and this means that one is never deterred by the idea of progress from continuing to wage "the fight for the oppressed past" (thesis XVIII)'.[47] *Itihasa* is the oppressed file awaiting to be retold and not always in line with the colonial historiographical modes of representations and narrations. The 'blast' produces a consciousness of an object beyond the object (object diffusion) that the world materially formulates. 'Rabindranath' has encountered the limitations of experience and the confinements that a dialectical materialist understanding of life produces. This has resulted in the unselfing of Tagore into 'Rabindranath' as an experience (another version of *yatra*) and subject position that exist outside the empiricist and conservative epistemology of mere subject–object understanding of life and history. It is a different kind of history of reason where the world 'looked at' and the world's 'looking back' are not necessarily congruent modes of experience. 'Rabindranath', for me, is the flaneur that all historicist self-possesses and Tagore's philosophy of *itihasa* knows its investments in the 'contrived corridors', 'cunning passages' and 'whispering ambitions' that constitute it.[48]

Out of Time

Tagore's understanding of and experiments with education owe to his sense of *itihasa*. Tagore analysed and lived his history; he meditated and performed *itihasa*. His distinct habits of experiencing time, distance, past, present, narrative, space, traditions and, hence, *itihasa* encourage me to argue a different aesthetics and politics of engagement with education. Tagore's manifest interest in and reasoned endorsement for India's past were not impervious to the cultural and sociopolitical imports from other cultures and civilizations. His transcendent problematic of the 'East meeting the West' was deeply constellative and diffractive – the rhythm of negotiation was nowhere close to a demure handshaking but alive with the throb of interference, infringement, entanglement, porosity and informed pervasiveness. For a man whose sense of *itihasa* cannot ignore the dimensions of cultural interfusion, capacious and the mediatory presence of the familiar and the factual, the collapsing of historical distances across cultural-epistemic paradigms and a unique sense of historical time and tradition, any critique of his educational philosophy and thinking cannot avoid drawing on the dynamic potential of his historical sense. How can a personal establishment and investment in a variety of role playing impact on his educational policy and philosophy? What happens when the visionary educationist meets the *kavi-aitihāsik* (poet-historian)?

This gets me to configure the book around what I have termed the (in)fusion-transcultural-now[49] which broadly is about questioning the limits of critical understanding and trying to understand how far and to what extent critical correspondences between contesting paradigms of thoughts and concepts can be explored and executed. It is based on a sound faith in epistemic entanglements and a happy refusal to see concepts as binarized or polarized. Here epistemological norms and the pleasure that emerge from conducting thought experiments and in pushing frontiers of conceptual understanding come together. Conjugating with the notion of a 'transcultural now,' the (in)fusion approach has the potential to become a new method of global comparison. Comparison is 'world-wideness', which implies 'intensified intra-action and a perpetually differentiating "world" – a "world" continuously in the making'.[50] So comparison in the sense in which Jean-Luc Nancy calls *comparution* is both immanent and planetary. This is a 'wandering' (*errance*) which does not show any rectitude but develops its own momentum across traditions, paradigms, cultures and ideologies. Elsewhere, I have termed this comparison 'worlding',[51] which feeds on what Wai Chee Dimock argues as 'diachronic historicism' that 'tries to engage history beyond the simultaneous, aligning it instead with the dynamics of endurance and transformation that accompany the passage of time'.[52] In fact, Tagore's historical sense makes itself available for such trans-(in)fusionist interventions. As such, conceptual competences or correspondences effected through trans-(in)fusionized comparison between Tagore, Tolstoy, Rousseau, Martin Buber, Jacques Derrida, Paulo Freire, and a host of other thinkers have serious traveling frequencies 'causing unexpected vibrations in unexpected places'.[53] So when I argue Tagore as existing in multiple operative nows – dismantling territorial time or a Newtonian mechanics of unified chronology and submitting to 'deep time'[54] instead – the global politics of comparative education is faced with a different methodology of understanding. It is through the '(in)fusion-transcultural now' that comparative educational philosophy needs to execute some randomness (it risks being misperceived as aberrative juxtapositions of thoughts) of critical thinking and surprising frequencies of interference resulting in worlding. This book argues that Tagore's educational philosophy and the subsequent execution of its dimensions and ideals are inscribed in *complexity* – from the 'Latin expression "complexus" (fourteenth century) and adopted from the modern French, the term derives from "cum" and "plectere", meaning surrounding, encompassing, encircling, embracing, comprehending, comprising. Originally denoting "embracing or comprehending several elements", its use in English tended to be akin to the sense of "plaited together, interwoven"'.[55] I argue for an organized complexity in Tagore's ways of education, a fractal dynamics that can be enunciated to have a connective productivity between a variety of systems of thought and traditions of understanding. Ingrained in an autopoietic system, Tagore's thoughts have an apparent simplicity which hides an entanglement; it is a 'complexity' thinking that involves an ethics of non-linearity, transphenomenal concerns and an 'always-evolving reality'.[56] However, this is not an easy collapse into rhizomatics which is why we needed an understanding of Tagore's historical sense. Non-linearities combine both the stochastic and the turbulent and, in fact, Henri Poincaré's understanding of 'phase space' argues for the nature of accidents by enrolling the attendance of chance. In explaining non-linearity, Gaponov-Grekov and Rabinovich see almost all finite trajectories as unstable, at large: 'after a sufficiently long time this leads to a loss of information on the past of the system (i.e. on its initial conditions) independent of the (finite) accuracy with which that past has been specified initially. Thus stocasticity – the chaotic motion of a dynamical system – is the result of the instability of trajectories located within a limited and yet sufficiently large region of phase space (and not just in the vicinity of equilibrium states)'.[57] The seduction of complexity thinking is acknowledged with caution because Tagore has certain explicit sources of epistemic anchorage that have nourished his thinking and ethics with unflinching devotion. So my reading cannot, to an extent, avoid the implosive strategization of deconstructive (im)possibility; it is also threaded, rather, hynoptized, by a fractality (the creativity involved in fundamental braiding[58]) and the innate power of non-linearity.

The project becomes an 'intra-active' investigation of Tagore's educational philosophy and is devoted to 're-diffracting, diffracting anew, in the making of new temporalities (spacetimematterings), new diffraction patterns'[59] like it has never been imagined or attempted before. This is not mere uncritical putting together of thoughts but a destabilization of sedimented binaries through a collapse of space and time ('spacetimematterings'), a kind of diffracted condensation which betrays *unease* in seeing Tagore in critical communication – set in play – with a diverse range of thinkers and thought patterns. The resultant unease through planetization of reading is the real profit that the field of comparative educational studies needs to garner and work on for its future. Trans-(in)fusionist philosophy of education must realize that Tagore and diffractive engagements with a variety of thoughts, cultures and thinkers cutting across time, history and tradition are not here only because of my ability to generate a conjunctural reading; importantly, my theoretical position urges readers to believe that portions of their thought have always existed in entangled spacetimematterings. My emphasis is on how we can make 'superpositions' matter and how we accept that paradigm meshing between Tagore and his unlikely Western counterparts is not always an applausive ingenuity but an agentiality or an *event* that was there for us to locate and experience. Instead of seeing comparative exegesis as juxtapositions, I recommend seeing them as aesthetic imaginary or resonant relationality.

The book, then, is fundamentally about radicalizing our habits of 'critical listening'. As an artist-intellectual Tagore had always argued for cultural refinement, an emancipatory ferment and a dynamic consciousness that connected the 'home' and the 'world' – the 'public' and the 'private' – and eclectically problematized the relation between tradition and modernity. He worked from within a tradition which was richly diverse, and yet was not unmindful of the ways in which other traditions in their heterogeneity impinged on his own. 'Tradition' always appeared to Tagore as creative: his appropriations have been aesthetic, dynamic, non-adversarial and dialogic.[60] He chose to settle on a busy confluence – a cross road of vibrant possibilities – to realize the universal nature of the artist in him, excavating in the process the transnational intellectual which he quintessentially was. Bundles of habits crack and crackle when the dream, the spirit of projection, has a sublime power and the inspiration to swim currents and not resist them. Arguing Tagore's transversality and potent versality within T. S. Eliot's intriguingly capacious concept of tradition brings us to rethink what Tagore means by *compatriot*: the disturbing and delectable art of seeing all authors and thought systems in a productive contemporaneity.[61] Tagore always sought to incorporate different strains of ideas, practices and perspectives, acknowledging and accommodating the hopes and pains of people from different races, nations, cultures and religions. His work was meaningfully opposed to 'hegemonic' universalism and deeply oppositional to the imposition of one local set of beliefs and customs on everyone else. Instead, he had an unwavering support for 'empathic universalism', a universalism that did not impose dogma but fostered a sense of common humanity across the many particularisms that define our daily lives. As an artist of creative humanism, Tagore believed that the final nature of the world does not depend upon the comprehension of an individual person; rather, comprehension is associated with the 'universal human mind' which has the power to comprehend greater possibilities of meaning. As an artist-intellectual, he went for pushing the limits of knowledge, power, love, and enjoyment, allowing himself to remain on course to approach the universal. The spirit of the artist is not an abstraction from the world; it draws upon the 'worldliness'. It feeds on a dynamic aesthetic of wholeness, working out a vision which refutes 'absolute divisions between body and mind, matter and life, individual and society, community and nation, and empire and the world'.[62] This is the artistic aspiration for the 'universal', the continual intellectual striving to partner the local with the global, and also the reasoned articulation emerging from a profound understanding of Indian culture which he always wanted to see as removed from self-containment and insularity.

Michel Serres keys onto this subject with this usual exhilarating sharpness:

> Consider a late-model car. It is a disparate aggregate of scientific and technical solutions dating from different periods. One can date it component by component: this part was invented at the turn of the century, another ten years ago, and Carnot's cycle is almost two hundred years old. Not to mention that the wheel dates back to neolithic times. The ensemble is only contemporary by assemblage, by its design, its finish, sometimes only by the slickness of the advertising surrounding it.[63]

Tagore's educational thinking, as I would like to argue, has a Hermes[64] who is mediatory, a traveller, making unexpected correspondences and serendipitous connections. My reading of Tagore's philosophy and vision of education qualifies as an ensemble, an assemblage, whose power is in connecting with thoughts and philosophies around, making every historical era 'multitemporal, simultaneously drawing from the obsolete, the contemporary and the futuristic', revealing 'a time that is gathered together, with multiple pleats'.[65] Tagore believed in an individuality that cannot do without the other – thoughtful departures from home are frequent and risking encounters are not infrequent either. True to the theoretical tenor of the book, I would like to build a connection – strange, though intriguing – between my argument here and a particular mating song used by African parrots as illustrated by Chilean biologist Humberto Maturana: 'these birds', explains Fritjof Capra, 'often live in dense forests with hardly any possibility of visual contact. In this environment parrot couples form and coordinate their mating ritual by producing a common song. To the casual listener it seems that each bird is singing a full melody, but closer inspection shows that this melody is actually a duet in which the two birds alternatively expand upon each other's phrases. The whole melody is unique to each couple and is not passed on to their offspring. In each generation new couples will produce their own characteristic melodies in their mating rituals'.[66] What this illustration demonstrates is that the thought melody produced out of Tagore's educational thinking is mostly about a 'duet', an inherent we-ness in thoughts and perspectives. His full melody of thinking is not executed and conducted alone; the song is best experienced through multiple inputs which expand on each other dialogically and deepen and ramify its vibrations and epistemic tonality. This clearly impacts on his pedagogical philosophy which refuses to work in departments but finds comfort in the imperious temptation to live in the 'we'. The troubadour Tagore troubles me by taking upon himself the affective task of producing aesthetic education, a counter education, calling for invention and imagination.

When he stood before the vast tract of land given to him by his father to set up his school project in 1901, Tagore dared the dream not because of the money he thought his wealthy father would leave behind for his project or the assistance he might have received from the colonial government if that was really a viable alternative, but for his imagination and intuition, a 'dazzling, obscure, hard to define emotion'.[67] It was a project of 'love' – education realized and desired through a philosophy. Balked and buffeted by conventional systems of education where memory and normed patterns of tests and eligibility were unfortunate determinants of one's worth and value – the failure to make oneself 'at home (*einhaust*) in a world', a school education, as Hans Georg Gadamer argues, that has a tendency to levelling and conformity[68] – Tagore cared to invest in an education not strictly governed by curriculum alone. The 'unrepresentability' outside the aporetic calculus of a classroom has its own haunting potential. Serres notes that 'the goal of instruction is the end of instruction, that is to say, invention. Invention is the only true intellectual act, the only act of intelligence. The rest? Copying, cheating, reproduction, laziness, convention, battle, sleep. Only discovery awakens. Only invention proves that one truly thinks what one thinks, whatever that may be'.[69] Tagore may not be as ambitious and radical as Serres is about methodologies of instruction and the milieu in the classroom, but he recognized the inventiveness in instruction and the dynamical function of the teacher. Serres looks into a 'secular miracle'[70] proposing an engagement of the student's intuition and invention with chaotic instruction. Both converge on the significance of dissipative learning – Serres chooses to mix the clown or the practical joker with the ideal teacher and Tagore enthrones the guru with his dynamic, disturbing and disseminative power. However, under the reality of becoming slaves to enlightenment – tutored and domesticated – the acts of revisioning the teacher, and, hence, the principles of learning were always going to be difficult. It is in the post-endist thinking about education – the reconstructed metaphysics of 'return of learning' – that the teacher and the philosopher become not simple pure reason. Teachers are not meant to serve the ends of human reason alone; they exist, as Immanuel Kant has argued, 'nowhere'. Nigel Tubbs points out that 'we are left only to discover his legislation. This is the universal educative import of metaphysics regarding the contradiction of the teacher as law and excess. Its transcendental and speculative experience negates all dogmatic models of enlightenment and offers, instead, a philosophical re-cognition of the prior complicity of enlightenment within experience. Enlightenment here becomes enlightened about its own illusions. It is an enlightenment with a metaphysical significance, given actuality in the struggle or relationship between possibility and necessity or law and legislation'.[71] Tagore, intriguingly, as the book tries to demonstrate, legislates in the liminality of excess and law.

In Time

Although the imports of Western education were generally favoured by a substantial section of Indian intellectuals in the late nineteenth and early twentieth century – Tagore was no exception – the manner in which Western educational reforms and principles were introduced through the colonial machinery incurred the suspicion and the consequent apathy of many of its endorsers. The British were accused of deploying their strategies of control and hegemony through educational policies and agendas. In the decades following the birth of the Indian National Congress (1885), the general feeling was that the decision to promote education in English, at variance with Hunter Commission report (1883) that supported the growth of indigenous education, was a mistake. Lord Macaulay's dominant emphasis on Western education or English as a medium of instruction (advocated in his famous Minute, English Education Act of 1835) was not delivering any desired returns. Educated Indians vied for too few jobs and the growing unemployment ('discontented horde of officer seekers'[72]) generated a massive disillusionment with British Raj's educational policies. This fuelled nationalist sentiments and, anticoloniality was built on the accusation that much of the effective resources of education were held in check and the Indian educational system under the British colonial rule was not provided with sufficient nourishment in the post-Hunter commission years. In 'Siksha-samskara' Tagore points out the colonial intent in the prevalent education system and by accentuating self-reliance proposes a different methodology of education. He quotes Tolstoy, saying:

> It seems to me that it is now specially important to do what is right quietly and persistently, not only without asking permission from Government but consciously avoiding its participation. The strength of the Government lies in the people's ignorance, and the Government knows this, and will therefore always oppose true enlightenment. It is time we realized that fact. And it is most undesirable to let the Government, while it is spreading darkness, pretend to be busy with the enlightenment of the people. It is doing this now by means of all sorts of pseudo-educational establishments which it controls: schools, high schools, universities, academies, and all kinds of committees and congresses. But good is good and enlightenment is enlightenment, only when it is quite good and quite enlightened and not when it is toned down to meet the requirements of Delyanof's or Dournovo's circulars. And I am extremely sorry when I see valuable, disinterested, and self-sacrificing efforts spent unprofitably. It is strange we see good, wide people spending their strength in a struggle against the Government, but carrying on that struggle on the basis of whatever laws the Government itself likes to make.[73]

Tagore saw certain enervating deficiencies in colonial education (one may refer to his 'Shikshar Her Fer', Vicissitudes of Education (1892) – a kind of lack that he felt his own principles of 'education for fullness' could only address.[74] Coming into contact with young men, Tagore was 'stricken with distress to notice their shallow mental outlook. They would readily lend themselves to agitation, and could take interest in a cause only if there was room in it for boisterous display. Taught by men who, with a few exceptions, looked upon their own work as more a trade than a profession, they lacked vision. Even the few ideas they had collected, for success in examinations, were not very useful, as these had not been brought into "chemical combination" with life, as he put it'.[75] He believed that education could never be successful through method only or the exclusivity of a system; education has always had its justice in teachers. Similar concerns were expressed in 'Sikshabidhi' (Principles of Education) about the mechanization of education where methods, through relentless skill and strategy, were templated to churn out dogmatic precepts of learning. Tagore argued that this statuesque means of learning could only generate 'clerks' where man became a porter of 'degrees'. In a rush for such institutional accumulation, man was far removed from the pride of 'living' and the nourishments of his soul. Schooling under the colonial regime and its pervasive influence, Tagore argued, had become a mechanism that made a child the target of dry lessons like 'hailstones on flowers'.[76] Learning was performed in 'borrowed cages' that treated 'the students' minds as captive birds, whose sole value is judged according to the mechanical repetition of lessons, prescribed by an educational dispensation foreign to the soil'.[77] Tagore had had his brush with formal schooling although he did not graduate of any. Nita Kumar points out that Tagore started with the Oriental Seminary, then went to the Normal School, 'supposedly a model school formed on the British pattern', then Bengal Academy and finally to St. Xavier's – 'he did go to school in England, but again, left without completing a degree'.[78] In his *Boyhood Reminiscences*, Tagore recorded his dissatisfaction with the modes of child education and how he grew up being a victim of a mechanistic system that never valued 'education of sympathy' (*bodher sadhana*) – 'I know what it was to which this school owes its origin. It was not any new theory of education, but the memory of my school days'.[79] In fact, through his own boyhood years, Tagore realized that the child must in a productive way stay connected with nature and his teacher (*guru–shishya*, teacher–pupil), a connection that did not conform to a template of professional, mostly predestined, growth but allowed for the development of both the body and the mind. Interestingly, Tagore was deeply accepting of 'experiments' in thought and ideals in education and he made it reasonably clear in 'Sikshabidhi'.[80] We needed rule and restraint as much as we required freedom and unboundedness. Since 'tension' and 'contradiction' in man were the uncontesting truths, Tagore believed in the ability of happiness to teach man and considered suffering and sadness as potential lesson givers. A variety of educational ways might inspire one to choose the 'middle path'; but, culling the course through the middle was insuperably difficult because life and its changing situations and contexts reckoned continual alteration and adjustments, making room for experiments and shifting centres of balance and achievements. So Tagore argued that 'desire' based on one's internal and external wants must determine the contour and character of education, preventing it from being domained in rigid timeless principles of understanding and knowledge. However, such thrust on the contemporanization of education did not disqualify Tagorean ambitions from including age-old principles of learning, working out the presentness of a past. His philosophical modernity was in reinventing what we generically call the 'contemporary'. This dynamic contemporaneity defeated itself in man's persistent tendencies to proliferate himself 'externally' – Tagore pointing man's blemished gestures in demanding 'Be a Brahmin, be a Sudra' – and attenuate 'internally', muffling his innate human potential to care, sacrifice and connect.

Tagore's dislike for certain parameters of colonial education did not preponderantly stem from a *swadeshi* or nationalist educational policy but certainly from an inherent dissatisfaction with certain fundamental principles of education that he considered were pernicious to the growth of a student. Tagore was not overtaken by any kind of nationalist pride in an ancient indigenous school system; he prudently prised out the merit of such a tradition instead and tried to execute a synthesis with the most effective imports from the British colonial education system ushering tradition and modernity into close contact and infusing experiment and inheritance into a gainful conjugation. Tagore never cultivated a precondition to any political ideology. His sense of security for one's own culture and ideology was quite apart from what had come to be commonly defined as 'nationalism'. Without encouraging emotionalism in excess, his 'nationalism' would problematise the communication corridors which it could possibly engineer with the 'greater' world by his *bharat chinta* (thoughts about India, home) as meaningfully integrated with *viswachinta* (thoughts about the world). He never deigned to be parasitic on a foreign tongue and his dynamic commitment to the values and wisdom of the *Upanishads* and Vedantic tradition came to hold a close, fecund and critical proximity to many of the ideals and ideas of Western thinkers – a synthetic cohabitation and assimilation of the 'vernacular' and the 'foreign'. So, when Tagore decided to establish a school for children seeped in his own ethos and values of learning and pedagogy in 1901 at Santiniketan,[81] it was not, rather, could not have been a simple project in *swadeshi* education.

Hunger

Tagore's notion of the school can be read alongside the Greek word *scholé* which means 'free time': rest, delay, study, discussion, lecture, school building. His school was envisaged through a fresh engagement with 'time' (not the destined time) and 'paedagogus' where 'complex' investments in educational philosophy and execution were clearly in prominence. Learning need not always be telic; education, on occasions, can act on the opinion of time. Schooling can often begin when the school is under suspension. Jan Masschelein observes that 'it is formative and transformative: a world takes place, "things" appear, but in their appearing also the individual is transformed and co-appears and an interest in the sense of *inter-esse* can develop'. This leads us to the vexed issue of caring for the self 'as being a care for what inter-ests'. For Tagore, within the metaphysics of *scholé,* knowing the world was as important as what the world *tells* me or us – a conjugality in 'being exposed together'.[82] Jean-François Lyotard writes about his dream of being an astronaut who lands on a distant planet where children laugh in splits hearing that on earth a school is compulsory and it comes with homework to attend to every evening. He decides to spend some time with the children on this planet. Lyotard writes:

> On the first day back at school in September David, aged seven and a half, comes home with the following homework: He has to learn this little story by Erhardt Dietl. In the space of one hour he can recite it in the right tone of voice without any mistakes. He has drawn the distant planet in his exercise book and the spaceship approaching it. The first thing that school makes him learn is the happiness of a world without school, with no obligations and no homework. This world exists on another planet. It is reached in a spaceship. The story does not say whether the little dreamer had to study to learn how to pilot the spaceship. It seems just as natural as climbing onto a bicycle.[83]

Education is about leading out: not always the outside but the far inside which cannot be reached 'by uprooting oneself but by plunging deep within towards what is most intimate, where lies desire'.[84] In that sense, Tagore's school was his own education, being led out of himself,[85] a dependence not on the colonial outside but his eros inside. Tagore rested on his desire for a far-off planet, listened to the invitation of a dream and did not allow the spaceship to rust. His journeys and envisagements, however, repeatedly narrated a new order without losing their connection with the world outside. Tagore's projects – primarily his ashram school, the university and institutions in rural reconstructionism – could not have been isolated workshops operated and perpetuated through megalomania, self-immunity and an indulgent harvest of a swellhead nativist. Ideas across continents and cultures have always expanded on each other, contributing in their depth and peculiarity towards a reflective and jointly architectured establishment which does not need historical and evidential approbation and corroboration always.

John Comenius (1592–1670), who might be called the father of modern educational theory, used the model of the printing press to explain how education took place. 'Instead of paper, we have pupils', Comenius wrote, 'pupils whose minds have to be impressed with the symbols of knowledge. Instead of type, we have classbooks and the rest of the apparatus devised to facilitate the operation of teaching. The ink is replaced by the voice of the masters, since it is this that conveys information to the minds of the listener, while the press is school discipline, which keeps the pupils up to their work and compels them to learn'.[86] As against the printing press model of transmission politics in education, Tagore executed a rare mix of vigilance, supervision, discipline, creativity and freedom – something that, to an extent, resembles A. N. Whitehead's identification of the stages of schooling as part of his aims for education: romance which brings wonder and joy, precision that inculcates values through self-discipline and freshness that teaching imports. It is possible to see in Tagore's ideas on progressive education a Deweyan emphasis on the 'life experience of the learner'[87] – a philosophy of education that is largely founded on a philosophy of experience. However, Tagore's emphasis on schooling was less emphatic about social progress and reform than John Dewey's faith in this direction. The interest in *swaraj* – the self-reconstruction – was more in keeping with Tagore's aesthetic schooling that thrived in a subtle mode through the dynamics of a reformative variant in emotion and sensitivity conflated with moral and ethical action and thought. But the meditative proximity of the two thinkers becomes pronounced when Dewey argues in *School and Society* that 'occupations in the school shall not be mere practical devices or modes of routine employment, the gaining of better technical skills as cooks, seamstresses or carpenters, but active centres of scientific insight into natural materials and processes, points of departure whence children shall be *led out* into a realization of the historical development of man'.[88] Dewey's paedo-pedagogy implicates the denial of complete freedom to the child in his or her development. The child's growth must have heavy reliance on supervision and an interactive engagement with the world of adults and principles of everyday pragmatism. Growth in education is a man–nature contact, a negotiation built around intergenerational 'transmission' of actions, thoughts, feelings and habits. The naturalness and socialization come into an adroit contact – natural outgrowth teaming with external direction. Tagore's idea of 'control' approximates Dewey's, but not without differences. His aesthetic education had more freedom, plasticity, romantic spontaneity and organic outpouring than Dewey was likely to admit or allow. Tagore gave more leverage to the mind as against Dewey's emphasis on trying to build more things into the mind externally. For Dewey, the environment of the mind is connected with the social environment – 'naturalistic humanism'. Tagore, like Dewey, endorsed the efficacy of the natural or native powers in initiating education but his reflective education would still admit that learning could not be a matter of the 'spontaneous overflow of the unlearned powers' alone.[89]

In *The Idea of History*, British philosopher-historian Roger Collingwood writes:

> Man, who desires to know everything, desires to know himself. Nor is he only one (even if, to himself, perhaps the most interesting) among the things he desires to know. Without some knowledge of himself, his knowledge of other things is imperfect: for to know something without knowing that one knows it is only a half-knowing, and to know that one knows is to know oneself. Self-knowledge is desirable and important to man, not only for its own sake, but as a condition without which no other knowledge can be critically justified and securely based.[90]

This is not an ethics of individualism but a way to know more about the system one grows into and lives within. Students must labour to know their tradition, their points of cultural emergence, to know about others and become knowledgeable about the world outside growing into 'an active and vigorous contributor to the life of the world'.[91] Self-knowledge for Tagore was a conscious dynamic activity, closely dependent on 'reflective education' with its stimulation derived from living experiences where 'reasoning is sharpened and perfected by disciplined discussion' and students are initiated into reflecting 'effectively on the values that are constantly being urged on them'.[92] On the inductive, instructive and transmission principles of education, Tagore's position is somewhere between Rousseau and John Dewey – not strictly the organismic model and the neo-Lamarckian, adaptive, problem-solving attitude that we associate with Dewey. Educational growth for Tagore was neither authoritarian nor overindulgent organicity as emphasized by Rouseau at the beginning of his *Emile*. Education must acknowledge growth as internal, organic, natural and, inevitably, adaptive to the changing environmental conditions – a complicated dialectic between education as task verb and achievement verb where, most often, Tagore sought the former.[93] Wonder, surprise and imagination must find their neighbourhood among crises, real problems, attrition and the adaptive modes of survival – a pedagogy of 'unselfing' where 'to attend is to care, to learn to desire to learn', a kind of Iris Murdochian way of integrating the 'intellectual' with the 'moral' and the *techne*.[94]

Tagore, however, could not have disapproved the organizational denomination in William James's view of education that saw habits, stream of experience and conduct as closely integrated.[95] Habits are formed within a revisionary aesthetic where learning is a continual pattern in behavioural novelization pertaining to changing contexts and voluntary functionality: 'We think the thing now in one context, now in another; now in a definite image, now in a symbol. Sometimes our sense of its identity pertains to the mere fringe, sometimes it involves the nucleus, of our thought. We never can break the thought and tell just which one of its bits is the part that lets us know which subject is referred to'.[96] Both Tagore and James saw effective education originating in experiences and in the formation of concepts and ideas. However, Tagore would not see all experiences as resulting in percepts and not all processes of learning as 'thinking'; education is perception mixed with an intangibility of learning, premised in a separate vein of values and aesthetic and adaptive valence. Individuality determines functionalities of education which for James connects with socialization and for Tagore with the social process and creative dynamics of *swadharma*. Learning evolves through life, the cultivation of individuality, reformation of habit that ensures pluralism in thinking and teleological possibilities of human fulfilment. So Tagore's educational system, I would like to argue, cannot overlook the Durkheimian emphasis on the socialization of education. Émile Durkheim writes that 'education is the action exercised by the older generations on those not yet ready for social life. Its object is to awaken in the child those physical, intellectual, and moral states which are required of him both by his society as a whole, and by the milieu for which he is specially destined'.[97] Although Tagore did not discount the innate powers and predispositions of students, the educative and acculturative emphases were conspicuously built into his system of aesthetic education – a Durkheimian stress on the transmission of culture and the delicate mutually endowing combination of the social and the individual, the conscious unavoidable impact of social growth and milieu and the differentiation that individual powers bring. The aesthetics for both then was generally processual.

Here Tagore's penchant for humanistic education, rather, an education that would closely appreciate the dynamics between matter and spirit, finds a *compatriot* in Robert Frost who was apprehensive of humanities losing out in the face of monistic materialism. Both the thinkers combined the poet and the teacher in them and argued for a complex exposition in creativity and pedagogy, a spirit of education built over conversation, through talks outside the formal domains of instructive learning.[98] Knowledge in the Baconian sense cannot be the sole means of empowerment. Education, both believed, had its own moral and aesthetic habit formation, contributing to the transformation of human nature – the nature of the student in particular. Close to Frost's 'education by presence' which denounced strict prescriptions of methodological class lectures and pedagogical stringencies, Tagore was all for infusion of creativity which, again, did not make the business of teaching reckless and misguided. 'Education by presence' evoked expectations among students by urging on the teachers to dilate the horizons of learning and rethink the syllabic aporias of pedagogy. Both the poet-educators demonstrated their anathema for the strangulating formality of education system that was built less on imagination and more on regulative reason. For both, education was poetry.[99]

Inhering in the Kantian questions – 'What can I know? What ought I to do? And for what may I hope?'[100] Tagore's schoolosophy had its own project of cultivating humanity. In the spirit of Socratic teaching and self-criticality, Tagore's educational projects questioned tradition, the complacence of the authoritative given and sought to overcome the deliberation deficit between cultures and traditions.[101] His ethics of teaching was not the terrorizing normativism of colonial cultures of instructions. It was a position without being the limit experience of a subject – a submission to the regulative regime of reality. Tagore sensed the terror of a reality and allowed education to work on a provisional self that encountered the world, the reality, its norms and forms, to develop the agentic individual. The ethics of education is about testing the gap between the given and the taken, the ferment of a Badiouian event that exclaims 'Keep going!'.[102] Faced with the reality and spectre of a dwindling hold over Visva Bharati in the 1930s, Tagore lamented about the ethical struggle to hold on to a 'dream' and the collapse before the consolidated regimes of knowledge in many of his letters. Educational truth cannot afford to lose the truth of the event, the supplement, the surprise and the seduction. In fact, Tagore's major educational projects are agential narratives in fidelity to the consequences and potentialities of event.

Tagore, the hungry artist, agonized over the ruins of learning, was alive with a conscience to rethink and, hence, relive what existed within the colonial machinery. He always encountered an 'alien' – the event of engaging with oneself in a deflatory mode, recognizing failures as points of recompense and rehabilitation. His 'I', on occasions, was his 'other' generating the difficult art of homecoming. Tagore's projects were exhaustive enterprises in homecoming slugged out with the *alien* at various levels of attrition, prejudice and incommensurability. This inhabits the interstitiality of Richard Rorty's 'systematic philosopher' who has 'one set of practices, and see it as the paradigm of human activity' and an 'edifying philosopher' who is reactive to tradition and suspicious of canonical truths. Closer to an edifying philosopher, Tagore desired to keep the conversation in education going, infusing more wonder and wander into educational thinking without denying the historicity of knowledge and the cognitive feats of epistemological clarity.[103] This configured Tagore within an eros of thinking. Eros inspired sharing, passionate coexistence that enlivened all powers of listening – the 'intersubjective vitality' – a sort of 'social climate generated when trust and sharing and participation through dialogue transforms academic work into a fully awake yet contentious enterprise'.[104] Tagore's growing up had its own discipline and restrictions but the aesthetic and emotive dimensions were never ignored, thus, proliferating a steady flow of desires, the eros of self-transcendence. This desire shaped the destiny of his educational vision and all his projects – the school and the university in particular – were signposts of eros, 'the radical of the educational moment, the square root of its power'.[105]

The tension generated by eros in the Tagorean scheme of things can be understood through the notion of 'palintropos harmonie'. It is a 'back-turning harmony' which Heraclitus points out as 'how differing with itself it agrees with itself'. Tagore's educational vision was taut, held in a tension of multiple forces (colonial, anti-colonial, Upanishadic, Vedantic, contemporary, *Tapovan*, etc.) that yanked out of each other and yet maintained a kind of structural solidarity – a bowstring held in tension 'the bow will never settle, for it is precisely in the effort of each element to return to rest that the other element is held tense, that is, it is precisely the frame's attempt to straighten that pulls the string tight, and it is precisely the string's effort to fall slack that will not let the frame stretch to its full relaxed length. The palintropos harmonie is this self-opposition that tenses itself through its very effort to relax, that is, it is a unity that is not capable of settling'.[106] Tagore could seldom settle within a permanent system.

His educational projects inscribed in eros came with a *withness*, a connective transformative richness that reshaped the relationship with our situations and contexts both pedagogically and performatively. Eros forbids living in a habit, developing the urge in the person who has 'seen the light'[107] to go back to the Platonic cave to help others open into a new poetics of becoming. Reaching back to the cave for rehabilitation of the people caught in settled habits of thinking and action is what Tagore's educational eros does. All his projects then were products of inherent tension, construction in and out of himself, palintropos harmonie. Tagore brought a self-sustaining eros that was not merely single minded and obsessive in trying to get what it desired; rather, the telos was a dream, a desiring fulfilment that took on many different shapes and influences beyond the realm of conscious choice and forms of formal impact. He was a positive victim of eros and my book saw its life in aestheticizing the eros.

It would then be almost a 'category mistake' if we were to read Tagore as merely a subcontinental thinker. His wide interdisciplinary interests, extensive travels in Asia, Europe and America and his extraordinary range of intellectual sympathy enabled him to absorb all that he found was essential and significant in Western and Eastern thought. Tagore's 'unbounded cosmopolitanism' combined an 'existential engagement with one's tradition and the constellations of traditions that constitute the world'.[108] Saranindranath Tagore rightly observes that the 'Tagorean conception of rationality does not merely yield postmodern toleration of alterity, but aspires to dissolve instances of otherness altogether by enriching one's own tradition through hermeneutic absorption and assimilation'.[109] Tagore's understanding of reason encouraged 'talks' across cultures and put the local in communication with the global, the home and world coming together into a cross-traffic of enabling discourses of knowledge and ideas. So the developmental philosophy of his educational projects can certainly be read as having deep connections (both epistemically and intra-actively) with the corresponding and congruent developments across countries, primarily in Europe, Tagore's predominant version of the West. His ethics and aesthetics of educational thinking and philosophy demand that he be read in the cross-traffic of traditions, knowledge systems and epistemic commitments. He has left behind a legacy of cross-traditional thinking and remarkable congeries of ideas that have percolated beyond his immediate context and culture of understanding. So reading Tagore now is more about reading Tagore 'with' – in a productive hyphen. My book is about throwing Tagore into the *open*, challenging any school-centric evaluation of his works and ways, critiquing the multiversity of his institutional and informational investments and ensuring that he roundtables his experiments, experiences and emigrations with the thoughts and doings of a riveting and apparently surprising gallery of thinkers. Rewriting Tagore is making him soak up the exhilaration and entropy of being with, a disturbing settlement in the trans-now. In the delightfully frustrating enterprise to wrap him within the conventional ends of a book, Tagore becomes an experience in disquiet. Reading Tagore and knowing him is theft, experiencing him is perversion, revisiting him is illegitimacy and ruin.

Notes

1. Rabindranath Tagore, 'Bharatvarsher itihaser dhara' (The Tradition of Indian History), in *Rabindra Rachanavali*, Vol. 13, (Kolkata: Government of West Bengal, 1990), 491 (Tagore 1990). All translations are mine unless otherwise stated.
2. Rabindranath Tagore, *A Vision of India's History* (Calcutta: Visva Bharati Bookshop, 1951), 13 (Tagore 1951).
3. Tagore, 'Bharatvarsher itihaser dhara', 491 (Tagore 1990).
4. Jitendra Nath Mohanty writes: 'The dictionary *Vācaspatyam* gives the following definition of *itihāsa* (the closest, but not exact, equivalent of "history"): *itahāsa* means "arranged in the form of stories and past happenings, conveying instruction in *dharma, artha, kāma*, and *mokṣa*, i.e. in [the goals of] righteousness, wealth, sensuous love, and spiritual freedom". Kautilya writes that *itihāsa* includes the *purāṇas* (tales of past ages), *itivṛtta* (dynastic chronicles; also accounts of men and times that are past), *ākhyāyikā* (short tales), *udāharaṇa* (exemplary stories), *dharmaśāsrta* (laws) and *arthaśāstra* (political economy). *Itihāsa* and *purāṇa* seem to be identified or at least closely juxtaposed as early as *Bṛhadāraṇyaka Upaniṣad*. An old etymology of the word *itihāsa* is given by Durga's commentary on *Nirukta* ii. **10**: it lets us know "thus it was". The *aitihāsikas* or historians were the traditional story-tellers'. See his *Reason and Tradition in Indian Thought* (New Delhi: Oxford University Press, 1992), 188 (Mohanty 1992).
5. Ibid., 508.
6. Tagore, *A Vision of India's History*, 38–9 (Tagore 1951).
7. Thomas R. Trautmann observes: 'Hegel theorizes the exclusion from history of cosmology, Darwinian biology (Hegel's nature has no evolution, only self-reproduction), the astonishing new finds of historical linguistics (excluded because the changes of language are unconsciously made), the

family (which Hegel thinks is natural and changeless), the working class (because it merely reproduces itself), gender and women, India and even China which, though it has many and extensive histories, lacks the sense of developmental change, according to Hegel, straining every nerve to find a way to exclude the non-West'. See his 'Does India Have History? Does History Have India?' *Comparative Studies in Society and History*, Vol. 54, No. 1 (January 2012), 195 (Trautmann 2012).

8. Amartya Sen, 'Indian Traditions & the Western Imagination', *Daedalus*, Vol. 134, No. 4, (Fall, 2005), 170 (Sen 2005).
9. Ibid., 123. Also see Tagore, 'Bharat-Itihasa-Charcha' in *Rabindra Rachanavali*, Vol. 15, 528. (Tagore 1994)
10. Ibid.
11. Ibid., 124.
12. See Tagore, 'Itihashik Chitra' in *Rabindra Rachanavali*, Vol. 15, 519–20. (Tagore 1994)
13. Rabindranath Tagore, 'Itihasa-katha' in *Rabindra Rachanavali*, Vol. 14, (Kolkata: Government of West Bengal, Saraswati Press Limited, 1992), 453 (Tagore 1992).
14. R. Radhakrishnan, *History, the Human, and the World Between* (Durham: Duke University Press, 2008), 223 (Radhakrishnan 2008).
15. Ibid., 230–31.
16. Ibid.
17. Tagore, 'Aitihāsika kathāsāhitya', 373.
18. Ibid.
19. John P. Sisk, 'The Literary Imagination and the Sense of the Past' *Salmagundi*, No. 68/69 (Fall 1985- Winter 1986), 76 (Sisk 1985/1986).
20. David Quint, '"Alexander the Pig": Shakespeare on History and Poetry', *boundary 2*, Vol. 10, No. 3, (Spring, 1982): 49 (Quint 1982).
21. Robert P. Goldman, 'Historicising the Ramakatha: Valmiki's *Ramayana* and its medieval commentators', *India International Centre Quarterly*, Vol. 31, No. 4, (Spring 2005), 85 (Goldman 2005).
22. See chapter two titled 'Rabindranath Tagore: *Viraha*, the Self's Longing', of Ananya Vajpayi, *Righteous Republic* (Cambridge, MA: Harvard University Press, 2012) (Vajpayi 2012).
23. Simon Schama, *Citizens: A Chronicle of the French Revolution* (London: Viking, 1989), 325 (Schama 1989).
24. W. von Leyden, 'History and the Concept of Relative Time', *History and Theory* 2, No. 3, (1963), 279 (Leyden 1963).
25. Kenneth K. Inada, 'Time and Temporality: A Buddhist Approach', *Philosophy East and West* 24, No. 2, (April, 1974), 172 (Inada 1974).
26. Ibid., 176.
27. Tagore's *A Vision of India's History*, 4 (Tagore 1951).

28. Mark Salber Philips, *On Historical Distance* (New Haven: Yale University Press, 2013), 3. (Philips 2013)
29. Louise Blakeney Williams, 'Overcoming the "Contagion of Mimicry": The Cosmopolitan Nationalism and Modernist History of Rabindranath Tagore and W. B. Yeats', *The American Historical Review*, Vol. 112, No. 1, (Feb., 2007), 90–1 (Williams Feb., 2007); also see her *Modernism and the Ideology of History* (Cambridge: Cambridge University Press, 2002), 120–35 (Williams 2002).
30. I have used Ranajit Guha's excellent translation of Tagore's essay; see Guha, *History at the Limit of World-History*, 97. Italics are mine. (Guha 2002).
31. David Baucher, 'The Creation of the Past: British Idealism and Michael Oakeshott's Philosophy of History', *History and Theory*, Vol. 23, No. 2, (1984), 196. (Baucher 1984)
32. See F. Ankersmit, *Sublime Historical Experience* (Stanford: Stanford University Press, 2005), 257–58. (Ankersmit 2005)
33. Ibid., 336.
34. Ibid., 125.
35. Ibid., 119.
36. Hans Ulrich Gumbrecht, *Production of Presence* (Stanford: Stanford University Press, 2004), 99 (Gumbrecht 2004).
37. Hans Ulrich Gumbrecht, *Our Broad Present: Time and Contemporary Culture* (New York: Columbia University Press, 2014), xi (Gumbrecht 2014).
38. Walter Benjamin, *Selected Writings of Walter Benjamin* (ed.) Howard Eiland & Michael W. Jennings (Cambridge, MA: Harvard University Press, 2003), Vol. 4, 390 (Benjamin 2003).
39. An insight into Nishitani's 'Sunyata and History' explains how Zen notions of history approximate Tagorean ideas of looking into the instant of history as a synthesis of creativity and historical present. Tagore, with the undertow of the Zen views on transhistoricality, has not been supportive of the demythologizing teleological view of history, looking, instead, into the innocence of emergence of things and emotions with a strong understanding of rhythm that human life provides and hides. This is not 'pseudohistory'. For Tagore all history is not interpretation, not eternal recurrence either; there are experiences which demand being left to the realm of imagination, emotion and sensibility. See Steven Heine, 'History, Transhistory, and Narrative History: A Postmodern View of Nishitani's Philosophy of Zen' *Philosophy East and West*, Vol. 24, No. 2, (Apr., 1994), 251–78 (Heine 1994). There is a complicated dialectic between *kal* (past), *kaal* (time) and *aaj-kal* (present/now-past)—*itihasa* in its dialectical and fictive incarnation, in intricate temporality, and as presence and presentification. Raimundo Panikkar notes that 'Adverbs of time, such as yesterday and tomorrow, the day before yesterday and the day after tomorrow, three days before and three days later, are in each

case the same word in Hindi, the essential point being the distance from the center without giving priority to an orientation toward the past or the future'. See 'Toward a Typology of Time and Temporality in the Ancient Indian Tradition,' *Philosophy East and West*, Vol. 24, No. 2, (1974), 162–63 (Inada 1974).

40. Walter Benjamin, *The Arcades Project* (trans.) Howard Eiland and Kevin McLaughlin (Cambridge, MA: Harvard University Press, 1999), 475 (Benjamin 1999b).
41. Benjamin, *The Arcades Project*, 470 (Benjamin 1999b).
42. Tagore's sense of the *itihasa* would carry with it 'a secret index'; like Benjamin he would love to question: 'Does not a breath of the air that pervaded earlier days caresses us as well? In the voices we hear is not there an echo of now silent ones?' See Eli Friedlander, *Walter Benjamin: A Philosophical Portrait* (Cambridge, MA: Harvard University Press, 2012), 196 (Friedlander 2012). Friedlander argues that 'because the image of happiness is so entrenched in the concreteness of one's life, future generations lie outside the space of wishes, expectations and envy. It is because the future is free from intricacies characteristic of present relations in the human world that a different bond between it and its past can be forged. This other bond can be explored insofar as we reverse the perspective and consider not the expectations of the present towards its future but the relation of the present to its past in remembrance' (197) 'Rabindranath' has freed himself from the future and all connect with public history to develop a happiness that does not redeem but merely contributes to his creative suffering, his *viraha* with the presentness of the past – the index of *itihasa* in the *aaj-kal.*
43. Werner Hamacher, 'Now': Walter Benjamin on Historical Time', in *Walter Benjamin and History* (ed.) Andrew Benjamin (London: Continuum, 2005), 41 (Hamacher 2005).
44. Ibid., 52.
45. See Ronald Beiner, 'Walter Benjamin's Philosophy of History', *Political Theory*, Vol. 12, No. 3, (1984), 425–26 (Beiner 1984).
46. Ibid., 427.
47. Ibid., 428.
48. See T. S. Eliot, "Gerontion" in Manju Jain (ed.) *T. S. Eliot: Selected Poems* (Delhi: Oxford University Press, 1992), 24 (Jain 1992).
49. See my *Thinking Literature Across Continents* (Durham: Duke University Press, 2016, with J. Hillis Miller) & *Transcultural Poetics and the Concept of the Poet* (London: Routledge, 2016) (Ghosh 2016).
50. Birgit Mara Kaiser, 'Worlding ComLit: Diffractive Reading with Barad, Glissant and Nancy', *Parallax*, Vol. 20, No. 3, (2014), 276 (Kaiser 2014).
51. See my 'Intra-active Transculturality' *Modern Language Notes*, Vol. 130, No. 5, December 2015 (Johns Hopkins University Press), 1198–1220

(Ghosh August 2015); 'Reading and Experiencing a Play Transculturally' *Comparative Drama*, Vol. 46, No. 3, (Fall 2012), 259–81. (Ghosh 2012)

52. Wai Chee Dimock, 'Theory of Resonance', *PMLA* Vol. 112, No. 5, (1997), 1062. (Dimock 1997)
53. Ibid., 1061.
54. Dimock, 'Deep Time: American Literature and World History', *American Literary History*, Vol. 13, No. 4, (2001), 755 (Dimock 2001).
55. Michel Alhadeff Jones, 'Three Generations of Complexity Theories: Nuances and ambiguities', *Educational Philosophy and Theory*, Vol. 40, No. 1, (2008), 68 (Alhadeff-Jones 2008).
56. Brent Davis, 'Complexity and Education: Vital Simultaneities' *Educational Philosophy and Theory*, Vol. 40, No. 1, (2008), 60 (Davis 2008).
57. A. V. Gaponov-Grekov and M. I. Rabinovich, *Nonlinearities in Action: Oscillations, Chaos Order, Fractals* (Berlin: Springer, 1992), 8 (Gaponov-Grekov and Rabinovich 1992).
58. For more on creativity and fractals see A.J. Crilly & R. A Earnshaw & H. Jones (eds) *Fractals and Chaos* (New York: Springer, 1991) (Crilly et al. 1991).
59. Karen Barad, 'Diffracting Diffraction: Cutting Together-Apart', *Parallax*, Vol. 20, No. 3, (2014), 168 (Barad 2014).
60. Tagore writes, 'The tradition which is helpful is like a channel that helps the current to flow. It is open where the water runs onward, guarding it only where there is danger in deviation. The bee's life in its channel of habit has no opening: it revolves within a narrow circle of perfection. Man's life has time-honoured institutions which are its organised habits. When these act as enclosures, then the result may be perfect, like a bee-hive of wonderful precision of form but unsuitable for the mind which has unlimited possibilities of progress'. See 'Art and Tradition' in *Angel of Surplus* (ed.) Sisirkumar Ghose (Visva Bharati, 1978), 50–1 (Ghose 1978).
61. 'I love India, but my India is an idea and not a geographical expression. Therefore I am not a patriot – I shall forever seek my compatriots all over the world'. Rabindranath Tagore, *Letters to a Friend. Rabindranath Tagore's Letters to C.F. Andrews* (New Delhi, India: Rupa, 2002), 119. (Tagore 2002b).
62. S. Radhakrishnan, *The Philosophy of Rabindranath Tagore* (Baroda: Good Companions Publishers, 1961), 408. (Radhakrishnan 1961)
63. Michel Serres & Bruno Latour, *Conversations on Science, Culture and Time* (trans.) R. Lapidus (Ann Arbor: The University of Michigan Press, 1995), 45. (Serres and Latour 1995).
64. See M. Serres, *Hermes: Literature, Science, Philosophy* (Baltimore: John Hopkins University Press, 1982). (Serres and Latour 1982).
65. Serres & Latour, *Conversations on Science, Culture and Time*, 60 (Serres and Latour 1995).

66. Fritjof Capra, *The Web of Life: A New Scientific Understanding of Living Systems* (New York: Anchor Books Double Day, 1996), 287 (Capra 1996).
67. Serres & Latour, *Conversations on Science, Culture and Time*, 99 (Serres and Latour 1995).
68. Hans-Georg Gadamer, 'Education is Self-Education', *Journal of Philosophy of Education* (November, 2001), 531–33 (Gadamer 2001).
69. Michel Serres, *The Troubadour of Knowledge* (trans.) S. F. Glaser with W. Paulson (Ann Arbor: The University of Michigan Press, 1997), 92–3 (Serres 1997).
70. Maria L. Assad, *Reading with Michel Serres: An Encounter with Time* (Albany: SUNY, 1999), 147 (Assad 1999).
71. Nigel Tubbs, 'Return of the Teacher', *Educational Philosophy and Theory*, Vol. 35, No. 1, (2003), 77 (Tubbs 2003).
72. Suresh Chandra Ghosh, *The History of Education in Modern India (1757–2007)* (Hyderabad: Orient Blackswan, 2010), 107 (Ghosh 2010). For the other side of the scenario primarily on Indian Educational Service see Clive Whitehead, *Colonial Educators: The British Indian and Colonial Education Service 1858–1983* (London: I.B. Tauris, 2003). (Whitehead 2003)
73. *Rabindra Rachanavali*, Vol. 14, 322.
74. See his 'Siksha Samskar' (322). Tagore points out that such acts of retaining educated Bengalees in the government-formed senate and syndicate does not necessarily devolve the power on the natives to run their own show. The government needs to account before the people rather than answer the demands of a mere clutch of educated Indians. Tagore laments how Indians have been responsible themselves to ensure the downslide of education where access to education is only about ensuring a job and completely oblivious to its potential in the formation of humanity and humaneness (322). If education since the first day that a child goes to school is not directed to such an end, Tagore fears our extinction is certain – we shall desiccate in mind, material, character and culture.
75. Jnanendranath Chattopadhyay, 'Rabindranath and his Asrama School', *The Visva-Bharati Quarterly* (May–October), 1947, 10 (Chattopadhyay 1947).
76. Quoted in Sanjay Seth, *Subject Lessons* (Durham: Duke University Press, 2007), 163 (Seth 2007).
77. Ibid., 165.
78. Nita Kumar, 'The Educational Efforts of Rabindranath Tagore', *Journal of Contemporary Thought*, Vol. 34, (Winter 2011), 122–23. (Kumar 2011)
79. Mukherjee, *Education For Fullness*, 52.
80. 'Sikshabidhi' *Rabindra Rachanavali*, 363.
81. Uma Das Gupta writes: 'Santiniketan was discovered as a lonely spot in the early 1860s by Rabindranath's father who was travelling in the area to visit a friend and fellow landlord of the Sinha family of Raipur in the district of

Birbhum in southern Bengal. Moved by the peace of the empty countryside dotted only by some tall palm trees, Debendranath bought some land there and built a guest house on it in 1863. Debendranath named the house Santiniketan, meaning an abode of peace. The place then took its name from the house'. Uma Das Gupta, *Rabindranath Tagore: An Illustrated Life* (New Delhi: Oxford University Press, 2013), 63. (Das Gupta 2013)

82. 'Éxperimentum Scholae: The World Once More . . . But Not (Yet) Finished' in *Making Sense of Education* (ed.) G. J. J. Biesta (Springer, 2012), 105. (Masschelein 2012)
83. 'Spaceship', (trans.) Rosemary Arnoux in *Education and the Postmodern Condition* (ed.) Michael Peters (Westport: Bergin & Garvey, 1995), xix. (Lyotard 1995)
84. Ibid., xx.
85. The word education is derived from two Latin words. 'The first one is *educare* (*educo, educare, educavi, educatum*), a first conjugation verb, meaning "to bring up", "to rear", "to guide", "to direct", "to educate". The second Latin word from which education derived is educere (*educo, educere, eduxi, eductum*), a third conjugation verb, meaning "to draw out", "to lead out", "to raise up", "to bring up", or "rear a child" '. See Michael B Adeyemi & Augustus A. Adeyinka, 'Some Keys Issues in African Traditional Education', *McGill Journal of Education*, Vol. 37, No. 2, (Spring 2002), 225. (Adeyemi and Adeyinka 2002)
86. See Henry J. Perkinson, *Learning from Our Mistakes: A Reinterpretation of Twentieth-Century Educational Theory* (Westport: Greenwood Press, 1984) 3 (Perkinson 1984).
87. John Dewey, *Experience and Education* (West Lafayette: Kappa Delta Pi, 1998), 92, 19. (Dewey 1998)
88. See Terry Hoy, *The Political Philosophy of John Dewey: Towards a Constructive Renewal* (Westport: Praeger Publishers, 1998), 58 (Hoy 1998). Italics are mine.
89. Ibid., 63.
90. R. G. Collingwood, *The Idea of History* (Oxford: Clarendon Press, 1993), 292. (Collingwood 1993)
91. R. G. Collingwood, *Speculum Mentis* (Oxford: Clarendon Press, 1924), 316. (Collingwood 1924)
92. Matthew Lipman, *Philosophy Goes to School* (Philadelphia: Temple University Press, 1988), 4. (Lipman 1988)
93. Gilbert Ryle, *The Concept of Mind* (London: Hutchinson, 1949). (Ryle 1949)
94. I. Murdoch, *Metaphysics as a Guide to Morals.* (New York: Penguin, 1992), 179. (Murdoch 1992)
95. See William James, *Talks to Teachers* (New York: Norton, 1958). (James 1958)

96. William James, *The Principles of Psychology* (New York: Dover, 1950), 480. (James 1950)
97. *Education and Sociology* (trans.) S. D. Fox (Glencoe: The Free Press, 1961), 71. (Durkheim 1961b)
98. As Louis Untermeyer observed: 'Frost was almost as preoccupied with teaching as he was with creating. As a teacher he dwelt almost entirely upon the creative impulse'. *Robert Frost: A Backward Look* (Washington, D.C.: Reference Department, The Library of Congress, 1964), 22 (Untermeyer 1964). For more on Frost's emphasis on conversation see Louis Mertins, *Robert Frost: Life and Talks-Walking* (Norman: University of Oklahoma Press, 1965).
99. Jonathan N. Barron (ed.) *Roads Not Taken: Rereading Robert Frost* (Columbia: University of Missouri Press, 2000), 88 (Barron 2000). Earl J. Wilcox writes: 'Frost was very fond of Mark Twain's short story "The Celebrated Jumping Frog of Calaveras County", both for its lyrical qualities as a prose narrative and for its essential theme. He interpreted the story as "a great parable in education" '. 35 When the frog was trained and sensitized to jump with only a featherlike prod in his rear, he outjumped all rival frogs set against him. But when the city slicker, who bet against his owner, secretly slipped a handful of buckshot pellets into the champion frog, even strong and persistent prods could not budge him, and very ordinary frogs were able to outjump him. Frost explained that before the frog was filled with buckshot he was 'like a poet... a free spirit' who had assimilated only as much knowledge as was needed to give him strength to jump far. But after swallowing the buckshot pellets the frog 'became a scholar... weighted down and ponderous with useless knowledge, and unable to jump'. Frost's own prototype of a ponderous professor was Dr. Magoon, in 'A Hundred Collars', a satirical portrait of a deadly introverted nervous academic who was rather too fond of calling himself 'Doctor'. When he is forced to share a hotel room with a half-literate French Canadian bill collector named 'Lafe', who mistakes him for a medical doctor, Magoon corrects him by saying, 'Well, a teacher'. Frost was favourably oriented to sound scholarship, but he despised academic affectation (91)'.
100. Immanuel Kant, *Critique of Pure Reason* (London: Macmillan, 1978), para. 805 (Kant 1978). Also see 'Purbaproshner Anubriti', in *Rabindra Rachanavali*, 451.
101. Martha Nussbaum, *Cultivating Humanity* (Cambridge, MA: Harvard University Press, 1997) (Nussbaum 1997); see Chapter Two 'Socratic Self-Examination' and Chapter Three 'Narrative Imagination', 50–112 from this book for greater elaboration.
102. Alain Badiou, *Ethics: An Essay on the Understanding of Evil* (trans.) P. Hallward (New York: Verso Press, 2001), 79. (Badiou 2001)

103. Richard Rorty, *Philosophy and the Mirror of Nature* (Princeton: Princeton University Press, 1979), 367–68. (Rorty 1979)
104. K. Burch, *Eros as the Educational Principle of Democracy* (New York: Peter Lang Publishers, 2000), 180. (Burch 2000)
105. Ibid., 2.
106. John Edward Russon, 'Erôs and Education: Plato's Transformative Epistemology', *Laval théologique et philosophique*, Vol. 56, No. 1, (2000), 114. (Russon 2000)
107. Ibid., 124.
108. Saranindranath Tagore, 'Tagore's Conception of Cosmopolitanism: A Reconstruction', *University of Toronto Quarterly*, Vol. 77, No. 4, (2008), 1081. (Tagore 2008).
109. Ibid., 1078.

CHAPTER 2

No Schoolmaster: Aesthetic Education and Paedosophy

'By the bank of the river Padma, in Shilaidaha, I lived a quiet life amidst my literary pursuits', writes Tagore. 'With a mission to create I came to Santiniketan'.[1] It was a sublime mission in that it endeavoured to realize an 'ambition' which largely knew the immense difficulties it had to encounter and yet which ceaselessly inspired him to turn an ashram into a school woven around with fresh ideals of education and a distinct aesthetics of pedagogy. This sublimity worked on the aesthetics of splendid waste, as opposed to the cringing pressures of economic gain, social prosperity and cultural recognition. The creative burst, its energy, which triggered the poet's dislocation, was the delightful 'irresponsibility' of the butterfly. Tagore writes, 'The silkworm seems to have a cash value credited in its favour somewhere in Nature's accounting department . . . but the butterfly is *irresponsible*. The significance which it may possess has neither weight nor use and is lightly carried on its pair of dancing wings. Perhaps it pleases someone in the heart of the sunlight, the Lord of colours, who has nothing to do with account books and has a perfect mastery in the great art of *wastefulness*'.[2] So the ashram-school was set up by courting values which could not have discounted the butterfly (the ideal, what is conventionally understood as impractical)[3] against the silkworm (*utilitas* and *potentia*). When Tagore brought together a few boys 'one sunny day in winter, among the warm shadows of the tall straight *sal* trees with their branches of quiet dignity, he started to write a poem in a medium not of

R. Ghosh, *Aesthetics, Politics, Pedagogy and Tagore*,
Palgrave Studies in Education and Transculturalism,
DOI 10.1057/978-1-137-48026-2_2

words'. Seeking to exorcise the phantom of his boyhood experiences in school where he was briefly enrolled, the poet sought to 'live in the lives of other boys, and to build its missing paradise with ingredients which may not have any orthodox material, prescribed measure, or standard value'.[4] He wanted a school away from the turmoil of human habitation which would be the site for 'quiet studies and teaching'; here his pupils would 'grow up in the sacred and profound atmosphere of learning' – a school inaugurated with five students and five teachers (interestingly, much to the chagrin of Hindu orthodoxists, among the five teachers Tagore recruited, three were Christians – two of whom were Catholics and the third his son's English teacher from Shilaidaha) with the ambition that 'man could become truly human by responding creatively and sympathetically to his environment'.[5] Tagore was perfectly committed to building a school that would be 'situated in a quiet spot far from the crowded city' having the 'natural advantages of open sky, fields, trees and the like. It should be a retreat where teachers and students would live dedicated to learning'.[6] Can the aesthetics of education be configured within the connections built between 'open sky, fields and trees' and a 'profound atmosphere of learning'? What kind of space did his ashram-school grow into by working on the potent network between 'becoming human', creativity and sympathy towards environment? And what was its lifeworld?

Presence Pedagogy

In 'A Poet's School', Tagore observes:

> In our highly complex modern conditions, mechanical forces are organized with such efficiency that the materials produced grow far in advance of man's capacity to select and assimilate them to suit his nature and needs. Such an overgrowth, like the rank vegetation of the tropics, creates confinement for man. *The nest is simple.* It has an easy relationship with the sky; the cage is complex and costly, it is too much itself, excommunicating whatever lies outside. And modern man is busy building his cage. He is always occupied in adapting himself to its dead angularities, limiting himself to its limitations, and so he becomes a part of it.[7]

The spectre of the 'encaging' predatory techno-infiltration left Tagore worried as he tried to find a way out for his school and the atmosphere that it promised to generate. This concern approximates Martin Heidegger's anxiety: 'No one can foresee the radical changes to come. But the technological advance will move faster and faster and can never be stopped. In all areas of his existence, man will be encircled ever more tightly by the forces of technology. These forces . . . since man has not made them, have moved long since beyond his will and have outgrown his capacity for decision'.[8] Through what Heidegger calls the 'technological way of revealing', humans, thus, have lost all claims to a 'simple nest'. The 'dead angularities' to which humans adapt is a sort of surrender of lives at source to an authoritarian system, that, in the words of Lewis Mumford, 'gives back as much of it as can be mechanically graded, quantitatively multiplied, scientifically sorted, technically conditioned, manipulated, directed, and socially distributed under supervision of a centralized bureaucracy'. The lure of 'automated superfluity' dehumanizes techno-loaded Mumfordian machine-addicts who are ready to relinquish 'their prerogatives as living beings: *the right to be alive*'.[9] Conscious of the right to be alive, Tagore ensured that his ashram-school allowed a life far removed from the pentagon of power – inspiring other possibilities of 'revealing'. However, Tagore, like Heidegger, did not harbour any hardened prejudice towards technology's non-aggressive benevolence. He accepted machines and yet urged men to understand the life that machines cannot deliver; our thoughts and imagination need not cease to function after we had spoken our last words with the machines.[10]

Tagore observed that the 'glorious march of cement-concrete' civilization in India did not begin in the city but grew out of the forest. Humans have not jostled and lumped themselves together to help create this growth. It happened because of the ways by which humans decided to conjoin with nature around them – not in fearful and perspiring congestion but through spaces that were both open and crowded. This openness, this decongestion, he argued, kindled the consciousness of India and prevented her soul from being a congealed immobile entity.[11] Tagore found an 'energy' in the forest – the cult of *tapovan* – which was dominantly independent and internal in its inception and dissemination. This was the energy that had not grown through extrinsic forces born out of necessity, contesting contingencies and overpowering centripetal material persuasions. This immense, immanent, immutable energy was a 'quiet power' that infused the spirit of the world; it was a power in solitude that, on most occasions, emerged in meditation. Tagore writes:

> the sub-conscious remembrance of some primeval dwelling place, where in our ancestors' minds were figured and voiced the mysteries of the inarticulate

> rocks, the rushing water and the dark whispers of the forest, was constantly stirring my blood with its call. (Some living memory in me seemed to ache for the playground it had once shared with the primal life in the *illimitable magic of land, water and air.*) The thin shrill cry of the high-flying kite in the blazing sun of a dazed Indian midday sent to a solitary boy the signal of a dumb distant kinship. The few coconut palms growing by the boundary wall of our house, like some war captives from an older army of invaders of this earth, spoke to me of the eternal companionship which the great brotherhood of trees have ever offered to man.[12]

This vital 'kinship' with nature determined the temper of the ashram and its enviable communitarian space. In 'Ashramer Siksha' Tagore makes an interesting point:

> Once I was a guest in the house of a Japanese friend. My host was a gardening enthusiast. He used to say: I love trees and plants. The power of my love enters into their being and comes out in the form of fruits and flowers. It goes without saying that his words are particularly apt for the gardener who has to look after the tender young shoots of the human soul. When one mind meets another in perfect harmony, the outcome is spontaneous joy. This joy is instinct with creative energy. Education in an ashram is the gift of this bounteous joy.[13]

This interdependence, this unconstrained relationship between the teacher and the taught, spoke of the core of ashram education where man, nature and the greater spirit were threaded together in 'joy' (Tagore writes, 'The gifts of nature, unconsciously, build the human race').[14] Education in the ashram was 'education for life at its fullest'. In a letter (9 May 1922) written to Patrick Geddes, Tagore pointed out:

> I merely started with this one simple idea, that education should never be dissociated from life. I had no experience of teaching, no special gift for organisation; and therefore I had no plan which I could put before the public in order to win their confidence. . . . I began anyhow. All that I could do was to offer to the five little boys who were my first students my company. I talked and sang to them, played with them, recited to them our epics improvised stories specially given to them by evening, took them on excursions into neighbouring villages. . . . we are fully aware of the absolute necessity of widening, across all barriers, the *human sympathies* of our students, – thus leading them to the fulfilment of their Education.[15]

Tagore made children realize that education was 'a permanent part of the adventure of life' and not 'like a painful hospital treatment for curing them of the congenital malady of their ignorance'; it was 'a function of health, the natural expression of their mind's vitality'.[16] Endowed by a 'curiosity' to establish 'contact with their immediate environment', students and teachers sought for worlds beyond the textbooks and desired to find 'joy' in direct experiences – a 'joy' that was creative. Tagore pointed out the importance of the child growing in soul and body through freedom and joy because going against nature would surely have its indisputable fall outs. Suffering must come from 'freedom' – it was the new politics under the spell of which the ashram had incepted and flourished – and never from imprisonment conducted under the sign of education.[17] The ashram-school grew an 'atmosphere' (a significant word in Tagore's philosophical vocabulary) which was responsive to 'colour, perfume, music and movement'.[18] Tagore complained that 'in his society man has about himself a diffuse atmosphere of culture. It keeps his mind sensitive to his racial inheritance, to the current of influences that come from tradition; it enables him to imbibe unconsciously the concentrated wisdom of ages. But in our educational organisations we behave like miners, digging only for things and not like the tillers of the earth whose work is a perfect collaboration with nature'.[19]

The 'green space' of the ashram fostered a 'teaching relationship' that kept the dynamics of human condition and its collaterality with nature firmly in place. It thrived in a dialectic of communication and conformity. The teacher, the taught and nature were caught in non-hierarchical gestaltic games of 'mutual domination' and 'interchangeable supremacy' involving imagination, empathy and tolerance. This could be argued as the deconstructed site of suffering that informed inter-species value generation, where teaching was not monological instruction in a power differential but a collective aggrandizement where no member of the suffering team survived and buoyed at the expense of the other – the *egregore*, the precipitation, which had its material advancement both at the level of the body, mind and milieu and at the level which was beyond the scope of teaching.[20] In fact, the beyondness in formal text-based pedagogy leaves us within the philosophy of 'presence'. This might urge us to rethink the connection that Tagore wanted to experience outside the academic meanability of experiences.

What did Tagore mean when he pointed out the 'signal of a dumb distant kinship' that a solitary boy in a 'dazed Indian midday' grows with the thin shrill cry of the high-flying kite in the blazing sun'? Is experience in pedagogy strictly subservient to textual meaning or do experiences outside the domain of ceaseless meaning effects contribute to experiential richness? Willie Pearson recorded an incident during one of his class lectures conducted under a tree (this practice continues to this day)[21] when a boy drew his attention to the song of a bird. 'I am quite sure,' he commented, 'that my class learnt more from that bird than it had ever done from my teaching and something that they would never forget in life. For myself, my ears were opened, and for several days I was conscious of the songs of the birds as I had never seen before'.[22] What did the class learn from the bird's song? How could learning go beyond formal teaching?

Thinking non-dualistically through the body and the mind is always an *achievement* – a mode of being that involves embodied meditation of the world and its consequent intellection. This is about psychophysically knowing a truth of education where, for instance, the act of knowing by the ear (song of the bird) is connected with refigurations of mentalization (achieved through a distinct experience of learning). So the lived body or the feeling body never becomes the whole because, as Jean-Luc Nancy argues, the parts of the 'corpus do not combine into a whole, are not means to it or ends of it. Each part can suddenly take over the whole, can spread out over it, can become it, the whole – that never takes place. There is no whole, no totality of the body – but its absolute separation and sharing'.[23] As a part of the corpus, the ear takes over the whole of a 'feeling and receptive body' generating a surplus of understanding that is difficult to explicate. The education for life at its fullest cannot be experienced simply within a system because without the surplus – in cogitation, in acts, in cognition – the 'fullest' can never be a realistic telos to achieve. By 'listening' to the same event, the body of the boy shared his experiences with other fellow bodies to produce a 'beyond the body' realm of experience. Education in the ashram was built on a complexity inscribed in metapsychics[24] – an intricate non-Cartesian system which ensured that physicality of learning was closely integrated with the development and intervention of the mind. Not disharmonious with each other, this ensemble of the body-mind generated the 'play drive' (in the words of Schiller) that challenged the dualist infrastructure of thought and feeling. Education in the ashram encouraged this difficult 'art' where the self of a student became an aesthetic subject, subjected to a variety of forces at once somatic and psychic.

The psychophysical mode of reading – learning being transgressive in its directness of somatic experiences and dialectical ways of intellection – is about, as Hans Ulrich Gumbretch argues, reading books and reading the world and not simply meaning attribution. Gumbretch observes that 'it is the never-ending movement, the both joyful and painful movement between losing and regaining intellectual control and orientation, that can occur in the confrontation with (almost?) any cultural object as long as it occurs under conditions of low time pressure, that is, with no "solution" or "answer" immediately expected. This is exactly the movement that we are referring to when we say that a class or a seminar "broadened" our minds'.[25] Experienced somaesthetically, this helps in the thriving of the mind. It is interesting to record Werther's experiences while walking the wood where the whir and buzz of the little gnats, tremulous rays of the sun, beetles springing out of the grass, the 'moss wresting its nourishment out of the hard rock' configure an experience that defies all Cartesian modes of analysis.[26] Tagore who believed that 'imprisonment' was the 'best way of making children confirmed criminals' wanted all education to be peripatetic – an engagement with the physicality of learning by releasing children from the confinement of 'same benches, chairs, walls, buildings, globes and kinds of games'. Tagore advocated that 'let them know other games'.[27] Gumbretch argues further that 'rather than having to think, always and endlessly, what else there could be, we sometimes seem to connect with a layer in our existence that simply wants the things of the world close to our skin'.[28] The closeness of the experience of the world to our skin helps us to avoid our compelling status as 'intercourse beings'.[29] The nakedness of skin is textured with deep social insertions that forget the psychophysical experiential directness of things under the influence of social encrustations and habitus of being and performing; these are much opposed to the vitality of connection with the world around. The consequent disability leaves one close to being a discursive being and not an embodied individual for whom 'broadening the mind' is not about gathering knowledge but surely about a fullness of experience. In trying then to grow an intense 'connect' with nature and objects, Tagore looked into the possibilities of 'intense joy' generated through efforts to discover a layer of existence beyond the mere cultural and material values of things – experiencing the 'things of the world in their preconceptual thingness'.[30] In his school, Tagore sought to introduce 'sparks' emerging from the mundane and the ordinary into ways of teaching and understanding – the amazement which moments of surplus could bring through a closeness with the everyday. This is Cezanne-like in that Tagore saw pedagogy as drawing upon the experience of a moment much in the same way Paul Cezanne desired to live in a 'minute' and 'become that minute'.[31] In such 'presences', Tagore wanted an alternative atmosphere of 'aesthetic intensity', such 'spots of time' (in the words of Wordsworth) within a non-Cartesian and pre-discursive 'presence pedagogy'.

The integration of the laws of nature (both its meaning effects and presence effects) and the laws of humans (in this case the inmates of the school) operated on 'possibilities' (something that Tagore liked to see as 'surprise', 'wonder', 'excitement', 'mysteries') beyond the exhaustion that technology provided. Indeed, heartless technological dominance and the growing rationalization and intellectualization had taken the wonder and mystery out of our lives and civilizational ways. Tagore saw a rift being opened up between the individual and the world – a Simmelian tragedy of culture – where the subject–object dualism worked on an internal logic of development that did not inspire a return to 'totality' or harmonic completeness. The 'disenchantment' that both Georg Simmel and Max Weber talked about was something that also disturbed Tagore.[32] Privileging the 'dispersion of mind' over 'concentration of mind', Tagore prepared the children for a 'real home-coming into this world'.[33]

The Child Question(s)

Working within the dialectics of fact and value, presence pedagogy submits to a different level of ethical understanding where a child's question, a child's wonder and curiosity are not always in apposition with adult explanation and rationalization. Pedagogy often refuses to see the meaning in the inconceivable – the relation that children might have with things around them or with nature – because the notions of facts in the adult consciousness cannot configure or appreciate the values with which children approach the reality that meets them. Tagore interrogated the compelling nexus between fact and value in education. Refiguring the post-intrusive school, he considered the existence of contradictions and multiplicity in the children as necessary elements towards the development of their 'inner' realities – the chaos, thanatos and the eros. D. H. Lawrence, in *Fantasia of the Unconscious*, rightly observes that 'A child will ask "why" often enough. But he more often asks why the sun shines, or why men have moustaches, or why grass is green, than anything sensible. Most of a child's questions are, and should be unanswerable. They are not questions at all.

They are exclamations of wonder, they are remarks, half-sceptically addressed. When a child says, "Why is grass green", he half implies, "Is it really green, or is it just taking me in?" And we solemnly begin to prate about chlorophyll'.[34] The truth of the chlorophyll is not the truth of the child's factual wonder. There is somewhere a presence value attached to the fact of the grass being green before him; this value transcends the apparent rigour of the fact and unconceals the inspiration that initially inaugurated the search for meaning. The hunt for meaning in the 'grass as green' resulted in the fact of the chlorophyll; however, the search based on the child's ways of seeing nature and his surroundings expire in a combination of both presence and meaning and fact and value conducted at various registers of experience. The green ceases to be monochromatic and becomes more colourful through the child's engagement with the grass – a reality redefined and values newly experienced.

Do such persistent 'whys' from children affect the understanding of science? Tagore disagrees. In his school, he associated science with curiosity and wonder – an orientation of learning that he believed did not necessarily have to be undergirded with reason, rationality, limits of precision and the live wire of clarity. Science for Tagore's children was not Matthew Arnold's insistent claim that it must be taught through the blackboard alone. It was more close to what John Ruskin meant when he wanted a child to 'assuredly learn the elements of Geometry, but she should at first call it "Earth-measuring" and have her early lessons in it in laying out her own garden'.[35] A well-known former student of Tagore's school (Patha Bhavan), Supriyo Thakur, who went on to become the school's principal, recounts his science lessons by pointing out how 'education of the senses' was essential to all kinds of pedagogy. Inspired to learn from nature, children roamed the ashram to observe plants and trees, learning their names, finding out the hour of flowering and fruiting and educating themselves about the time of the fall of leaves and consequent denudation. Whether it be the distance between things or places or weight of an object, children were first taught to guess out the measurement and then 'playfully' encouraged to use the measuring tape to find how precise they had speculatively got. Thakur observes that 'science was indeed so lively'.[36] This further approximates what young Wilfred Owen while teaching in an elementary school wrote to his mother in January 1913: 'Teachers in colleges talk of studying a child. And they go about it with moral microscopes in their eyes and forceps in their fingers. Not the way at all children are not meant to be studied but enjoyed. Only by studying to be pleased do we understand them'.[37] Tagore observes that children:

> have their active sub-conscious mind which, like the tree, has the power to gather its food from the surrounding atmosphere. For them the *atmosphere* is a great deal more important than rules and methods, building appliances, class teachings and text books. The earth has her mass of substance in her land and water. But, if I may be allowed figurative language, she finds her inspiration of freedom, the stimulation of her life, from her atmosphere. It is, as it were, the envelopment of her perpetual education. It brings from her depth responses in colours and perfume, music and movement, her incessant self-revelation, continual *wonders* of the unexpected.[38]

Within the 'atmosphere' of the ashram the surplus in the child had its own desire and reason. This surplus is generated through an *aionic* growth where childhood, as Walter Kohan has argued, seems 'to be a possibility, a strength, a force, an intensity, rather than a period of time'.[39] Tagore saw in the 'atmosphere' (he specifically uses this word as a qualifier of his school's potential) of the ashram a 'play' – moments of ecstasy (*ex-stase*) – in the conjuration of *basileus* (realm) which eluded *chronos* (the continuity of successive time). *Basileus* was both his ashram and the atmosphere that he tried to develop. Tagore believed that childhood was not always a period of time conceived as preparation for adulthood. It had its own 'play' outside the chronic time into the *aion* which was 'just one singing, speaking, breathing world'. This resulted in a specific experience of life which was unteachable and stayed untutored. Kohan notes appropriately that 'childhood might be a kind of experience where questioning opens experience to the not-experienced, thinking to the not-thought, life to the not-lived'.[40] Indeed, Tagore became a child-like questioner in that his questions as to the working of the ashram had, at times, the wonder, unreason and desire with which the child chose to transform the adult world. A 'good' child was one who did not have any significant questions. Tagore was the 'bad child' whose questions destabilized the adult world and made the adult feel, without any superiority, the difference it had from the world of the child. Tagore, deeply opposed to the Aristotlean or Platonian ways of looking at a child[41] where he was qualified as subspeciation (Latin. *infans*, or *qui fari non potest*, 'who cannot speak'), thus, identified a moral agency – a happy capacity to make choices – in the space that was provided to the ashramites. The commonly prevalent

Erasmusian urgency in the adult to 'instruct' and 'mould' the child was alien to Tagore for whom a child was never the 'unproductive brute' obligated to a 'process of intensive instruction'.[42] Children, at his school, were never elements of coercive and telic transformation, but possibilities and projections that enjoyed an ontological privilege of existence in instincts, desire, in the conscious and the unconscious, in the ego and its metamorphosis. He believed that children brought up in disciplinary technologies were never allowed to dialogue with their parents for they carried parental projections in their growth conducted within structures of learning that were strict and non-liberatory.[43]

The child knows what the adult does not (speaking about schoolmasters, Tagore observes that a typical schoolmaster 'does not understand that the adult mind is many respects not only differs from, but is contrary to, the child mind'[44]). Tagore knew that he stood to gain a lot out of an intensive interface with the children of his school: he was certain that the wonderful productive exchanges, most often built on the liminality of their relationship, would benefit the 'atmosphere' of the school in every way. Tagore persistently questioned the limit conditions of the children – looked at with unitary interest, the child was an unfinished organismic being which was neither wholly a post-adult utopia nor eminently an integrative preparation to adulthood – and the life work of the school through a transrational intersubjective system. Institutions cannot be mechanisms to develop, as John Dewey has argued, 'a docility to repeat and conform'. Tagore writes:

> There is no room for surprises in the schoolroom, only the perfect symmetry which can be of non-life. Every morning, exactly on the stroke of the clock, the pupil must attend school, must come to a particular class, to hear the same subject taught by the same teacher of forbidding aspect. Exactly at a particular hour he finds his freedom. The holidays are all on the calendar long beforehand, and everything is mechanically accurate and perfect.[45]

Tagore then was deeply opposed to the one-dimensional growth of the ashramites that society and its forces usually sought to execute through the disjuncture between habit and thought, action and soul. This dualism, as Dewey observes, enables social monopolists to 'do the thinking and planning, while others remain the docile, even if awkward, instruments of execution'.[46] The child, thus, to Tagore, was not Edenic or a product of romantic genius but, a wonder – a self-inventive enthusiasm – that kept on discovering itself as it transited to the socially denominated period termed 'adulthood'.

In this context, William Godwin's mode of laying emphasis on child education forms an intra-active correspondence with Tagore. Godwin's statement that 'the true object of education, like that of every other moral process, is the generation of happiness'[47] approximates the ethics of the ashram. Caught between Locke and Rousseau, Godwin tried to wrestle out a premise that viewed the child's mind as the 'empire of impression'.[48] The mind is indeed a terrain that requires fine preparation. It cannot be a deposition ground of knowledge but a repository of 'real contents', interesting and imaginative – the mind of the child seen not as a 'white paper, as a piece of wax, to be moulded and fashioned', but as an active, reflecting individual. The teacher for him ceased to be a mere schoolmaster with a 'torpedo effect'. A similar crisis can be traced in Tagore's restlessness to fashion the balance between 'careful education' which assumes, to an extent, that a child's mind has a peculiar ductility – not something as wholly pregiven and preoriginary – and the need for instruction. Nothing for the child can be a habit; the child comes evidently with certain traits in him or her before care and concern help grow certain things leading to a harmonic development. Godwin notes:

> It is of less importance, generally speaking, that a child should acquire this or that species of knowledge, than that, through the medium of instruction, he should acquire habits of intellectual activity. It is not so much for the direct consideration of what he learns, that his mind must not be suffered to lie idle. The preceptor in this respect is like the incloser of uncultivated land.... In a word, the first lesson of a judicious education is, learn to think, to discriminate, to remember and to enquire.[49]

This again comes diffractively close to what Leo Tolstoy suggests in his discussion on the 'curriculum'. For Tolstoy, curriculum needed to be a response to questions posed by life: questions that spring not from issues which schools pedagogically repeat with uniformity but arise from the intellect of the child and also the events which usually schools ignore in *mechaniser l'instruction*. Tolstoy's words are a kind of attestation of Tagore considering his ashram-school an educational laboratory:

> The compulsory structure of the school excludes the possibility of all progress. And yet when we consider how many centuries have passed in

answering the children's questions – questions it did not occur to them to ask – and how far the present generations have departed from that ancient form of culture with which they are inoculated, it becomes incomprehensible to us how it is that these schools still exist. School, so it would appear to us, ought to be an implement of education and at the same time an experiment involving the young generation, constantly giving new results. Only when experiment is the foundation of school – only when every school will be, so to speak, a pedagogical laboratory – will school not fall behind universal progress, and will experiment be able to lay firm foundations for the science of education.[50]

Was ashram-school an 'experimental school', something that Johann Heinrich Pestalozzi had in mind while writing *Views and Experience*? Even Kant in his *Lectures Upon Pedagogy* (1803)[51] emphasized the need for setting up such schools before 'normal schools' could come up. Pestalozzi saw the need for experiment and the value of experience: setting a project up with mere reason might prove a mistake because experience can teach us lessons contrary to what we hoped at the point of inauguration. So perhaps there cannot be a model school. Both Pestalozzi and Kant disapproved the idea of the 'model school'. Tagore did not consider the school he built as not 'normal': for him, it was a way of learning – experimental and 'normal' at the same time – and not an experiment awaiting graduation to the next stage of normality. He never suggested modelizing his ashram for posterity. Both Tagore and Tolstoy combined experimentalism and the acquisition of experience in the working out of aesthetic education in their schools: a sensitive inquiry into an examination of the demands of the child in processes of learning and emotional and intellectual maturity. Mistakes and necessity contribute to the experimentations of learning experiences. Tagore's students were made to rethink situations, encounter crises, without being instructed about ways to exit trouble. In *The Absorbent Mind*, Maria Montessori writes:

Supposing we study the phenomenon of error in itself; it becomes apparent that everyone makes mistakes. This is one of life's realities, and to admit it is already to have taken a great step forward. If we are to tread the narrow path of truth and keep our hold upon reality, we have to agree that all of us can err; otherwise, we should all be perfect. So, it is well to cultivate a friendly feeling toward error, to treat it as a companion inseparable from our lives, as something having a purpose, which it truly has.... Whichever way we look, a certain 'Mr. Error' is always to be seen! If we seek perfection, we must pay

> attention to our own defects, for it is only by correcting these that we can improve ourselves.[52]

But the freedom emerging out of mistakes of the kind Montessori speaks about has less to do with experiment and innovation. Though not a strict theorist, Montessori's instructions in a cultish atmosphere have not been amenable to any change since they were formulated more than a hundred years ago. Very different from Montessori though the governance in the ashram looked at the teacher as 'directress' who supplied 'desired help' by waiting upon the students to grow with freedom and intelligence.[53] Tagore's ashram-school, importantly, was not a kindergarten in line with what Froebel, Pestalozzi, Minna Shelhorn and Adolph Diesterweg advocated; rather, it came very close to the sign that Tolstoy hung from the door of his school: *Enter and Live Freely*. What was this nature of freedom within the bounds of permissive pedagogy?

Tagore looked into discovering the 'soul' above the strains of learning a syllabus, into the cultivation of a life force which while accepting opposition and dialectical growth refused to flourish within the template of a 'factory'.[54] He was more keen on building a 'culture' than making his pupils learn the trick of passing exams, disciplinizing themselves into covering a certain syllabus and thinking about the advantage that such an education could bring in getting them gainful employment. This culture did not always come with a set standard of values and codes endorsed through coercive means of execution: not always a clear guide for activities or performances of students which got wrapped on both ends by the violation-punishment principles. The culture spoke of independence: a freedom to think and wish beyond a pedagogical dependence on their educators. This was where the guru (Tagore has mentioned Satish Chandra Roy and Ajit Chakraborty as the great ashram-teachers)[55] vitalized the connection between life and pedagogy and explored the joy between knowledge and learning, leading to self-respect, self-restraint and powers of integration and peace. The guru cannot be wholly subordinated to a method because education is about man learning better from man; just as a water tank can be filled only by water and fire can be kindled with fire, so life, Tagore insists, can be inspired with life. 'The mere pill of a method instead', Tagore observes, 'shall not bring us salvation'.[56] The culture of education that Tagore proposed can risk being perceived as chaos; but, Tagore inscribed an order – implicit and delicate – into the forms and methods of learning and instructions, making education in phronesis 'rise above education'. In 'Siksha and Sanskriti', Tagore argued for the need of inner reconstruction – a *sanskriti*, a culture or dharma – which infused enthusiasm among children, making them conquer their immediate poverty (Tagore points out how being ashamed of the poverty in his ashram was considered shameful; in the space thrown open by culture one may harm oneself but must not self-debase) and the limitations in self-confidence; they developed the strength of character and the ardour of commitment to say 'we can achieve everything'. Tagore observes that 'there are no provisions of such culture and *sadhana* in ordinary schools' and in his ashram 'different kinds of work are undertaken in different departments and there must be an arrangement to apply energy and enthusiasm to each one of them'.[57] In a compelling mix of prudence, fortitude and reflection, Tagore's ethical deliberation, without discounting the methodologies of instruction (*unterricht*), did not forget its integral conjugation to life activities. He writes, 'since an incubator is not an easy machine, we get to hear extended description of its mechanism and expenses. But the life-activity of the hen laying her eggs is an easy natural act and, thus, does not bring over much discussion. Yet this is outstandingly remarkable'.[58] Learning in the ashram was the calm cheer of the hen naturally incubating the eggs to hatch and prosper.

Unlike Tolstoy, Tagore distinguished between good and bad method of instruction and worked out, with confidence and perseverance, his own version of aesthetic education. More pragmatic and wise than Tolstoy in paedocentric education, Tagore saw in the formation of the 'culture' of the ashram a continuance of historical heritage not in an obligatory passing down of values and traditions – a kind of Hegelian determinism – but as a revitalizing force which, in investing motivation and energy (Tagore mentions it as *siksha-sadhana*), sought to initiate currents of difference and self-revision. Like Tolstoy, Tagore was never in support of inventing a new method that would annihilate the old (*Tapovan* continued to sustain his educational ideals). In truth, his religion of pedagogy – *sadhana*-centric – was under continual interrogation.

Was Tagore trying to be Lockean in the sense of seeing the mind of his students as 'a blank sheet of wax' upon which his ideas could be inscribed or stamped?[59] Was he, in line with Descartes and Locke, looking into a progress from the 'simple' to the 'complex'? Perhaps not. The Lockean emphasis on child education as a 'process' – mechanically controlled and always consciously inculcated – could not have demonstrated any equivalence, both principally and praxially, with how Tagore saw the atmosphere of his school and the attendant growth of his pupils. Tagore, undeniably influenced by the notion and tradition of the 'romantic child', could not but differ from Locke in his understanding of 'human malleability' and the dialectic of nature and nurture. He did not see the teacher as having an absolute control over the mind and life of his students; the teacher would not consider his students as morally passive and merely impressionistic without a mind and consciousness of their own. This need not be misread as obviation of all rules and decimation of all methods and an exclusive exhortation to follow nature alone. A child's reason is not of the same order as that of an adult and, hence, Tagore developed a synthetic method – a natural method – where learning was both an effort and effortlessness. Tagore's school was not Doctor Blimber's school in Dickens's *Dombey and Son*, not Mr. Gradgrind's model school in *Hard Times* either. It is interesting to dwell on the description of M'Choakumchild:

> He and some one hundred and forty other schoolmasters had been lately turned at the same time, in the same factory, on the same principles, like so many pianoforte legs.... Orthography, etymology, syntax, and prosody, biography, astronomy, geography, and general cosmography, the sciences of compound proportion, algebra, land-surveying and levelling, vocal music, and drawing from models, were all at the ends of his ten chilled fingers. He had worked his stony way into Her Majesty's Most Honourable Privy Council's Schedule B, and had taken the bloom off the higher branches of mathematics and physical science, French, German, Latin and Greek.... If he had only learned a little less, how infinitely better he might have taught a little more![60]

Students could not be made to feed on facts only – what Dickens abhorred as 'object lessons' – and considered as 'little pitchers' ordered in rows. Tagore wanted to preserve what Louisa Gradgrind says lamenting to her father: 'What are my heart's experiences? ... You have been so careful of me, that I have never had a child's heart ..., never dreamed a child's dream ..., never had a child's belief or a child's fear'.[61] The atmosphere of the ashram made allowance for the child's heart and his dreams, belief, fear and play – the heart firmly protected to flourish but not completely without reason. Aware of both the wants of nature and the desire of fancy, Tagore could neither have agreed to a state of absolute purity in the child whose primordial innocence may be left untainted by any trace of discipline nor subscribed merely to a Lockean technique of rational and moral education which was predominantly a process of habituation inflicted on an 'empty organism'. The natural order of Tagore's *brahmacharya* in the ashram-school, his notions of malleability, 'innateness' and spiritual education were all braided into a rare combination.

So more than being learned, it is more important to learn how to learn. Tagore did not have the complete support for 'negative education' – the kind of education where, as Pestalozzi insisted, the educator did not have much role to essay, where his abilities to render life or breath to children were discounted – 'he only waters the dry earth that the roots may not strike it as stone. He only drains away the standing water that the tree may not suffer'.[62] Resistant to an Aristotlean 'growth model', Tagore refused to see child education as a mere technology whose every function was enacted with an eye for the next developmental terminus. He could not have agreed with Froebel that the unfoldment of the child has to be teleological always. Without a strict Hegelian bias, Froebel writes:

> We grant space and time to young plants and animals because we know that, in accordance with the laws that live in them, they will develop properly and grow well; young animals and plants are given rest, and arbitrary interference with their growth is avoided, because it is known that the opposite practice would disturb their pure unfolding and sound development; but the young human being is looked upon as a piece of wax, a lump of clay which man can mold into what he pleases.[63]

However, this should not make us miss the point about Tagore's emphasis on the child's 'original nature' – '. . . first leave the germ of his character free to show itself, do not constrain him in anything, the better to see him as he really is'.[64] A child certainly has an inner directed growth – self-realization and self-interest acting as motors for the growth principle – which cannot, however, ignore the shaping external principles that the educator, and here the guru, is capable of importing. Through his principles of 'freedom cure' Tagore looked at a mechanism of assimilation and accommodation which was not always formulaic and instructive: an aesthetics of living the life out where passivity and a few categorical exhortations under 'right' situations (not always enforced attention) were destined to bear productive fall outs.

Tagore's idea of growth was not subjected to reason and rationality only, and it did not call for a stoical ordering of the human–nature relationship.

The ashramites were not merely living a life enacted in reason alone; rather, it was an amplitude of existence that hailed both freedom and law. Tagore gave us the evidence of a 'plan' which he wanted to execute but not without a non-mechanist understanding and experience – a denial of obsessive modes of perfectability and mechanist psychology which, we know, have received support from Thomas Hobbes and Baron de' Holbach down to the materialists of the nineteenth century. There was no Helvetius-like educational 'engineering' but some experiments that put certain foundations of education and learning under trial. Education could not have grown without 'friction' in the way, perhaps, Comenius, the seventeenth-century reformer, envisaged the functioning of education: as smooth as the movement of a clock whose motive power is supplied by weights and an education where failures, like mechanical contrivances, are never considered as possibilities. The child's education should not show much strain and method. His first education – purely negative – is to have a rule without the apparent stress that a rule inflicts. Rousseau in his *Letter to Christophe de Beaumont* writes about his opposition to positive education in the manner of Helvétius where the child's mind is lumbered with things that the adult wants her to learn and possess.[65] Tagore showed a unique position on the growth of reason in the child's mind. For him education could not be made possible every time through explanation and the art of reasoning[66]; it came through as repetition and also through things that were left unexplained and allowed to grow in the mind of the child. Tagore never considered the child's curiosity and query as irritants in the formation of reason – progressing from the sense (*une raison sensitive*) to the intellect.[67]

Tagore made children learn to acknowledge the principle of 'waste' in growing up. This was about an understanding of an 'abandon' and a 'random' in learning and experience which could be identified in Goethe's young Meister. The world was not lost on Meister and yet he was not symptomatic of 'human engineering'. Tagore's idea of education worked out the comfortable space between mechanical naturalism and idealism; this was not a deleterious dichotomy of thought and matter. His ashram embodied a philosophy of living that was completely alien to the abstractions in the nature–matter divide and the strict schism in sensation and reason. Education, he believed, did not always come from 'outward forms' but had a clear allegiance, in the words of Samuel Coleridge, to 'the passion and the life whose fountains are within' ('Dejection: An Ode'). Indolence created its own diligence and, Tagore, perhaps, in senses that were greater and wider than John Keats, knew this perfectly well. This indolence subsidized a life where the heart 'watched and received' and the meddling intellect was not always allowed to murder and dissect to produce what Bertrand Russell qualified as 'despair'[68] – the despair that was the only possible religion for free men. Indolence for Tagore had the power to cultivate sensibility against 'pure reasoning' and made room for 'solitude' in education and creativity.

Aesthetic education, then, as C. S. Lewis would have liked to see, becomes a project to become 'human'.[69] The solitude of the ashram was 'contemplative' in nature – the experience that came from communication with one's inmost thoughts. The work at Santiniketan, as Tagore emphasized, began as an enterprise of 'gladness'. Tagore's idea of solitude was built into his insight and egoism (the productive *amour de soi*); it was not merely the natural quiet but the quietude that difference usually generated, outsiderhood might encourage and the prospects of removal from human company could bring. He writes that birds who build their nest on a huge tree do not bother to find the diversity and seasonal variations that come to the tree which houses them. They stay happy knowing only about their nest. The ashram was never meant to be so in that it demanded knowing the 'life' of his school – the rules which governed it, the life that no rules generated, the materiality of growth and the spirituality of possession.[70] This knowledge made his school a classroom, workshop, pasture, prayer room, playground, a home, all welded into one. This bred 'peace' – a sense of quiet – which, Tagore knew, by his choice of the locale and through his ideals of learning, was essential to all forms of education. Indeed education became poetry.

Tagore wanted to see objects as they exist and not merely as 'objects for use'. Such an attitude *created* 'possibilities' out of the impossible. This was the poetics of indwelling – the attainments from dwelling in a variety of configurations – which considered a student reading a book sitting on a branch of a tree as no less significant than his sitting on a chair or a bench while reading and learning. Tagore was for breaking limits – the 'dead angularities' and the 'constraints of education' – deconstructing the impositions of use value and object value that modern, mechanistic society has clamped on us. He endeavoured a release from a 'denial' of our possibilities, the heavy load of certainties and normativeness that 'systematic conveniences' of existence had brought in their trail. Children in the ashram needed a world capable of surprising them and a world whose projection supervened on mutual knowing and seeing. The ashram, thus, conjured a space close to the Heideggerian 'homeland' where 'the powers of nature around us and the remnants of historical tradition remain together'.[71]

The Topos of Tapovan

Although John Dewey accents the necessity of a qualitative social life he does not overlook 'man's home in nature'. Dewey argues for a 'unitary conception of nature' which is out of character with the human–nature dualism in traditional philosophy where man and nature are seen to have held distinct realities.[72] Nature contributes to the foundations in human education; the development of values and the dynamics of social existence owe in significant measure to the abiding charms and influences of nature. Tagore did not subscribe to a strict dichotomization of nature and culture into mutually exclusive categories of reality. Rather, he was in favour of promoting a version of education that saw both the social self and the eco-self of his students in a dynamic interaction. He had always sought a balance but the search for which was never easy. Dewey points out in *Democracy and Education*:

> For this associated life, with its experiments, its ways and means, its achievements and failures, does not go on in the sky nor yet in a vacuum. It takes place on the earth. This setting of nature does not bear to social activities the relation that the scenery of a theatrical performance bears to a dramatic representation; it enters into the social happenings that form history. Nature is the medium of social occurrences.[73]

Dewey rues man's inability to see the living whole of nature and man's failure to avoid seeing nature as only 'an object of control, alteration and exploitation' where nature becomes a force to be subdued and not as a territory to be respected with certain boundaries.[74] Probably, the 'modern understanding of nature' predicated on objectivity and differently attitudinized towards the non-human nature – what Neil Evernden calls 'the epistemological policing of nature'[75] – does not leave much room for an empathetic connect with nature. Tagore's naturalism seeks to reverse the attitudinal legacies under which nature has continually been bracketed for disinterested examination. This can be seen as something that falls in line with Dewey who finds geography (the place) and history (the human) coming together to study the same reality. The connection between the two thinkers does not go too far beyond these points. Tagore is more 'deeply' ecological[76] than Dewey whose methodologies of problem solving and intelligence are directed towards a critique of culture and less at life-affirming traditions that connect man with nature integrally.

What is the nature of a biocentric way to pedagogy? Tagore looked into the 'ecological self', a self that could transcend both individualism and holism. This non-Cartesian process of learning amidst nature – human consciousness as an extension of the environment – is an energy flow where individuals are like 'local perturbations' having an awareness of individualism and a sense of being a part of the whole. Endorsing *friluftsliv*, Tagore's ecosophy would see this learning amidst nature as partaking of the energy flow – the *lila*, the *ananda dhara*, the joy, whose nature is not one of domination, not self-gratification, but communion (*sahit*). This is a joy whose foundation lies in *tapasya*, the mediation of restraint (*bodher tapasya*, cultivation of feeling); it is the inscribing of an awareness of a greater movement that often eludes us in our atomistic consciousness of things and existence. John Seed has argued that '"I am protecting the rain forest" develops into "I am part of the rain forest protecting myself"'. I am that part of the rain forest recently emerged into thinking. The thousands of years of separation are over and we begin to recall our true nature'.[77] This is not *unio mystica*, rather a separate investment in transpersonality with nature – an 'earth wisdom'.[78] Tagore vindicated the growth of an 'ecological self' necessary to the 'pedagogic' and complementary to the 'cultural'. I would term this the 'ecological capital', the intervention and poaching both of which can end up in multiple personalities – green low, green high, green deep. Without being 'partist', Tagore accented the 'relational' aspect between holism and individualism – dividualism. Within the collective cooperative of the ashram, Tagore intended to fasten a green sky over all but not in a reductive way which would have disabled individual experiences from speaking out in different tones.

Tagore's proposition that the 'beauty and sap' of learning inhere in one's closeness to nature met with a chuckling indifference from many of his contemporaries who characterized it as acutely poet like and far too imaginative to become a feasible and rational way to education. Tagore responded by saying that 'nature does not sit before a desk in a classroom to teach, but opens her classroom to the domains of water, the air and the sky. This enables our minds to grow in intense power which a mere schoolmaster can scarcely think of imparting'.[79] The ashram created 'personal moods, values, aesthetic and philosophical convictions which serve no necessarily utilitarian, nor rational ends'. In a deep ecological way it formed itself around goodness, truth and beauty of the natural world, and of a human being's biological and psychological need to be fully integrated into it.[80] Although largely concerned with the deep interdependence between nature and culture, Tagore saw a certain 'human need' to affirm ecological interdependence. Within such a metaphysics his students needed a certain order of growth and maturity drawing upon a conviction of their embeddedness in a vast web of life, in the efficacy of a co-evolutionary perspective. It is, to an extent, an act of being let loose in nature with a purpose (a freedom that is both mindless and alert); this cultivated a 'conscience' that extended from people to land, from commodity to community, from clothes to nakedness, from knowledge to mysteries, changing intellectual emphasis, affections and fealties. The 'sacred' that Tagore proposed for his ashramites and the ashram-campus to touch was transformative, vital, rejuvenative and resuscitatory, requiring what Alpo Leopold termed as 'intelligent tinkering'.[81] This 'sacred' denied anthropocentric mastery and disclosed on the students a charm and a mystery that non-human nature could only unleash – an act that was not mere intuitive-instinctive in nature but required the growth of a 'conscience' whose understanding of bio-egalitarianism was of a different order and degree. The ashram-campus had a world view grounded in ethical and spiritual appreciation of interrelatedness – ecopsychological, ecosophical and ecotechnological – which was, also, a 'participant consciousness' (in the words of Morris Berman) and a 'transpersonal identification with life'.[82] This was not merely the world produced by material objects but an energy whose production was of a different character and consequence.

Tagore's vexed 'deep' ecological position, however, had nothing to do with the mystical. The governance of the ashram had a basis in material human practice (the ashramic rituals, prescriptions and injunctions) rather than unmixed contemplation. The connection that Tagore wanted to imbibe was both material and non-material, psychological and corporeal, mediated and non-mediated and yet not 'mystical'. His deep ecological base to pedagogy was performative, reflective, transformative and non-utopic. Tagore's distinctly deep ecological perspective was informed both by an inheritance (the ideal of the *tapovan*) and irreversibility of the present ashramic practices that included specific historical and material circumstances. *Tapovan* as a 'minority tradition' is said to have appropriated nature reverently where 'richness of ends was achieved with material technology that was elegant, sophisticated, appropriate and controlled within the contest of a traditional society'.[83] In fact, nature was controlled and motivationally instrumentalized by men in *tapovan* too, something that Tagore was aware of. Without submitting uncritically to the principles of *tapovan*, he made a wise appropriation (like the act of 'meditation' which Tagore so obsessively emphasized as part of his ashram-school curriculum) of certain principles keeping in view the pressures of the changing times. So the relevance of the general principles of *tapovan* education in the growing up of a modern-day ashram stood questioned and his ashram was not a tangled misappropriation of premodernity and modernity. The ashram, thus, was both professionalized and domesticated. But his somewhat obsessive reliance and celebration of *tapovan* was redolent of a basic belief in a 'minority tradition' which Devall and Sessions claimed focused on 'personal growth within a small community' and selected 'a path to cultivating ecological consciousness while protecting the ecological integrity of the place'.[84] Did the ashram, its circumambience and principles, run the risk of being critiqued as univocal 'minority tradition'?

The submission to nature in the ashram, however, was not a commitment to return to a pre-technological age. The difficulty of sundering science and nature into mutually conflicting discourses is not the norm of 'progress'. For Tagore, nature spoke not amidst the muteness of science but in the background of consistent throes of the abuse of science; it did not signal any intractable divide between the science-blessed human and the science-hurt non-human but projected an embodied self-nourished in the duality of the two forces. Is this the provocation to reinterpret the 'use value' of existence in nature? Does Tagore direct us to redefine 'self-preservation' beyond the domains of the instrumental reason? Tagore's appropriation of nature in his understanding of green pedagogy had a kind of internal limit to it. Under a regulative idea of reason he chose to minimize the opposition between nature and man. For me, Tagore by his choice of the 'locale' made nature available to his students in a 'liberating' way, reducing considerably the dichotomy between *res cogitans* and *res extensa*. The use value of nature in this new found space (Santiniketan) where mastery was not subordination but a striving to reach a point of cohabitative mutuality, influenced methods of pedagogic learning. But if education benefits from closeness to nature and swells a kind of 'knowledge accumulation' that Jurgen Habermas has pointed out, does it not fail to dismantle the 'anthropocentric framework of a discourse ethic', the discourse that Tagore's ashram sponsored and vindicated? Habermas notes that 'proper norms of regulating the relation between society and nature would somehow follow from the communicatively conceived idea of the human good life without reference to nature as an end-in-itself'.[85] Tagore envisaged a 'human good' within the discursive ethics of the ashram but could not deny the anthropomorphic ends to it ('soft anthropocentrism'). The ashram, as a discursive space, was not a green submission to autotelic nature but the extrapolation of a space which declared the continued 'knowledge accumulation' that human and the non-human have always developed through negotiation and opposition. It was a 'human settlement' in nature which clearly emphasized that nature could not have been left in her inviolability. Hence, the ethics of 'use value' and 'mastery' begged consideration within Tagore's principles of aesthetic education. As sites of power and in refigured polarities of value and practice, the students worked and corresponded with nature through a 'discipline' and 'punish'.[86]

But I would demur to reset Tagore's concerns here wholly with what Habermas has ascribed as 'nature-in-itself', an understanding that considers the 'opposition' between human and nature from principled apercus of anthropocentrism. Liberation in nature is about 'allowing' nature the space to articulate back its values – both intrinsic or extrinsic – and the ashram accommodated them in its infrastructural bareness, spartan life habits, and remarkably conscious ways of connecting with the 'earth' (for instance, the ashram students walked bare feet on ruddy muddy roads, students sat on the bare earth underneath the tree for their classes, a part of the teaching between the teacher and student was conducted while walking between the rows of trees). Tagore's resurgent motives to help create a space in the ashram that would respect the intrinsic values of nature was, however, a little different from the Naessain school of deep ecology. As 'culture amidst nature' the ashram was not a post-enlightenment programme of 'disenchantment of the world'. The ashram had its own laws of governance, a protocol, the footsteps of science, and, yet was not free from the touch of fancy and myths that led students to the philosophical and religious level of knowledge accumulation and formation. It was less intellectual and more experiential. But for me the ambiguity over Tagore's alleged romanticization of the *tapovan* remains. So the relevance of *tapovan* as 'minority tradition' to the institutional praxis of the ashram is questionable.

Disinvested of 'shallow environmentalism' and yet not completely espousing of a post-anthropocentric ecosophy, Tagore came close to redefining his own 'biospherical egalitarianism'. Tagorean ecosophy saw *sanmilan* (communion) of nature and human forces, not in a piecemeal, shallow approach to problems of integration and opposition, but within the framework of a philosophico-religious world view. So it is out of order to see any dissolution of reason into nature. Rather this reasons nature out in a meaningfully consonant dialogue with man achieved within a separate truth and value regime. This is no 'de-development' (in the words of Ted Trainer),[87] but prioritization of the non-instrumental reason which, without being extremist in its interpretation of nature as either a space for wholesome consumption or brute untainted vitality, treats nature as a text of meaningful 'suffering'. The aesthetics of learning through 'suffering' – the labour, pain and consequence – is inscribed within nature whose 'suffering' is a reality that disappeared under man's promethean instrumentalist and consumptive modes of behaviour. Tagore wanted his students to acknowledge this reality. Education in the ashram afforded space to revitalize the 'principles of cooperation in our daily life', providing children opportunities to 'give play' to their 'creative joys by inventing things with the help of whatever material lies ready at hand'.[88] The positive suffering generated out of the inconveniences of an ashram-life[89] – a certain deprivation in material comforts and endowments in the life of the ashramites – ensured that their needs were simplified. This assisted in the development of a sense of responsibility that forbade grumbling over deficiencies and made students look into their 'lack' with more thought and energy – for instance, to improve their dietary, as Tagore pointed out, they realized the importance of applying 'extra zest on their vegetable patches'.[90] This suffering owed to Tagore's deep belief in enjoyment that came through sacrifice and not from avarice.

Negotiations built around the ethics of 'suffering' – the dynamics that provided the ethos of imaginative reconstruction and non-aggressive mutuality – leveraged the post-technological or non-substantive reason. This reason – humanist and green in nature – acknowledged the self-preservative dimensions of existence and yet notionalized a 'freeing up', an unboundedness, that argued for a life beyond self-preservation. Tagore claimed that easy accessibility and ready availability could not be creative. Suffering and 'lack' fostered creation. He wanted in our schools, in every possible manner, 'the ideal of reducing the unnecessary in our life'; he believed that we lose our power once we make the 'unnecessary' indispensable to us. Tagore writes:

> An institution of this kind should not only train up one's limbs and mind to be ready for all emergencies, but to be attuned to the response between

> life and the world, to find the balance of their harmony which is wisdom. The first important lesson for children in *such a place would be that of improvisation, the ready-made having been banished in order to give constant occasion to explore one's capacity through surprise achievements.* I must make it plain that this implies a lesson not in simple life, but in creative life.[91]

Education amidst nature then was worked out through 'sacrifice and resignation'; this resulted in agonistic suffering to find a point of 'peace' (*santarasa*) in the traffic of contending forces. This peace in *Santi*niketan was not the 'tranquillity' in nature, but a suffering – an inherent disquiet – to sustain an interdependence which did not become a habit mechanism but turned into a synergy requiring continual attendance and alert commitment. Tagore, thus, proposed a new ethic of 'being' and 'doing' – an ethic that never lost sight of conflicting and conflating persuasions and principles. This redefined 'biocentrism' through modes of self-realization in students who then tried to connect themselves to the 'pleasure of real freedom'. Tagore writes that '. . . boys are happy to live in the discipline of nature. The discipline helps them to develop fully and taste the pleasure of real freedom, and it makes their bodies glow with the vigour of their sprouting minds'.[92]

Realizing a dream, an ideal, cannot simply happen on its own and cannot frame its own course merely on the strength of a supposed self-ignition. Tagore proposed a 'freedom' but this freedom was not purposeless; it was not a freedom devoid of method. The discipline of *brahmacharya* was green bureaucracy. The issue was less about allowing freedom to reign *per se* and more to do with a distinct kind of freedom formulated around the notional boundaries that *brahmacharya* had set out to achieve. Tagore's demand to install a specific structure into the functioning of the ashram-school betrayed a discursive rigidity whose inflexibilities were concealed within apparent freedom and creativity. Ashram education worked within a bureaucratic green shot through in an ecological ethic of survival. Tagore termed nature's method of discipline as 'freedom cure'. This was similar in essence to the doctrine of discipline by natural consequence formulated by Rousseau and later, developed by Herbert Spencer. But 'freedom cure' was more human in spirit. Tagore observed that when mind and life were given 'full freedom' they achieved health. The philosophy of 'freedom cure' allowed his boys to run about, to climb difficult trees, often to come to grief in their own, get drenched out in the rain and swim in the pond. This was a freedom, a suffering, a disquiet, that was not without method. Environmentalizing pedagogy then was pivoted on a 'biophilia' where the man–nature dialectic contained the poet's I within the 'we-ness' of the green discourse. So within the habitus of the ashram-school, Tagore unleashed a kind of green democracy, a discourse of green politics.

Would this system and philosophy have a logic to it? Working outside the Baconian and Benthamite dimension, Tagore saw, to an appreciable extent, a Coleridgean conception of 'coalescence'[93] that submitted to a balance between reason and thinking, passions and feeling. This is also close to what Cardinal Newman made of 'logic' under the Lockean tradition by avoiding abstractions from experience and notionalizing fact and knowledge beyond the ken of utilitarians. For Tagore, as with Newman, experience was both subjective and objective but Newman, more than Tagore, was wary of working outside the 'coalescence' resulting in the endogenous development of the self. Tagore, by imbibing a more expansive and accommodative consciousness, did not always choose the strident middle path. If Newman was Catholic, Tagore was Vedantic. This, however, did not imprison both within an obtuse dogmatism; rather, they evinced liberal sensibility in their idea and in the actuation of the ideals of education. Both of them ignored the flip side of liberalism by thrusting ahead in positive liberal knowledge achieved through a different interrogation of tradition and faith. This brought the logic of the ashram within the being–becoming bind where empirical knowledge consorted with post-materialist ideas and achievement fraternized both realizations and sensations.

The ashram, without being an 'ecotopia', was Tagore's 'aesthetic space' which had both the technological and post-technological rationality, becoming in the process an 'art of life'. It was a space of resistance, of a struggle against instrumentalist and exploitative societies and, also, speculative and restitutive in its generation of life-enhancing forces of nature.[94] Fritz Schumacher argues in *Small is Beautiful* that 'we are estranged from reality and inclined to treat as valueless everything that we have not made ourselves'. The use-value capital bequeathed through our post-enlightenment inheritance has unwisely blinded us to 'capital provided by nature and not by man – and we do not even recognise it as such'.[95] Tagore looked into the generation of an eco-aesthetic capital and the ashram was to be a space for 'meditation' unmediated by what Max Horkheimer has termed 'pragmatic intelligence'.[96]

Talking Body, Speaking Mind

When Nietzsche found the sedentary life as the 'real sin against the holy spirit',[97] he was looking into a separate biospherics implicated in a negotiation conducted with an 'openness' that had its own control, rationale and consciousness, had involuntariness and impulse, and surrendered to emotionality. Education or pedagogy is not mere art but pleasure too. Tagore's idea of the 'freedom cure' is fun, a 'letting go'. Freedom cure is crucial to self-construction that mere textbooks cannot bring – the 'leaps of self-abandon',[98] as Richard Shusterman calls it. It makes learning a fluid dynamics of imagination, wonder and curiosity. Unlike Stoic thinkers for whom reason had to be insulated from affection and unlike Plato who was sceptical of the soul conjugating with the body to produce clarified thinking,[99] Tagore saw imaginative reason as arising from our bodily experiences. Freedom cure was meant to guide the child to the realm of the variable and the vital, creating 'body emotions'. Learning in the ashram was not essentially about thinking but also about 'touch', affect and dependence on material things. Kinesthetic education – combining both kinesis and aesthesia – cannot rule out proprioception also. Proprioceptic aspects of body pedagogy demanded attunement to the situation and atmosphere enabling a cluster of skills and modes of accommodation which the ashramites worked hard to develop. Tagore, thus, ordered a 'body knowledge', a 'body behaviour', informed through the principles of *brahmacharya*. The harshness of setting and the compulsive inconvenience of living brought forth a unique *sambandha* between the body that endured and the mind that provided the strength of endurance. The Spartan bareness of *brahmacharya* made children peg their education on a 'Why' – questions as to what difference (the more, the surplus) this would bring to their learning when thrown against conventional forms of schooling. Children became enfleshed learners. Opposed to 'spectator theory of knowledge', freedom cure came to emphasize, in a Deweyian way, an embodied understanding that replaced the Cartesian asomatic type with a post-Darwinian one.[100] Freedom cure could not simply have submitted to the prioritization of sight, and hearing for it then would only lead one to objectivity (the act of watching and thus believing), detachment (sans involvement in the phenomena or the reality before man) and passivity (relishing the role as a receptor). Premised in an embodied mode of existence, it worked through experiences in a living world that simply could not be understood through a pure mind alone. The ashram-school behaved like an 'organizing' society, a cooperative, the kind that Durkheim has called 'a small society'.[101] The 'spirit of discipline' through *brahmacharya* involved regularity of conduct, obligation to be obedient towards the fulfilment of a moral order of Tagore's small society. Tagore employed a system that schooled the body into appreciating human dignity and, as Durkheim has argued, the fullest possible development of humanity.[102] The physicality of living (the ritual, manual and the formal) generated bodily emotions and desires which, in the process, got connected with the movements of the mind, resulting in education both at the level of carnal sociology and 'lived body' (*Leibkörper*). Durkheim notes that education cannot merely operate both at the level of the intellectual and the emotional to shape the personalities of pupils. This kind of education is not intended or employed to endow the mind with some theoretical ideas or speculative notions; it is designed to usher a 'principle of action'. The flesh of Tagore's ashram became a site or acted as a location for intellectual, emotional and psychical inscriptions (both the *Körper* and *Lieb*)[103]; this resulted in habitual actions, imagined expressions and 'aptitude' for sympathy which, as Durkheim notes, is predominantly social – for Dewey it is sociocultural – but for Tagore was both social and aesthetic (*sambandha*). For Durkheim, as much as for Tagore, 'communal life' contributes to schooling and corporeal processes contribute to the moral realization of society whether it be the one that a student grows into or the small society in which a child learns the art of self-development.

Deeply invested in variety and variability, Tagore did not want education to rationalize every segment of its manifestation, reining in emotions in matters of inquiry. Trying to live through the bodily memories of living, Tagore points out in his *Boyhood Reminiscences* how school education affected his mind through the contraction of the body and how he desired to free himself from dogmatic learning and stereotypical systems of instructions. This made possible an 'enselfment' realized through resonant and resistant experiences. Enselfment realized itself in experiences where the body was continually in *sambandha* – body being always the other. Bodies outside *sambandha* are impossibilities and in such relational realities the mind does find a place to grow and get endowed. Education then was being with others: an alterity which took into account both the human and its non-human counterpart – a contact where students were made to invest in the other, not suppress oneself in the other. By establishing 'other landscapes besides my own'[104] they made the life of education in the ashram a contested site, a flesh which Merleau Ponty would qualify as an elemental medium where the self and world are constructed through mutuality. Education through the body reverses what the body is fundamentally known for and experienced as – not as a mere object simplistically understood as something which when cut renders pain or aches when empty of food. Body is both a material organism and a metaphor as Le Goff has argued – 'it is the trunk apart from head and limbs, but also the person [as in "anybody" and "somebody"] . . . The body is at once the most solid, the most elusive, illusory, concrete, metaphorical, ever present and ever distant thing – a site, an instrument, an environment, a singularity and a multiplicity'.[105] As a site for subjectivities and consciousness, the body of a student in the ashram became a 'locus of sensory-aesthetic appreciation (*aisthesis*) and creative self-fashioning'.[106] This self-stylizing, autopoiesis, worked on several factors which Tagore wanted the atmosphere of his ashram to cultivate: character, integrity and sensitivity. The self was considered to be in transition: seeking a movement from what it was to what it purposes to be. In a somatic-affective way, education built around books, bird cries, the shrill cry of the kite in the sky and touch and smell of bare earth could not be non-reflectional and non-pragmatist always. The doings, sufferings and enjoyment of the world could not be shifting portions of a student's experience. Invested in a 'fullness', education as enselfment was a combination of multitude of dispositions ranging from curiosity, wonder, reason, instinct, sympathy and circumspection. There was, thus, an 'undoing' where structures of understanding the world were destabilized and formations of knowledge emerging in their wake created new epistemic openings and voluminosity.

Stanley Keleman writes, 'The body you have is the body you live'. It is the living body that shapes the contours of our minds and eventually our lives. He observes:

> In the name of knowledge we dampen and channel aliveness. Our current system of education creates spasms. We cramp our children's bodies so that we can form their minds. The school system institutes a social contract between the kids and the teachers, and between the kids and adult authorities in general. And the model is a contraction model. Learning becomes painful. Learning becomes a chore that requires discipline.[107]

'Aliveness' undergirded by emotions and passions did not extirpate the claims of reason and the prudence with which the ashram was built and nourished to survive. Tagore made his students realize the need of a body that knew how to reason; in fact, the psychophysical principles of learning in the ashram worked on a 'reason' whose fundamental structure emerged from the embodiment of its students. Emotions (*affectus*, Spinoza's *Ethics*), Tagore advocates, are closely allied to actions without which education cannot find its limbs. He saw a power in emotion influencing both the corporeal and ideational processes in consequentializing certain ideals of learning. Emotionalization of the body in education helps in enselfment (a reconstructive process which is surplus generative) where primates signs in the flesh and the mind help to create a discourse and narration. This is from where the primary sources in the life of education are derived. Tagore wanted 'moodhoodness'[108] to prevail on the aesthetic of his ashram, its works and ways: a kind of knowing – sensory cognition – that knew how both the mind and the body would get wounded or refigured in our learning and edulcoration; this was a kind of biocritical hermeneutics. The being in the world was Tagore's *sambandha*, the spirit of love. This unconcealed truths of human existence and Tagore admitted being interested in such disclosures. This was a life of the body and not the transcendent reality or truth or something derived out of the zones of the pure abstraction. In Tagore's system of thought, relational understanding created realities as much as realities created thinking in his ashram. Tagore effectuated a *sambandha* between the 'necessity' (need) and the 'spiritual' (desire). In the continuous dialectics between reason and sensing, an awareness of the perceptive sensual body was built – the living body with a mind of its own. So Tagore's aesthetic education in the ashram, its moodhoodness, was a way of conjugating the students to think and act with a responsibility for themselves and the world in which they lived.

Tagore observes:

> We can grow into full manhood only if we have been *nursed* by earth and water, sky and air, and nourished by them as by our mother's *breasts*. So let the children *play* under the open sky which is the playground of sunlight and clouds. Let them not be taken away from *Bhuma*, the Supreme Spirit. Let them *see* the sun unlock the day with bright *fingers*, and the tranquil glow of evening merge into the star-studded darkness of night.... Let them *hear* the roar of thunder and *see* the massed clouds darken the woods before bursting

> into rain. When the rains are over, let the children *see* the green and dewy fields waving in the wind and overflowing with corn as far as the horizon.[109]

He believed that the primal energy of life residing at the heart of Nature was the motive force that actuated a child and allowed for his rhythmic connection with the universe. Tagore saw a 'necessity' of the human body interacting with earth in its candour, its 'nakedness' and in an unabashed state of communion. He emphasized the nakedness of the child's body interacting with the nakedness of nature assigning, in the process, a separate dimension to the notion of 'shame'. Education in the ashram was envisaged as a kind of 'shamelessness' – an unclothed, unwrapped state of being encountering the 'random' and what Tagore qualified as the infinite. Tagore knew that book-bound education imparted knowledge of the world but not the earth, of our culture but not our nature, of our intellect but not the soul; it required reinvestments through an intense connection with the circumambient nature. This enabled both an exposure to the visible and created a possibility for the 'invisible' to disclose itself on the ashramites. Tagore moans, 'We do not touch the world with our mind, we touch it by books'.[110] He, like Emerson and Montaigne, believed that books alone would never be able to contribute to the development of the children in his ashram; a resonant contact with society and nature, with men and things, needed to be cultivated.[111] Here the object of his education was Emersonian in that he evinced deep faith in self-trust, an interest in oneself and a curiosity to touch one's own nature – 'acquaint him with the resources of his mind'.[112] Emerson's accusation against the limitations of education closely resembles Tagore's belief on the subject: 'We are students of words; we are shut up in school, and colleges, and recitation rooms, for ten or fifteen years, and come out at last with a bag of wind, a memory of words, and do not know a thing. We cannot use our hands, or our legs, or our eyes, or our arms'.[113] The ideals of aesthetic education as much as the spirituality of education were thwarted. For both, an attunement to a power mightier than the children and yet not inimical to their existence determined the spirituality of education: 'Yonder mountain must migrate into his mind'.[114] This created the reverence for education.

The logic of books (inductive, agonistic, declarative) and the logic of 'body-processed' (both human and earth, elemental and candid) education are different. This is not to misconstrue Tagore as suggesting a collective disapproval of books. This is about education that connects in vital terms the 'flesh of our body' with the 'flesh of the earth', a lived, animated, body-subject processing meanings for the consumption of mind and the industry of intellect. He notes that 'children with the freshness of their senses come directly to the intimacy of this world. . . . They must accept it *naked* and simple and never lose their power of quick communication. For our perfection we have to be at once *savage* and *civilized*'.[115] The impersonality of education achieved through books is contrasted through live, gestural, 'talking' ('movements of the eyes, modulation of the voice, signs of hands and fingers'[116]) in education which for Tagore has 'life' – 'speaking' lessons, rather, than 'reading' lessons; education is lived through the body and then allowed to settle in the intellect, avoiding, thus, the 'world-weariness'.[117] Resonating with Merleau-Ponty's words – 'I am not the spectator, I am involved . . .'[118] – Tagore's methods of body education can be eclectically interpreted through the interactive processes involving 'environed/conceiving subject' and the 'environing/conceived objects'. Somaesthetically, the politics of embodied learning solicited as much interplay from the agency of the children as it did from the contribution of the dynamic surrounding. Tagore wanted the body to reach out for nature, her inherent lessons, radiance and meanings through a manifestation that was to be dynamic, joyous and self-revisionary.[119] This emphasis on being educated at the primary stage through the pores of a body untrammelled by tropes of shame and culture is, for me, Tagore's 'talking body' that creates paths for the emergence of the 'talking intellect'. It is the 'savage' that he wants us to be sensitive about. His school 'had for its object a continual reclamation of the non-civilized'[120] and the 'peripatetic method' of learning worked on the correlation between the locomotion of the body and activity of the mind.

Bunyard and Morgan-Grenville argue that 'in modern farming the farm worker is increasingly isolated from the soil he is tilling; he sits encased in his tractor cab, either with ear muffs to shut out the noise or with radio blaring, and what goes on behind the tractor has more to do with the wonders of technology than with the wisdom of countless generations of his predecessors'.[121] The disconnection from the 'earth' in accumulation of knowledge – life experiences in screened off glass cubicles of self-contained technological incarceration – created vacuities which Tagore chose to refurbish by reclaiming the notion of 'interdependence'. Tagore writes:

> when they are not engaged in study, the students should work in the garden, loosening the soil around the roots of trees, watering plants and training

> hedges. Their contact with nature would thus be both manual and mental. In favourable weather the classes should be held in the shade of big trees. Part of the teaching should be in the form of discussion between teacher and student while they are walking between the rows of trees. In the evening recess the students should read the stars, cultivate music, and listen to legendary and historical tales.[122]

This mode of intersubjective existence is not born of the tilled earth or the blue sky or the green fields alone but through a life-consciousness – a diffusive sense-generation, a churning of the soul – which is impossibly difficult to explicate substantively. The body in education is a 'responsive' subject alive to the powers of transcendence achieved through a changing consciousness – responding to non-human bodies through touch, hearing and seeing and resonating, in the process, with others. As Didier Anzieu points out that 'from before birth, cutaneous sensations introduce the young of the human species into a world of great richness and complexity, a world as yet diffuse, but which awakens the perception-consciousness system, forms the basis for a general and episodical sense of existence and opens up the possibility of an originary psychic space'.[123] Within an evolving perception-consciousness somatic system, the child made to function in the *brahmacharya* system, in psychophysical experiences of being exposed to the heat and dust of an open classroom underneath a tree, in lessons rendered while undertaking long walks down the ashram roads, quite often bare feet, experienced the existential transfigurations that initiated at the level of the skin before it transported its messages, both organic and imaginary, to the skin of the mind. Education then at the ashram found its inroads through the skin – the 'skin ego' – which acted both as a barrier and a site of permeability that created experiences, produced psychical differentiation and engendered a surplus of understanding. Education, both as communication and communion, could not do without an excess: a loss of distinction between bodies and minds and yet a coming together in difference (identity-in-difference) that constituted a force field where separate bodies (teachers, students, natural objects) co-functioned both tangibly and intangibly, became present and unveiled presence. In a delicate art of 'reversibility' (not strictly in the Pontian sense of the term though), the students 'touched' the world with their bodies and were touched back through a chiasmatic nature of involvement. This reversibility was a kind of vulnerability (in the sense of *vulnus*, wound) towards the embodied experiences of learning and knowing or 'minding' the world around. It resulted in an indeterminacy of understanding, a kind of learning that was not pressed into shape through a syllabus but allowed to take its own direction and volume both touch-formatively and disembodiedly. Within the flesh of existence, a student, thus, became both a subject and an object to oneself.

The ashram, thus, created a space for what Merleau-Ponty calls the body schema and motility. Children in the ashram were aware of their bodies in different relational configurations be that with their teachers, the dietary schedule, the lessons, the leisure hours, the co-curricular activities and other coordinates of its environment. However, motility helped them to exercise agency by incorporating capacities to think and expand the quality and quantity of movements and experiences – 'a project towards movement or "potential movement", further orientate the body in space'.[124] So the awareness of the world was actively embodied constituting a being towards others; it means that we operate through the body in our functions with the world investing a particular emotional patterning. The abstraction from the corporeal world was denied and the perception was structured within an understanding that included the experience of the world – the earth – achieved through the body and through things which hid themselves behind other things ('We rob the child of his earth to teach him Geography, of language to teach him grammar. His hunger is for the Epic, but he is supplied with chronicles of facts and dates. He was in the human world, but his banished into the world of living gramophones'[125]). This mode of being, made Tagore and his young students engage with the uninhibited and uncultivated forms of experiences (unpremeditated too) in nature and the world. Such engagements, appealed primarily to the body, generating a freedom to choose and realize one's being within a depth that an immersion in culture could rarely help us achieve. Tagore knew how this prevalent perceptive mode in the ashram would allow 'invisible' lines of force to influence the 'becoming' of his students – the secret life of the wind, the shadows of the scudding clouds, the rhythm of the cricket-songs, the power of fragrance, the movement of the buds into bloom. (Tagore observes that 'children love the earth with its dust and its dirt, and they love the sun, the wind and the rain. They do not like to be dressed up, they enjoy themselves most when they are discovering the world with their senses, and they are not a bit ashamed to be their natural selves'.[126]) Before education could move into the domain of the intellect, the hidden power of the overarching nature or the horizon-dipping world was disclosed upon the students who then tried to measure the secret kinship between the sky and the ground in a non-conflictual axis, in a mutuality of excitement and incorporation. In fact, through 'the flesh of the ashram' the students encountered inter-subjectivities which clearly demonstrated secrecies and codes of 'nakedness', of glances, gestures and traces whose visibility was unconcealed on them through certain modes of transcendence. Tagore ensured that the elementality and eventality of the interactive non-human was never lost on the young ashramites. This precipitated a surrender whose motives were not assessed through determinable categories or intelligible psychophysical paradigms and whose constitution and voice were, most often, irrelevant to the experiential logic of culture and society.

Leisure is a significant component in Tagore's educational psychology. He emphasized the need of leisure as a means to educational development where work did not merely contribute to the formation of the child's mind and personality. Since the mornings passed busily with classes and lessons, leisure among the ashramites was experienced primarily in the evening when children engaged themselves in singing and listening to songs, preparing plays, reading mythical tales and walking in groups down the roads in careless abandon, and, sometimes, huddling under the starlit night sky. This is strictly not the Aristotelian way of understanding leisure where the emphasis is inflexibly on growing the capacity to reason and where reasoning, even though that be in times of leisure, can help actualize the potentialities of man. Man, for Aristotle, cannot be veriphobic and in his love for truth lies the key to intellectual and moral virtue.[127] The idea is to make leisure worthwhile and turn it into another means of attaining virtue. It is neither rest nor recreation but a cultivated exercise whose intrinsic worth determines the character and value of work. Tagore believed that recreation prepared the mind to perform superior work. This is close to Aristotle's idea that leisure and work for children exist to enhance the performance value and leisure contributes to the delicate uplift of work. Tagore saw leisure both in its recreational and instrumental value (not just non-work time) consolidating the art of good education. But it is not completely clear whether Tagore, like Aristotle, considered work as inferior to leisure on the grounds of it being ulterior which leisure is not and, as incapable of providing happiness which indeed leisure can, and being enslaving when leisure can be liberatory. This parsing of values related to work and leisure – polarization of merit – could not become an integral part of the 'fullness' of Tagore's educational project. Tagore saw as much intrinsic and extrinsic worth in work as he saw in leisure and connected both without hierarchizing one over the other. Endorsing an atmosphere that militated against 'leisure lack', Tagore chose a subtle middle line that fenced out education *as* leisure and education *for* leisure; this choice did not structure leisure with particular telic ends and disallowed 'anything goes' principles of experiences too. This became a mode of liberal education where work demanded that students stayed formally connected with knowledge and reason and leisure became knowledge and happiness that students chose to engage voluntarily without any pedagogic and performative mandate. Tagore knew that there were fewer opportunities for 'error' in work than in leisure; he believed that achievement and meaning in life have a separate dynamics and purchase in work and leisure.[128]

Indeed, 'open space' both as the politics and aesthetics of work and leisure, mattered to Tagore. Margaret McMillan, in her book *The Nursery School* (1919), saw the need for children to be in contact with light and space as much as they needed food and air. McMillan and Tagore spoke nearly in the same voice on the subject of privileging 'free activity' over anything else towards the development of the child's mind and body: an inviting unbarred space which generated love, joy and freedom removed from the heft of daily routine. She writes that 'to move, to run, to find things out by new movement, to feel one's life in every limb, that is the life of early childhood.... Bare sites and open spaces are what we need today'.[129] Tagore's freedom cure comes close to what McMillan emphasizes as 'outdoor learning', the play developed through contact with fresh air, sunshine, physical activity, music and movement (stories, play and free movement).[130]

Whether in work or leisure, children at the ashram were taught to 'wake up' to nature as much as to a self-consciousness which determined their relationship with the world. This was about making the sky and the flowers 'speak' because Tagore had always tried to respond to 'speaking nature' and its virtues. Anne Dillard in 'Teaching a Stone to Talk', introduces Larry and 'palm sized oval beach cobble' in a prospective conversation where the stone is being taught to speak. This is a commentary on our inefficiency and insensitivity to hear the silence of nature, the silence that we need to be attentive and a witness to. Tagore recommended 'waking up' to the silence. The bird's song which halted the class that Pearson was teaching was also a testimony to this waking up to 'silence' – an effort to teach the bird to talk. The acuity of Dillard's perception is worth noting: 'We have drained the light from the boughs in the sacred grove and snuffed it in the high places and along the banks of sacred streams. We as a people have moved from pantheism to pan-atheism. Silence is not our heritage but our destiny; we live where we want to live'. She agonisingly points out that it is 'difficult to undo our own damage.... It is hard to desecrate a grove and change your mind.... We doused the burning bush and cannot rekindle it.... Now speech has perished from among the lifeless things of earth, and living things say very little to very few'.[131] Tagore tried to make this silence speak through his ashram, encouraging his students into the difficult art of learning to be patient and sensitive listeners. Tagore could not have agreed more with Dillard when she notes that 'silence is not actually suppression; instead, it is all there is'. Ashramites were encouraged to 'live' and ritually watch the 'connect' grow on them – appropriately, in the words of Dillard, 'quit your tents'.[132] Incidentally, Tagore encouraged his students during their moments of leisure to look metapsychically at the night sky dappled with stars. Somewhere, in such acts of engagements, students were trained to 'wake up' and, in the process, the stars found occasions to break their silence. [133] The starry sky is provocation enough to quit the tents. Is Tagore then recommending a leisurely approach to education, an approach that recognizes the subtly creative, though faint, voices inherent in leisure? Are these voices usually smothered under the attendant compulsions and responsibilities that routine work brings? Organic education, Tagore argues, is not about external accumulation; he believed in giving back to education what we hold inside us. The way food grains are stored in a granary and the ways in which the body accepts food are not similar. The granary keeps a close tab on every item that it stores and collects. Our body does not merely accept but assimilates them towards greater substantiation and health. It is not about transporting the food out of the granary for material gains, but allowing food to work its way into providing more strength, blood and mass.[134] Tagore was aware about how modern-day education had come to closely resemble the granary and how important, thus, it was for him to make his school work within the organic metaphor of the body that he repeatedly cited and explicated.[135]

Tagore compares contemporary education to an act where one goes out to buy clothes but ends up buying socks and then tears them up to pieces to see whether they can be stitched back to fit like a dress.[136] The ashram installed to challenge the oddities and obtuseness of educational policies and achievements happily grew to internalize education and humanize its connection with the world.[137] Education in the ashram then was a continual fight against the philistinization of learning and was enacted to protect in the children what Emerson qualified as 'gleam of light'.[138] Tagore's serious anxiety over modern-day education comes close to Lawrence's concern to protect naturalistic education from the conspiracy of society and capitalism. Lawrence writes: 'Education means leading out the individual nature in each man and woman to its true fullness. You can't do that by stimulating the mind. To pump education into the mind is fatal. Every extraneous idea, which has no inherent root in the dynamic consciousness, is as dangerous as a nail driven into a young tree'.[139] The 'young tree' has its own *dharma* (in the words of Sri Aurobindo)[140] which is ceaselessly harmed by the anxiety and dread of the regnant habits of colonial education. Tagore, like Dewey, feared the 'tragedy of the "lost individual"'[141] and considered this increasingly atrophic situation as 'moral subjection', a loss of 'mental freedom which is a condition of creation'.[142] In a reconstructive bid to stem this derailment, to prevent the ashramites from becoming 'uncommunicating atom, an icy rock',[143] to make his students realize that being a 'good boy'[144] (in the words of D. H. Lawrence) was not always an achievement but an incarceration, Tagore sought to evoke and acknowledge the 'whim' – the constructive energy. It was the harmonic sense that bulwarked against stupor and 'hollowing out' and brought ashramites back to connect with nature and themselves again. This came with a 'mindful awareness'[145] which was not strictly 'virtue education' but a growth of the self – predominantly the compelling 'heart and body' education where 'the inmost in due time becomes the outmost'.[146] Embedded in freedom (leisure) and discipline (work) the 'whim' addressed a prophetic drive to make students what they *are* and not look similar in the future (the monochrome 'we') through a mechanism of 'railway track' education, the killing of the golden snake as Lawrence suggests.[147]

The School as Tirtha

Was the ashram a space for the ethics of reverence for speciesism? Is morality only about being able to 'maintain and cherish life' ('it is *evil* to destroy and to check life') as Albert Schweitzer argues?[148] What moral worth in biospheric interdependence and sentiosis did the ashram teach? Was Tagore trying to instruct and inculcate an intelligible conception of what *good* nature could be?

It is not the non-sentientism of the non-human world that mattered; ashram held together a consciousness that valued the 'teleological centers of life' (in the words of Paul Taylor).[149] This brought forth a coherence that drew upon a deep interconnectedness of things and an organic wholeness which deserved reverence for what it is: not necessarily what humans make them out to be, but essentially for what they *are*. Tagore's ashram was a projective, formative, generative process about 'growing together', forming a living system, that hyphenates autonomy with mutuality. It would not be very disanalogous to see Tagore's insistence on building an 'atmosphere' for his ashram-school in the light of Aldo Leopold's holistic land ethic. The land ethic spoke of a moral extensionism that included soils, waters, plants and animals and also the transformative self of the humans changing his predatory, plundering identity to become a citizen of the holistic community. But, also, within such a land ethic lay the development of the school with its appeal to cultural value. His school was both a part of nature and culture whose rationalities might differ and where one accented inclusiveness and the other emphasized historical particularity. This was the complicated ethics of 'moralizing the biological given'. It led to an inclusivity in a 'historically objective world' whose land ethic was nature-culture in nature, inscribed in certain forms of eco-essentialism, anthropo-constructivism and perspectivism on well-being. Tagore's ashram was about 'humane holism'.

A disturbed Tagore, discommoded by the growing encroachments of materialism and threats to the province of the child's mind, came close to accenting the Emersonian 'gleam of light' in his children. Emerson's instance of the rose is succinct:

> Man is timid and apologetic; he is no longer upright; he dares not say 'I think,' 'I am,' but quotes some saint or sage. He is ashamed before the blade of grass or the blowing rose. These roses under my window make no reference to former roses or to better ones; they are for what they are; they exist with God to-day. There is no time to them. There is simply the rose; it is perfect in every moment of its existence.[150]

It was the 'self-reliance' which connected the children productively to their suffering: a connection which taught them self-reliance not simply in the running of the ashram but in the conduct of their lives too. The self-reliance spoke to an inner sense of being to which Tagore wanted his students to submit. This was both spiritual and pragmatic. The aesthetics of 'labour' in the ashram – the generated labour capital – stressed a quietistic attitude to life. Students laboured, not arationally though, to adapt to a harmony beyond the choric order of things; they aestheticized labour (another version of soft anthropocentrism) to achieve a sense of quiet. Energy in units is expended to maximize a synergy – Zen Buddhism calls it *mono no aware* ('sensitivity to things') – leading to the perpetuation of 'greater energy' which Tagore refers to as integration to the tune of the 'Flute Master'. Looked at from such a perspective, the ashram became a *mandala* – approximating Hua-yen Buddhism it became the jewel net of Indra whose centre was not clearly determined and where relationship was of simultaneous mutual identity and mutual intercausality.

Tagore's ashram then embodied a 'being', a being located in its inhabitants, that took note of the manifestation of one object on the other in the functioning of the circumambient nature. This was a Heideggerian way of looking into the authenticity of his ashramites who, in the process of conducting a spatial and temporal clearing, manifested themselves, often, to each other in a non-utilitarian way (Tagore points out that humans have the rare ability to commingle with all. This commingling is at the level of the 'soul', the clearing of spaces with species-being, which, thus, is founded on 'joy', *ananda*).[151] Tagore notes that 'perfect freedom lies in the harmony of relationship which we realize not through *knowing*, but in *being*. Objects of knowledge maintain an infinite distance from us who are the knowers. For knowledge is not union. We attain the world of freedom only through perfect sympathy'.[152] This sympathy is being-with-the-world. Heidegger clearly emphasizes, as does Tagore, the importance of *besinnliches Denken* (meditative thinking) as against *rechnendes Denken* (calculative thinking). Nature in the ashram was allowed to *be*: ashramites learning to let things be. With the stress on 'meditative thinking', Tagorean ecosophy clearly underlined an essential relatedness where diminishing the prospect of a being-with-the-world was diminishing oneself. This being demanded care (*sorge*) where understanding one's authenticity within the prevalent biocentrism led the way to a sense of peace, the *santarasa*, as argued earlier. Ashram accredited 'survival' not as prevention from the danger of the techno-maniac 'calculative' inroads but in 'freeing' objects into their essences, unchaining them from man-imputed uses. Tagore tried to make his ashram a place where the intrinsic values of non-human entities were allowed to 'exist' unmediated. The authenticity lay in realizing the 'sacrament of co-existence', an ontological democracy where nature demanded being seen as being-in-itself (and not as object-for-something-else) and human as being-with-the-world. This bears an insight into what the Japanese ascribe as *shi-zen* (nature), translated literally as self-thusness and *fūdosei*. Clearly, as to Tagore, as is to the Japanese tradition of looking into 'nature', the communication is effected through the 'poetic' (music, poetry and imagination) where sensibility and 'sympathy' power a participatory dialogue. Augustin Berque translates *fūdosei* as *médiance* which speaks of an eco-centrism that arraigns place to both the subjective and the objective, assigning and creating spaces both for the human and the non-human.[153] Berque writes:

> Lexically, this word [*médiance*] simply derives from the Latin root of milieu, and as such it is related to the already existing adjective medial. I define milieu as the relationship of a society with space and nature, and I define *médiance* as the sense of this relationship.... The logic of the Japanese medial process, or *médiance*, tends both to blur the identity of the self and, at the same time, to enhance the identification of the self with what is not the self: environment both social and natural. These processes involve not only psychological, social and ecological relations as such (eg., self and others, self and environment) but, more, generally, the relation of the subject with the object.[154]

The ashram-space was 'trajective'[155] where within the nature-culture dialectic there existed certain 'structured structures' that were inscribed functionally as 'structuring structures', something that I have tried to argue as 'green bureaucracy' of the ashram. The 'trajection' of the ashram was a *médiance* where society related to nature in ways and at levels that were different from the self's relation with the environment.

Tagore writes that man realizes his greatness in two ways: one in his individuality, in his separateness from others, and the other through union with others: one through gratification and the other through connection or communion.[156] This brings us to understand what Tagore means by *tirtha* (pilgrimage). *Tirtha* is the point of transformation which leaves the site and the person sighting it in a protean matrix of harmony and humaneness. It is less about visiting the site and more about the transformation (processuality) that it brings. *Tirtha*, men conventionally think, comes from certain objects – water or portions of earth – which, in fact, decimate the 'soul substance' in the heart of those objects of desire. Ablution does not bring peace and redemption when the water the devout dips in is merely considered in its objecthood (water considered only for drinking, bathing and washing). It is a separate level of connection and interdependence that the water sprinkled over the body grows through a certain holiness springing from the 'soul substance' – a triadic integration in earth, human and the divine. Here *tirtha* becomes the point where water as an object of necessity becomes a transformative power leading to man's self-cultivation and inner emigration. Tagore, in a neo-Confucian way, sees nature and man as interconnected and interpenetrating, something close to what Tu Wei-ming considers as a 'continuity of being'.[157] Tagore's idea of energy as continual, connective and communicative is *ch'i*, the material force or psychophysical element of the universe, an integrative dynamism which ensures deep reciprocity between the human and the non-human world. Wang Fu-chih writes:

> The fact that the things of the world, whether rivers or mountains, plants or animals, those with or without intelligence, and those yielding blossoms or bearing fruits, provide beneficial support for all things is the result of natural influence of the moving power of material force. It fills the universe. And as it completely provides for the flourish and transformation of all things, it is all the more spatially unrestricted. As it is not spatially restricted, it operates in time and proceeds with time. From morning to evening, from spring to summer, and from the present tracing back to the past, there is no time at which it does not operate, and there is no time at which it does not produce.[158]

The ashram was founded in *ch'i*; it was a transformative matrix built not merely through connections of knowledge but modes and networks of sensibility. Students in the ashram-school were taught to have faith in 'relations of sensibility and realizations' that outbound sensate experiences provided by the 'logic of the senses' ('. . . it is not just knowledge through education, education of sensibility, of sense-generation, should hold the primary place in our school'[159]). The growth of such a realization led to the formation of an 'identity' – the identity that did not come from learning technological skills or qualifying exams in schools and colleges. It was the result of a *tapasya*, a *tirtha*, whose core existed in the triadic unity explored as sedulously as possible and experimented within the confines of the ashram. As *tirtha*, the ashram, in a rather post-utilitarian metaphysics, became more a journey than a junction of definite eventuality; it was a processing of possibilities leading to the 'impossible' (which is not to be interpreted as unachievable or unrealisable). It was never inscribed in 'force' or 'coercive power' (Tagore calls it 'probolata'; he writes that circulation of air in its quietness is more powerful than the storm; storm cannot last forever, it rages and confines itself to a limited area. But the quiet movement of air embraces the whole earth). Ashram was Tagore's *sadhana*, a way, the site of what Chu Hsi has termed as 'humaneness', a praxial ground of interpenetrative processes, almost always in the making, on the move, quietly in attendance.

The Politics of Twinhood

Tagore could not have been a strict endorser of Vico's concept of development (cf. *Developmental Psychology*) based on psychogenetic law by which, as Elio Gianturco argues, 'the individual develops through a certain series of phases, the sequential order of which is immutably fixed by nature'. But he believed in the child's powers of sensation and imagination followed by his development of memory before he attained the powers of reason and reflection. Tagore believed in these 'culture stages' and 'language stages' where the 'single individual recapitulates the entire process of development of the species'.[160] It was a separate vein of being and performing where language, representation and meaning have to be different – in the words of Vico the divine and the mythic will have to be different from the human.[161] Being human was essentially dependent on how well imagination, sensation and memory could work synergically towards the development of the human. Tagore's experiments in aesthetic education, thus, stand vindicated under Vicoean pedagogical system or force field which sees a profound complementarity between *verum* and *certumis* and a fine balance between the rhetorical-pathetic and the logico-rational. Unlike Descartes and Vichy, Vico's insistence on poetry as having an enriching curricular co-existence with mathematics shows the humanist foundation of knowledge, contributing to the development of a separate character of learning which demonstrates respect to a variety of disciplines. The child grows into playing up the imaginal and the deductive against each other. Working on the rhetorical-pathetic mode, Tagore, like Vico, humanistically integrated knowing with communication, sensation and imagination – the art of knowing was in the *sense* of knowing and participating in things which directly and quasi-directly connected with the child, was marginally incidental to his development and had imagined realities contributing to the construction of experiences that led to maturity. Learning was both veridic and reconstructive, creating and living in the things that children were made to learn and which they ordinarily experienced. The non-mathematization of Tagore's aesthetic pedagogy was revealed through the celebration of items of imagination – poetry, plays, painting, music – and reason that were worked out in forms of various experiments for survival and sustenance against the odds of the situation and the atmosphere. This comes close to walking the line which Vico suggested. However, the success of Tagore's walk down the delicate middle path was never immune to interrogation.

Despite Tagore's declarations that he had no knowledge of any development related to child education (philosophy of pedagogy and learning) outside his own school, the ashram could not have remained as one huge space at once isolated and unique, aseptic and removed. So the developmental philosophy of the ashram can certainly be read as having deep connections with the corresponding and congruent developments across countries, primarily in Europe (Tagore's predominant version of the West). In Germany, around the same time that Tagore was wrestling with his ideas on paedo-centric education and the eventual establishment of the school, Georg Kerschensteiner (1859–1932) made education amenable to the child's natural development through the idea of the *Arbeitsschule*. The intersecting issues pertaining to both the thinkers network around the understanding of the potential relationship that a child has with a teacher, the function of the teacher in relation to the impartment of education and the nature and learning among children as distinguished from adult education. Kerschensteiner emphasized an educational model which could mould a child to a particular 'life form' in congruence with one's inner nature, attending to the development of the child's interest.[162] Character formation was integral to the 'freedom' that a child got and, most often, the limitations of the classroom awaited to be transcended through the ideal of creativity and virtues of action – a vein of thinking which caught on more substantially through Hugo Gaudig (1861–1923) and Berthold Otto (1859–1937).[163] Gaudig's insistence on developing the psychological potentialities of the child and Otto's emphasis on rendering the child as an active agent were directed to foster the child's independent activity, expression and experience.[164] Diffractively resonant with such ideas, Tagore's paedo-centric education explored both consciously and reflectively the 'life processes' and vitality of phenomena that it was expected to generate. Character formation, for Tagore and these thinkers, owed as much to the child's independence and creativity as it was to the teacher, the pupil's immediate other – the nature and nurture working through a twinhood which was a solidarity formed and invented through the intervention of the teacher and the taught.

The difference in knowledge and understanding from his German counterparts starts to surface when Tagore points to the inadequacies of the teacher and seeks a terminological and functional substitute through the introduction of the concept of the 'guru'.[165] Ashram-education was a strong alchemy of the guru and the students – the I-Thou – and Tagore spent years contemplating the role in which he might see the guru in such a scheme. The lack that a teacher has, Tagore argues, is complemented and problematized by a guru. The formal competence of a teacher requires to be substituted by the resourceful potential and power of a guru who *will* give much more than what he is usually expected to deliver. The dry interactive and pedagogical laws of a teacher await rejuvenation at the hands of a guru who would, as Tagore writes, 'devote his whole mind and spirit to the service of his students', earning from the students a 'devotion that owes nothing to the fear of being punished, and is deep enough to be called religious and genuine enough to be called natural'.[166] Here within the trans-(in)fusionist 'spacetimematterings', an unexpected interference with Tolstoyan thought frequencies are difficult to ignore:

> The best teacher is the one who can instantly recognize what is bothering a particular student. This ability in turn gives the teacher a knowledge of the greatest possible number of methods; the ability to invent new methods; and above all – rather than the blind adherence to one method – the conviction that all methods are one-sided, that the best possible method is the one that answers best all the possible difficulties incurred by the student. This is not a method, but an art and talent.[167]

Tolstoy writes, "I as a teacher in my school was at once confronted with two questions: (1) What must I teach? and (2) How must I teach it?'.[168] This 'what' and 'how' that prepare the grounds for aesthetic education of both is the most important affair of life.[169] It cannot be 'a deliberate moulding of people into certain forms' which is 'sterile, illegitimate and impossible'; rather it should be a 'human activity, having for its basis a desire for equality, and constant tendency to advance in knowledge'.[170] If Tagore was deeply disturbed by the system under which he had to perform as a student, Tolstoy, after having travelled to various countries in Europe, attending Dickens's lecture on education and meeting Matthew Arnold, was profoundly affected by the school system that promoted 'prayer for the king, blows, everything by rote, frightened, paralysed children'.[171] The children in their schools were taught to be 'free' – 'the only method of education is experiment, and its only criterion freedom'[172] – where education never became wholly instrumental, oriented merely to 'gain an advantage in the world'. Education, for both, encouraged 'creativity' and 'joy' that did not come from punitive fears and caged morals of certain forms of learning. Tolstoy writes, 'How is the best relation to be established between given people who want to learn and others who want to teach?'[173]

The twinship is built on the 'spirit of active love'.[174] If Tagore believed in the role of the *guru*, Tolstoy laid deep faith in the charismatic teacher and his abilities in free pedagogy whose spirituality was unfailingly dynamic and inclusive. Tolstoy notes:

> The spirit of the school is something that is rapidly communicated from pupil to pupil, and even to the teacher, something that is palpably expressed in the sound of the voice, in the eyes, the movements, the tension of the rivalry, – something very tangible, necessary, and extremely precious, and therefore something that ought to be the aim of every teacher. Just as saliva in the mouth is essential for digestion, but is disagreeable and superfluous without food, even so this spirit of strained animation, though tedious and disagreeable outside the class, is a necessary condition for the assimilation of mental food.[175]

Although both disfavoured violence on the students, an educational regimen was never ruled out. Tolstoy observed that out of sixteen waking hours in a student's life, half were apportioned to carrying out necessary chores and recreation and the other half was directed to studies. Studies involved encouraging the student's desire to choose, learn and experience the joy of avoiding military impositions; it made allowance for spaces to educate teachers through the consciousness of one's errors. Through their pedagogical experiments both wanted to address the question as to how one should live her life: how does spiritual education connect with science, our moods and emotions? How does one learn 'by heart'? Tagore's idea of education, unlike Pestalozzi's, (the principle of *Anschauung*, where the concrete must come before the abstract), held that concepts of 'natural learning' were more flexible and had a randomness about them. Tagore was conscious of such indulgences and unlike Pestalozzi, never trapped himself into a pedagogic premise based on number, form and word. He knew that these principles could not assist the inner development of children; this development was like a synthesis where the saliva and the food needed to work together for all kinds of endowment: natural learning needed the instinct and spontaneous inevitability of saliva and the reason and prudence of food because ingestion of all kinds of food might just impair the assimilative processes, resulting in serious indigestion.

Within the trans-(in)fusion-now, Tagore's notion of the guru here connects with Don Simón Rodríguez's writings where we encounter again the significance of 'thinking' and the difference that he draws between a teacher and a lecturer ('bocinas').[176] Walter Kohan explains Rodríguez's thesis on the three different types of teachers: 'that which resolves to show that he knows and thus does not teach, in other words, the conceited one; that which wants to teach so much that he confuses his disciples (these two types would be a form of "catedrático" or "bocina" teachers); and lastly, others that put themselves at the reach of EVERYONE, they consult with him for his capacities. These last ones are the ones that achieve the goal of teaching, and the ones that perpetuate their own names in the schools'.[177] Teachers in the ashram inspired and induced excitement and desire in others and put themselves as Rodríguez argues 'at the reach of Everyone'. The guru goes out in search of a student's attention, 'seduce it, incite it and invite it to place itself on what is to be questioned, understood, thought about, and invented – that is, to get attention to tend to what it is that life needs to live'.[178]

Continuing on the subject of guru, Rousseau, like Tagore, agreed to an outward stewardship in the teacher helping the course of the inner development of the child. 'We are working in agreement with nature', writes Rousseau, 'and while she is shaping the physical man, we are striving to shape his moral being'.[179] The pupil is her tutor's 'work',[180] but this does not make her a captive denied of all kinds of freedom to think and talk. The freedom is both an indulgence and device ('prepare from afar the reign of his freedom' as Rousseau points out in *Emile*) and has its own logic inscribed in imagination and reason, restraint and license. Rousseau observes:

> Take an opposite route with your pupil. Let him always believe that he is the master, and let it always be you who are. There is no subjection so perfect as that which keeps the appearance of freedom. Thus the will itself is made captive. The poor child who knows nothing, who can do nothing, who has no learning, is he not at your mercy? Do you not dispose with respect to him, of everything which surrounds him? Are you not the master of affecting him as you please? Are not his labors, his games, his pleasures, his pains, all in

> your hands without him knowing it? . . . It is then that you will be surprised by the subtlety of his inventions for appropriating all objects he can attain and for truly enjoying things without the help of opinion.[181]

A correspondence with Emile's growth can be identified in Tagore's insistence that children should not lose touch with the sense-given facts. In such an attitude, 'thought' is not mere abstraction but a process that comes from its connection with sense-experience. Rousseau's philosophical tutor is Tagore's guru, someone who is not a mere schoolmaster and, whose contribution is in linking the life of the child with the life of humanity and nature. Both are assumed to understand the 'natural developments of the human heart', study man and the individual and know 'beforehand what will bend your pupil's will when he confronts all the objects of interest to his age that you will cause to pass before his eyes'. Rousseau notes: 'Now, to have the instruments and to know their use well, is that not to be the master of an operation?'[182]

This brings me to the important voice of Martin Buber in the back of the revolution that German school education was undergoing in the second half of the nineteenth century. Buber's idea of the teacher is caught between the one who allows the student to grow in spontaneous abandon without much teacherly intervention ('symbol of the pump') and the one who is conspicuously impositional and representative of a system of educational values ('symbol of the funnel').[183] The politics of attachment and commitment conflated with freedom and creativity that Buber raised is strongly relevant to Tagore's understanding and the mechanics of his guru. How does the guru become both the inspiring and the directing spirit without being careless and coercive? Imbibed in the spirit of a tempered freedom, Buber observes that 'this almost imperceptible, most delicate approach, the raising of a finger, perhaps, or a questioning glance, is the other half of what happens in education'.[184] Tagore was largely engaged with the meaning and ramification of freedom and, through repeated revisions, configured the margins of inner and outer freedom, the delicate divide between permissiveness and the desirable. Freedom, for Tagore, was an emergence of possibilities. Buber observes that 'compulsion in education means disunion, it means humiliation and rebelliousness. Communion in education is just communion, it means being opened up and drawn in. Freedom in education is the possibility of communion; it cannot be dispensed with and it cannot be made use of in itself; without it nothing succeeds, but neither does anything succeed by means of it: it is the run before the jump, the tuning of the violin, the confirmation of that primal and mighty potentiality which it cannot even begin to actualize'.[185] Tagore's ashram was deeply functional in its acts of 'communion' (the *sambandha*) at different levels which generated responsibility, care and responsiveness. Instinctive growth was undergirded by what Tagore calls 'shashontantra' (rule of governance) where the 'released instincts' needed to meet. Students cannot be thought of as prisoners in jail, writes Tagore.[186] Though not wholly identical to Froebel's Gliedganzes, Tagore ensured that his students developed individually to connect with humanity at large, pointing, thus, to a continuity in education. He emphasized how a student might grow and be made to grow. Eugen Baumann, the refugee turned teacher in disguise in Berthold Auerbach's *Neues Leben* that had a strong sway over Tolstoy, makes a pertinent point: 'you are executing something hallowed, never hesitate, and when you become anxious, think, that to all who know of you or will once hear of you, you will give the faith in mankind and the finest act of sacrifice, you must not, you cannot wear down and desert, you would destroy the finest faith and would become a traitor to the hearts which will be edified by you. Never forget your holy profession, which reaches far, far beyond the closed space of a school room'.[187] So in addition to his duties inside the classroom, the guru had a life with his students outside the classroom too. Eugen envisages students and teachers to develop their method together because 'all abstract methodology is nothing but system-raging mirror fencing; the best a teacher can achieve in his school comes from his personally, from the pure drive of nature'.[188] Buber sees the child as having 'pure natural association' where the other for him cannot be inimical to his growth. The child as self-interlocutor needs the distance to develop the dialogue. Education at the ashram gave the child the desired distance from the categorized schemata of the adult-centric world to grow his own mechanism of understanding and insights. The child always has the desire for the 'new' and Tagore's educational principles wisely ensured that the 'new' was kept fresh.

Tagore's enframing of the guru and the taught can be worked out through some interesting investments in Martin Buber's I-Thou paradigm. Buber, who saw the pupil and the teacher relationship through both inclusivism (*Umfussung*) and empathy, through mediation and passiveness, tried to locate the 'becoming I' through the Thou. Tagore tried to locate the dialogics in such a relationship where 'each of the participants really has in mind the other or others in their present and particular being and turns to them with the intention of establishing a living and mutual relation between himself and them'.[189] Tagore, like Buber, saw the engagement of the teacher and the child as an 'event' where each one lived through the common event and contributed to the standpoint of the other.[190] This also approximates Dewey's understanding of education as shared activity in which 'the teacher is a learner, and the learner is, without knowing it, a teacher and upon the whole, the less consciousness there is, on either side, of either giving or receiving instruction, the better'.[191] The inclusion spelled out through the relationship diffused identities and became constitutive. Schaeder calls it 'an elemental bipolar experience' in which the common situation is experienced with the entire person from the standpoint of the other.[192] Like Buber, Tagore saw education as an event of dialogue. But learning just could not merely be achieved through the teacher only. The truth of learning also needed some direction and could not be merrily abandoned to arbitrary acquirements. Education, for Tagore, then became 'personal' – a positive attitude of imaginative concern for the personal needs of his students. But how close do Tagore's aspirations for such an 'event' come to Buber's belief that in dialogism of this nature the relationship is more one sided than harmoniously mutual? Buber, however, does not deny that the teacher cannot learn from the personal experiences of his pupils – 'Our students teach us, our works form us... How are we educated by children, by animals! Inscrutably involved, we live in the currents of universal reciprocity'.[193] Emerson also finds the secret of education as existing in acts that believe in respecting the pupil. He points out that 'it is not for you to choose what he shall know, what he shall do. It is chosen and fore-ordained, and he only holds the key to his own secret. By your tampering and thwarting and too much governing he may be hindered from his end and kept out of his own'. So Emerson recommends respecting the child, not trespassing 'his solitude' and not become too 'much his parent'.[194] Both Emerson and Buber, however, could not attest to a full partnership in the sense of a well-proportioned mutual contribution that might implode the relationship, spelling disaster to learning. It would be a failed friendship, an abortive twinhood. Tagore could not have disagreed with these concerns. The guru understands both himself and his students and, in fact, to expect students to know their guru in all his dimensions is tantamount to making a huge demand on the dynamics of inclusivism. But despite the comparative advantage in the ability of the teacher to swing into the life of the student, the twinhood breaks into 'friendship' which is what Tagore had always aspired in every form of education in his ashram.[195] This friendship, pragmatically, is incompatible with complete mutuality. Tagore knew that such incompleteness resulted in learning and it is in such normative limits to mutuality that the guru had always found his worth.

In Hegel's educational theory the acts to initiate children into dispassionate indoctrination and memorialization are singled out with aversion. Children are suggested to be spared from arid lessons thrusted endlessly down their unprotesting throats. Clearly, in line with Tagore, Hegel sees an 'independence' in learning which approbates the voice of the children unhappy with a pedagogic asylum. This unhappiness is not provocation to indiscipline; rather, it defeats the purpose of learning which cannot be mere receptivity and memory work performed under an assemblage of laws and strictures. Tagore's ashram had discipline without subjugation and bondage. It induced, in a Hegelian framework of pedagogic function, love and reverence whose severity was not stultifying, but, regenerative. 'Thinking' cannot be pedagogised for it is a phenomenon that requires freedom and inspiration. Hegel notes that truth 'is not a minted coin that can be given and pocketed ready-made'[196] and a teacher cannot think for a student any more than he can eat or drink for him.[197] This ability to 'think' is the significant prelude to 'creativity'. Like Hegel, Tagore vouchsafed for a knowledge which could not be rooted to and roted from textbooks and academic curriculum alone. However, the difference with Hegel begins to surface when the philosopher-teacher, as Hegel observes in his enunciation of a 'system', assumes a masterly knowledge over the pupil's activity, a kind of preordained wisdom for his or her good. If Tagore's *guru* in the ashram led the children with a 'thought' which then called on the participation of the little folks, Hegel's philosophy teacher pre-thinks, ordaining the 'views of the young on essential objects' as still 'totally deficient and empty but in part – in infinitely greater part – they are opinion, illusion, half-truth, distortion and indeterminateness'.[198] This results in dominance over the students which only a 'system' can generate. Tagore could not deny a 'system' (*brahmacharya*) in his ashram either (during its years of inception the school was called *Brahmacharyashram*). But Tagore refused to accept the 'discipline' that Gandhi's Phoenix school which was briefly housed at Santiniketan in 1915 introduced. Tagore observed that the school had 'discipline where they should have 'ideals'. They are trained to obey which is bad for a human being; for obedience is good, not because it is good in itself, but because it is a sacrifice. These boys are in danger of forgetting to wish for anything and wishing is the best part of attainment'.[199] Although Tagore pointed out that he was never much of a disciplinarian,[200] discipline, interestingly, never became foreign to the system of the ashram-school. In a 20-page letter to Kunjalal Ghosh on 13 November 1902, Tagore spelled out the constitution of the school. This constitution[201] made both physical and mental demands on the students. Bratin Chattopadhyay observes:

> The school bell ringing under the system of codes used to regulate the quotidian routine at Santiniketan. Remarkably, such codes were not only meant for regulating the learning activities alone. The alarm calls or congregation calls were meant for the community at large . . . the routine presented a very interesting case for studying the 'pastoral' attributes and its integration with the average daily activity cycle of the well attended children. Such a routine seems very similar to the routine followed by the lonely boy at Jorasanko joint family-house with of course the addition of school hours. If the codified time blocks were the restrictions, the spaces filled in were the moments of freedom. The child in the school at Santiniketan was never seen as an individual with personal choices and problems. Personal choices and problems were subsumed by the distinct pattern in the routine and even more by the compulsions of joining the congregations, and most of all by the heavily value loaded teaching.[202]

Yet Tagore's system and discipline had more reciprocity, inter-human space and opportunities for procreative activities than what the Gandhian and the Hegelian system would allow. Tagore's guru was not sovereignly wise and hubristic as to deploy a system in the nature of what Paulo Freire calls the 'banking education'. There existed a challenge to the ways in which students and teachers confronted their limits through 'suffering' which, again, was the power of 'thinking' – exceeding one's self and situation. This suffering came from the doubt that the teacher had about the perfection of his lessons and his ways of 'mastering' of the students; it also emerged from the curiosity (an important faculty in Tagore's aesthetic education) that students were expected to have beyond the pedagogic premises of their academic acquirements. The suffering made them 'slaves' to their own drives of curiosity and, on certain occasions, this showed the creative mastery of the guru over things which he sometimes missed out on inculcating. So caught amidst creative suffering both the students and the teachers kept configurating, to an appreciable extent, their master–slave relationship in a complementariness devoid of the one-sided grammar of coercive domination, power and sovereignty. This made room for the life-enhancing 'conversations' (to employ Michael Oakeshott's pregnant metaphor)[203] in the ashram.

Tagore's ashram imbibed, to an extent, the spirit in *Taittriya Upanishad*[204] where we find the urge to know, grow and integrate with the Brahman – it is realized from the root *brh* which means to 'burst forth', to 'grow'.[205] Seeing the 'bursting forth' of the student under the inspiring tutelage of the guru, how can we interpret the character of the ashram? Where does that refigure the politics of 'friendship'? Tagore's Vedantic training notwithstanding, the ashram, and, subsequently, Visva Bharati, were not allowed to work out their investment-return dialectic with a Hegelian strictness. What this means is that Tagore saw certain limitations in the Upanishadic growth network between the teacher and the taught. The Hegelian tension with which knowledge and learning are seen to inscribe the teacher–taught relationship in *Taittriya Upanishad* does not work in Tagore's ways of aesthetic education. Less about integrality as harmony and more about plurality as generation of knowledge, Tagore's ideas about seeing the tension between institution and knowledge garnered significant attainments that got manifested in pleasure, delight and passion. Largely non-Platonic in nature, duty was pegged onto urge, desire and curiosity as promising determinants of knowledge formation. Also, austerity conjugated to devotion and renunciation formed a part of learning and acquirements and, hence, the Upanishadic formations achieved through self-realization, quietude and self-control invariably impacted on the growth of the life of ashramites in relation to their gurus. Tagore struggled to realize the middle ground generated through tensions between the tyranny of the senses and overpowering asceticism. Learning, thus, in the ashram became an embattled space whose apparent tranquillity concealed the restlessness of the experiments of a man whose learning had always extrapolated new areas of experience and understanding. Could knowledge be solely generated from the guru only, as Patanjali insisted? Or would the two be cooperators of a larger scheme of things where harmony comes from varying investments and diverse levels of endowments? The philosophy of living in the ashram fed on *Tattriya Upanishad's* formulations of giving nothing without faith: of giving in plenty, with modesty, fear and sympathy.

Intuition in educational pedagogy was as important a subject to Emerson, the pragmatic mystic, as it was to Tagore who wanted learning to be integral to the tragicomedy of human life. For both there was as much a deep force, 'the last fact behind which analysis cannot go' as there was the external nature which demanded that we educate the bodies, that we trained the 'eye and the hand'. Tagore and Emerson saw the 'deficit' of learning in the 'bookworm', the lack to see a 'fine barn as well as a good tragedy'.[206] Reading for both was indispensable – 'history and exact science he must learn by laborious reading'[207] – and inspiring but over-dependence on books was discouraged for that would replace in children their 'powers of intuition and reason': books should never be valued as such, not related to nature and human constitution, making them, thereby, a sort of 'third estate'. Tagore, in an Emersonian way, saw both 'drill' ('A sure proportion of rogue and dunce finds its way into every classroom . . . and the *gentle teacher*, who wished to be a Providence to youth.., knows as much vice as the judge of a police court'[208]) and 'intuition' in education, the importance of habit ligatured with curiosity and the growth of self-sufficiency embedded in a strong humanistic ideal. The 'gentle teacher' is Tagore's guru who ensures a communication – 'the method of nature' – between the one eager to disclose a new fact and the one awaiting to hear and experience, qualifying teaching as 'tranquil ministry'. The guru's function, in the words of Emerson, is to inspire – 'it is not instruction, but provocation that I can receive from another soul'.[209] The guru does not fail to introduce discipline but, as Emerson has argued, needs to cherish 'mother wit' whereby courses of learning should also learn to 'smuggle in a little contraband wit, fancy, imagination, thought'.[210] Ways of knowing – the dynamic gestalt of teaching – in the poet's school were deeply emotional and personal, bringing insight and emotion into a close communion. This built the legacy of childhood which empowered the child as he gained in on years and prepared to enter the next stage of learning and reading in the university.

Once again we encounter Godwin and Tagore in deep time (in)fusionizing to the point of creating unexpected travelling frequencies. William Godwin observes that master–pupil relationship is clearly about trust and goodwill and never pretence and insincerity. Tagore's guru does not have any 'trickery' Godwin accuses Rousseau of where the master strategically holds the reins of domination without making an ostentatious show of mastery. The guru makes allowance for the child to enjoy his claim 'upon his little sphere of empire and discretion'.[211] There was a kind of 'honesty' that Tagore sought to appreciate in the guru; this honesty made good measure of the child both by encouraging the growth of a romantic and reflective mind prospering on its own to adulthood and by tempering the mind with rationality and acumen – both a 'sheet of white paper' and a self-generative mind. Was Tagore his own self-portrait of a guru? I see this 'guru-ness' in both Godwin and Tagore, who by choosing to write for children, sought a way of intervening on the young minds and their requirements. Godwin writes, 'A child is not to be reared as that precious thing that no wind may blow, and no sun may scorch . . . . He should begin to stand by himself and respect his own dignity, as soon as he is able to utter an articulate sound'.[212] Through their writings both Godwin and Tagore proceeded to protect the children from censorious parents puritanizing their growth for a future measured only through certain yardsticks of material success. Their writings (like Tagore's *Sahaj Paath* or Easy Reader, his primer for children and Godwin's rewriting of the fables) helped children to travel freely into a world of their own, with inhabitants and things they would independently suffer and enjoy with. Both these thinkers mixed delight with education – an indulgent stretch that a guru would entertain to develop the reflective and imaginative faculties of a child. Godwin rightly notes, 'If we would benefit a child we must become in part a child ourselves. We must prattle to him: we must expatiate upon some points: we must introduce quick unexpected turns which if they are not wit, have the effect of wit to children. Above all, we must make our narrations pictures, and render the objects we discourse about, visible to the fancy of the learner'.[213] Books are consciously fashioned to entertain and develop a child intellectually and to avoid cluttering their tender minds with details that excite no passion and emotion.[214] Learning is both anticipation and advancement of life. Even John Ruskin disapproves what Arnold disparagingly terms as the 'ladder' which parents always consider as education in the life of their children. Education cannot merely turn into an instrument to secure social power and position buttressed by certain set of values and enabled by the 'Goddess of Getting-on'. Ruskin, like Tagore, disapproved the motive of 'competition' afflicting a child's points of engagement with education through the 'vice of jealousy' and 'strain and anxiety' and considered the prevalent examination system as 'miserable confusion and anxiety'.[215] Both Ruskin (*Elements of Drawing*, 1857) and Tagore, working in two different continents, advocated a freedom in the child's learning of art where rules, veracity of representation and decorum do not weigh in much. Ruskin's stress on preparing a child for its life's works and Tagore's insistence on connecting the child with the earth and 'living' correspond with Arnold's awareness of not overdoing the Hebraist virtues of 'doing' and not underperforming at the same time the Hellenic virtues of 'knowing'.

Contesting Minds, Contrasting Systems

The understanding of Tagore's philosophy of education is likely to suffer if we try to critique his experiments and thoughts in isolation, removing them from some of the ideas of European thinkers, particularly Rousseau and Froebel. Tagore's appropriation of Rousseau's ideas in *Emile* (Tagore mentions his acquaintance with Rousseau in his novella *The Broken Nest*, 1901) owes to the tradition of the 'natural order' in French education in the seventeenth and eighteenth centuries. Tagore's choice of the locale of his school, away from the broiling city, corresponds with the change that came over Rousseau when in 1756 he decided to settle on the borders of the Forest of Montmorency, far removed from the hubbub of Paris. This closeness to nature brought significant changes in Rousseau, stubbing out the indignation that city life bred in him. He admitted to have ceased despising men as soon as he lost sight of them. Whether it is 'Project for the Education of M. de. Sainte Marie' or 'Discourse on the Origin of Unequality among Men', Rousseau proposed a return to the state of 'nature', emphasizing the formation of the heart, mind and the judgement in children. The idea of the 'Natural Man' is not about a retreat to primordial savagery; but, an urge, a desire, to fight oneself free from the travails of civilization and the stultifying injunctions of society. For both Tagore and Rousseau, this freedom in nature determined a major part of their educational ideals. In the laboratory of his ashram, Tagore adopted Rousseau's 'return to nature' but attached importance to both the world of nature and the world of man; return to nature included human nature as well as external nature and both were founded on a primal sympathy.

Tagore's education was 'negative' as was Rousseau's. He recommended 'fullness of experience' by creating an 'atmosphere' of ideas. Education based on deep societal norms is no-education; rather, education guided by natural laws, through enabling procedures that enhance physical, emotional, moral and mental capacities become the reliable foundations of action. This contributes to the harmonious development of personality. Rousseau sees the natural man as greater than the citizen in whom education becomes a development from within and not merely an accretion from without. So like Tagore's guru, Rousseau's 'teacher' does his best to get the innate dispositions of the child to the fore, working on a pattern where the senses become one's guide. It articulates a life of the child where the sign can never be allowed to substitute for the thing itself except when it is impossible to show the thing. This prevents the child from getting absorbed in the signs and forgetting the thing represented. Nuanced disjunctures besides, Tagore's freedom-cure and the play-way method of Rousseau address the judgement of the child in her pursuits and choices of learning: in their patterns of natural education both know that childhood has its own ways of thinking, peculiar to itself, remarkably removed from both the norms and forms of adult thinking and understanding.

The dismissiveness with which Rousseau treats education as a kind of perversion of society in *Discourse on Inequality* finds some redemption later when in *Emile* he comes to believe in a plan of education based on nature. But the niggling crisis as to the reconcilement of the man in nature and the man in society does not show much signs of abatement. The constitution of man in nature – his education, values and achievements – is clearly faced with contradiction when man resorts to a different kind of adaptation of and compromise with values to survive socially. In the first book of *Social Contract*, Rousseau writes:

> The transition from the state of nature to the social state produced a very remarkable change in man by substituting justice for instinct as the principle of conduct, and so imparting to his actions the moral character which they originally lacked. It was only after that change, when the voice of duty took the place of physical impulse, that man, who had hitherto thought only of himself, was compelled to act on different principles and consult his reason before listening to his inclinations. Though in this state man loses many of the advantages he derives from nature, those he gains from the exercise and development of his faculties, the broadening of his ideas, the ennobling of his sentiments, and the elevation of his whole soul, are so great that, if the evils of the new condition did not often degrade him beneath that which he had left, he would have cause to bless unceasingly the happy moment that took him from it forever, and made an intelligent being and a man out of a stupid animal beset with limitations.[216]

But these conflicting principles derived from the savage nature and civil society put man against himself all the time for he needs to make prudent and prescient adjustments to restore the imbalance generated through the binaric tension. And the near utopic harmony among 'education of nature', 'education of men' and 'education of things', deeply intended by Rousseau, seems difficult to achieve. Both the educationists have similar anxieties on this subject but they are not oblivious of the limitations of an education that is independent of society. Children growing with the ashramic values were expected to be 'extraordinary' in combining both the natural and the social in them. Tagore believed in overcoming this seemingly inflexible antithesis (Rousseau calls the 'double man') through an education whose purpose would be to feed on both the natural and social dimensions of development – the man-in-nature shaking hands with the man-in-himself. Here individuality – formed, valued and inculcated – warded off the idiosyncrasies of the society and also the dull brutishness of natural man, and introduced a configuration embedded in balance, sensibility and judgement. Rousseau observes:

> If we want to form a man of nature, there need be no thought of making him a savage and banishing him to the heart of the woods. Assuming him to be shut up in the whirl of social life, it is enough that he should not allow himself to be drawn into it either by his own passions or by the opinions of men; that he should see with his own eyes and feel with his own heart; and that he should be governed by no authority but that of his own reason. It is clear that in this situation the multitude of objects which impinge on him, the frequent sentiments by which he is affected, the diverse means of providing for his actual needs, are bound to give him many ideas which he would never have had or which have come to him more slowly. The natural progress of the mind is accelerated but changed in direction. The very man who would remain stupid in the forests is sure to become rational and acute in the cities, even if he is a spectator of what goes on.[217]

Children were taught to keep their connect with nature undisturbed and yet not be wholly prejudicial to urban life and social institutions. The struggle in Rousseau to bring together imagination and fact is not merely peculiar to him; it is evident in Tagore too because mixing the two in education with care and discretion does not happen easily. The romantic in Rousseau as much as in Tagore pursued a quaint blend of alienation and isolation to carve a road to happiness. His later writings, especially, show both his isolation and alienation, and some paths leading to happiness. In *Reveries of the Solitary Walker*, Rousseau writes:

> But if there is a state where the soul can find a resting-place secure enough to establish itself and concentrate its entire being there, with no need to remember the past or reach into the future, where time is nothing to it, where the present runs on indefinitely but this duration goes unnoticed, with no sign of the passing of time, and no other feeling of deprivation

> or enjoyment, pleasure or pain, desire or fear than the simple feeling of existence, a feeling that fills our soul entirely, as long as this state lasts, we can call ourselves happy, not with a poor, incomplete and relative happiness such as we find in the pleasures of life, but with a sufficient, complete and perfect happiness which leaves no emptiness to be filled in the soul. Such is the state which I often experienced on the Island Of Saint-Pierre in my solitary reveries, whether I lay in a boat and drifted where the water carried me, or sat by the shores of the stormy lake, or elsewhere, on the banks of a lovely river or a stream murmuring over the stones.[218]

Tagore possessed a similar soul and this brought him into configuring the 'atmosphere' of the ashram – quiet and serene. In an extremely revealing passage in the *Confessions* Rousseau writes, 'My obstinate nature is unable to bow to facts. It cannot beautify, it must create. Realities appear to it nothing more than they are; it can only embellish the objects of imagination'.[219] If Rousseau was reacting to the over rationalism of the eighteenth century, Tagore was responding to the growing mechanization resulting from obsessive industrialization. However, the facts of everyday reality punctured inevitable holes into the deeply romantic sensibilities of both. Rousseau's suffering, much less in Tagore, would have lessened if he could bring the fusion of object and the subject as romantics later in the day were able to accomplish. The split in the object–subject which Rousseau found difficult to bridge led to an agony – a rankling spirit that impeded his efforts to argue the case for the natural man who is expected to work his life out on an 'inner light'. This light clarifies the doubt which usually blinkers the principles of mutual dependencies between man and society. Tagore, in my view, is more enabling in balancing out the impertinencies of society and the voice of the inner light (the essential sensibilities which make man cherish his savageness). This is not to be judged as a regression to primitivism but a conscious art to protect the attributes of the 'natural man' – some quintessential conception of manhood. The poet's principles of education for the ashramites were never distanced from the contemporary strains and stresses which a historically evolving British colonial education was expected to provide. By initiating significant departures in the forms of learning experiments and pedagogic innovations the poetmaster demonstrates a sensible critique of the educational realities of his times.

The ashram then was not constructed with the pronounced aim to produce better citizens or best standards of social living, not what generally we encounter in say, Locke's *Thoughts Concerning Education* (1693) and Fenelon's *Treatise on the Education of Girls* (1689). Rousseau stands apart from such well-entrenched ideals by purposing through Emile a growth which is both civilized and savage. This development is not oblivious of a stoicism which can contribute towards the building up of one's own society through a 'spiritual education'. Tagore was more astute in his understanding of the 'natural man' in that he was aware of the inadequacies of the simplicity of existence and also alert to the complexities and incongruities of human development. Although Tagore endorsed 'freedom cure', he was not blind to the disadvantages of both nature and society. Unlike Rousseau he opened up a space for natural and social negotiations allowing for more freedom that Rousseau would probably not have sanctioned – the transition from the *raison sensitive* to *raison intellectuelle*. Rousseau believed that the environment in which the child would grow was to be selected with care and authority; but such a milieu continuously trembled with the threat of social contamination because the belief in man's innate goodness (Emile's education is seen as highly egotistic) unabatedly encouraged the sceptical thought that the sources of evil lay in the 'other'. The responsibility for the generation of evil was disingenuously apportioned to the other, something that Tagore never supported in the organic development of the child.

Tagore's ashram, conceptually and pragmatically, reinvents itself in its negotiations with Frederick Froebel's school at Keilhau (he styled it as Universal German-Institution in 1820). Froebel's school had a variety of aims which, au fond, wanted to train children for humanity and create 'men in the image of God'. He, under the influence of Fichte, resorted to education as the cardinal means to inculcate a sense of nationality. Not much in sympathy with the subject of nationality, Tagore, through his school, amidst other patterns of training, sought the restitution of a cultural past which he thought was nearly lost to the hegemonic intrusions of the colonial West. However, through the ashram and the school respectively, Tagore and Froebel, brought about a rarely achieved harmony of life. Froebel points out that his plan was 'very simple' and what he wanted was 'a happy family school, and a peaceful life with nature' around him. When Superintendent Zeh visited Keilhau in 1825, he reported discovering a thoroughly and intimately united family of at least 60 members living in quiet harmony.[220] Froebel's school created a non-coercive atmosphere where the teacher and the student grew together in mutual trust and students built their community (in the sense of the *garten* which intones transformation) through solidarity, contributing to the successful functioning of the institution. It was the 'play' – the 'active representation of the inner necessity and impulse' – that became the article of faith in the life of the students in both the schools. The 'play' made allowance for the recognition of their skills and the freedom – the principle of *darstellung* encourages thinking, doing, work – that creativity and expression provide.[221] Play as a form of beauty, knowledge and life resulting in experiences, pattern and tangibility overlaid the notion of the *garten*. Students were encouraged to work in gardens and harvest agricultural produce not merely with an eye to relax a financially overstretched institution but, preponderantly, with the purpose to grow a connection with the earth and to cultivate the individuality required for a wholesome upbringing. Both the schools functioned with the dominant emphasis on a vernacular education and at the end of the day's work children were eased into meaningful leisure. Children chose their occupation in singing, staging plays, organizing musical functions, listening to and reading mythological tales – Froebel's persistent project in 'making the inner outer'.[222] Leisure had a purpose for both these men because they aimed to awaken the children into a different circulation of existence and understanding of good which could not merely be left to chance. Leisurely activities were made both recreational and subtly regulative to contribute to their organic development. Froebel's idea of kindergarten was built around the components of nature contact, divinity, self-activity and accomplishable social and moral ends. Tagore, however, executed a more thoughtful and delicate mix that had an acknowledgement of the ways in which Pestalozzi emphasized the importance of children over all other dimensions of a school, Johann Hebart's accent on teachers, and Hegel's stress on curriculum.

Froebel in *The Education of Man* observes that 'the child would know himself why he loves the thing; he would know all its properties, its innermost nature, that he may learn to understand himself in his attachment'. A child would invariably experiment and learn in ways different from an adult:

> A child has found a pebble. In order to determine by experiment its properties, he has rubbed it on a board nearby, and has discovered its property of imparting color. It is a fragment of lime, clay, red stone or chalk. See how he delights in the newly discovered property, and how

> easily he makes use of it. Soon the whole surface of the board is changed. At first the boy took delight in the new property, then in the changed surface – now red, now white, now black, now brown – but soon he began to find pleasure in the winding, straight, curved and other forms that appear. These linear phenomena direct his attention to the linear properties of surrounding objects . . .[223]

Tagore saw the significance of a child's way (play) of understanding the surroundings both in linear and complex modes of thought, instinct and inferences. There was an aesthetic in their 'play'. Tagore's point of intellectual contact with Froebel lies in conceiving the educator as a facilitator who makes education a kind of realization and experience of one's essential nature. Froebel's philosophy of education is predicated upon a conviction of the constancy of human nature and a belief in developmentalism which is organic and unitary. Educators are obligated to inspire the development of essential nature within a structure that combines the rational, the volitional and the affective dimensions of a child's activity. Is Tagore looking at a perfectibility that makes the child the 'adult's child', logically intervened and pedagogically prepared to develop as a fully determined individual? For Tagore, perfectibility is an error of judgement because inner logic of growth does not always 'listen' to the exactions and arguments of the adult world. Froebel's negative education corresponds with the 'freedom' that Tagore's ashram provides, but the growth in the ashram within the politics of the bureaucratic green generates a positive tendency to combine natural impulses and instinct with well-reasoned resistances to recklessness. For both these men, personal harmony is not in letting 'nature' run out of control because nourishment is dialectical in being attentive both to the 'ground of being' and the forces that discipline brings. The plant metaphor[224] need not always be the appropriate analogy in our understanding of the development of a child. Freedom is not in being limitlessly reflexive; it is also in earning the space to create new ideas through intellectual and existential unfettering. Education then for Tagore becomes a kind of 'striving', a freedom that self-activity and a certain cultivation of autonomy through the inner principle of growth can bring. Tagore, in the spirit of Whitehead, lamented the neglect of 'attention' to the rhythms of life. Whitehead notes that 'the most complete achievement of varied activity expressing the potentialities of that living creature in the face of its actual environment. . . . Each individual embodies an adventure of existence. The art of life is the guidance of this adventure'.[225] Freedom is an adventure in understanding the subtle stages of the child's engagement with education which can at once be normed and normless: an art of life where futility of knowing (all knowledge is not utility and future specific), disciplinization and impulse education contribute to the development of personality. This is the romance of education where the self grows by being aware of its limitations and conscious of adventurous transcendence.

The Romance of the Place, Resonance of the Space

Questions about the efficacy of the place and space were thrown at Tagore and he was at pains to explain his position and convince the world of the dynamics and pragmatics of a poet's school. For someone who had not had a full innings in a 'proper' formal school, this particular brand of green moralism and eco-pedagogy became an enormous challenge to execute, sustain and, eventually, defend. Although we encounter conceptual differences as to the hierarchical politics of place and space – Yi-Fu Tuan sees space and place as an inseparable dyad continually feeding each other through a productive complementariness,[226] Edward Casey's phenomenological geography talks more to the power of place than it does to space,[227] there is the primacy of space over place in Kantian epistemology – Tagore scarcely allowed any prioritization, making one complement the other. The poet's school was cosmos and hearth[228] – the hearth was the ashram that was integrally connected with the cosmos. The immediate setting, the hearth, was integrated to the greater truth that Tagore qualified as the infinite, cosmos. Choosing a place (Bolpur, a small town, now in the district of Birbhum in West Bengal) and constructing it (Santiniketan) was a combination of a mind and matter – material and mental. The experience of place, as Anne Stenros has argued, is essential, 'the feeling of place, and its origins, since place is the most unique experience of space, and it is man's deepest experience of the environment'.[229] Tagore's choice of place, his 'owning' it and his description of its landscape and environment show his engagement with the politics and dynamics of how a 'place' contributes to the construction of the space. He writes:

> All round our *ashram* is a vast open country, bare up to the line of the horizon except for sparsely-growing stunted date-palms and prickly shrubs

> struggling with anthills. Below the level of the field there extend numberless mounds and tiny hillocks of red gravel and pebbles of all shapes and colours, intersected by narrow channels of rain-water. Not far away towards the south near the village can be seen through the intervals of a row of palm trees the gleaming surface of steel-blue water, collected in a hollow of the ground. A road used by the village people for their marketing in the town goes meandering through the lonely fields, with its red dust staring in the sun. Travellers coming up this road can see from a distance on the summit of the undulating ground the spire of a temple and the top of a building, indicating the Shanti-Niketan *ashram*, among its *amalaki* groves and its avenue of stately *sal* trees.[230]

In his construction of Santiniketan, Tagore evinced an awareness of the 'where' (Aristotle has announced in his *Physics* that 'the power of place will be remarkable'.[231]) and then constructed something 'beyond the place', the 'post-placeness' (if I may make employ a not-too-pleasant neologism). The ashram became a potential space where the mind invested its own ideas into matter and matter in its sociocultural and eco-spiritual mobility contributed to the growth of the mind (its consequent and constructed meta-locations). As a potential space it constituted itself within a continuity that existed between the selves of the ashramites and the setting. (*Shanti-Niketan* is a composite of *niketan* which is place, matter, and *shanti*, peace, which emerges from the mind). This becomes a complex experience in that the visibility of matter (*actualité*) and the invisibility of affective and imagined realms of experience evolved, at times, a choric space subjected to the continual experimentation of Tagore. Indra Kagis McEwan in *Socrates' Ancestor* points out that the word *chōros* not just means the dancing floor (place) but the dance as a process (the mentalization, the imaging and the imagining), with *chora* being a place 'which admits not of destruction and provides room for all things that have birth . . . it is somehow necessary that all that exists should exist in some spot [*en tini topoi*] and occupying some place [*ketachon choron tina*] . . . '.[232] The poet's school had a setting, a place, and also, isomorphically, the making of a place. Tagore's romantic desire to break free from the pedagogic enchainment of his boyhood years, his winsome dwelling in the tradition of the *tapovan*, his choice of proximity to nature and his anxieties over the relevance of a system nourished by *brahmacharya* – design, desire and dream – rendered the ashram as an 'unveiling'. This became a phenomenon that was born out of the power to *own* a place, making the physicality of owning correspond with certain unconcealments of mind. It also provided the fecund 'supplement' that the mind, in its construction of spaces, supplied to the place *per se*. The ashram was Gaston Bachelard's 'eulogized space', the 'lived in' space not inhabited neutrally but with 'all the partiality of the imagination'.[233] The ashram-school discourse implicated how strongly Tagore defended both the space and the aesthetics of the place. So his school became both a 'geometric space' and a 'lived space'[234] – 'geometric' in its externality and uniformity of laws and ways and 'lived' in its values, opportunities and emotional investments. This lived space was personal, embodied and intimate. It engaged students in a network with teachers, peers, living and learning conditions; it transformed values and ideas and generated meaning through a lot of activities which were more physical than mental. Yet the abiding principle of *shanti* helped students to locate and anchor themselves within a dynamics of meaning that removed the apparent rivalry between the priorities of space and place. Perhaps 'naming' the place (*shanti-niketan*) was an important act in that it determined the space to a large extent and called for the enduring appeal of its character. Tagore chose a place which had *shanti* – his own 'Isle of Innisfree'[235] – and the *shanti* of the place was allowed to grow in conjunction with the peace and tranquillity of the mind which he encouraged and engendered among his pupils.

Tagore's ashram-school was, thus, geo-spiritualized between a mind that constructed and a body that experienced. It was constrained (rather, 'closed') by the limits of its chosen physicality that topophilic Tagore would never have compromised with; it was 'open' because of the projections and prolepticism that Tagore's mind could not have avoided importing. This is not about grasping space only by our senses as, Matoré has argued, but is also about living in it – 'we project our personality into it, we are tied to it by emotional bonds; space is not just perceived. . . . it is lived'.[236] Tagore had strapped an idea to a place; he introjected an idea into the making of a place, allowing the release of its aesthetic virtues through culture, nature, order and equilibrium. He, thus, interiorized it and made the matter the possession of the mind. Within its physical domain and liminality, the ashram became a site of negotiations among people of various caste and religious affiliations (Tagore clearly points out: 'We have fully admitted the inequalities and varieties of human life in our ashram. We never try to gain some kind of outward uniformity by weeding out the differences of nature and training of our members'.[237])

which, thus, turned into a site of 'sympathy' (*sambandha*). The school graduated into a space of *harmonia* of inter-enveloping selves. This made the ashram a geo-sophical space which did not simply create conceptual spaces but also acknowledged different kinds of values, feelings and experiences. Space, therefore, became both a 'spectacle' and 'receptacle'. Tagore effectuated a complex mechanism (ways, wishes, wants) which worked itself out within the apparent closure of the place and the consequent disclosures of the space: the 'palpable landscapes and impalpable mindscapes continually intermingle and form internal relations with each other'.[238]

The Picture of Hope

Speaking of hope Tagore observes that life does not definitively premise our limits and energies of hope. It is the 'right' to hope that enhances man's strength – the greater the expanse of hope, the more are the chances of empowerment. It is hope that clears out the way ahead and any project that shows and evinces seeds of hope alerts us to the possibilities and power that hope can bring into our lives.[239] The ashram was Tagore's utopia, his eros, and the metaphysics of his hope (both ultimate and absolute)[240] – hope existed as creativity, as 'anticipatory illumination', a 'pre-appearance',[241] as a Heideggerian refiguration of the present and as openness to possibilities. Hope in Tagore and for most of the teachers in his school who believed in his enduring experiments and dream, was 'alive'; it resulted in 'planning'.[242] Tagore's hopes in and for the ashram were not evangelistic but dialectical (Tagore had his own doubts about the continuance and fructification of his experiments[243]) in finding its anchorage in the suffering and delight of the present (Tagore was not carrying a past model into the making of his ashram and did not have a future model to achieve and emulate). His intense engagement with the 'present' of his school formed the hopes for its enduring 'presence' in the tomorrow. The school, Tagore confessed, was an intensely critical project of finding outlet for his long nurtured expressions. It was the manifestation of a self which found its fulfilment in the tortured twigs of ceaseless deficit – the exiguousness, the implacable murmur of an idea whose practicality was minimal and the joy of indulgence which braved a prospective economic ruin. He points out how immense courage (he even admitted to facing resistance from his own members of his family) was needed to inaugurate the project without the certainty of fund, resource and sustenance because the road ahead was unfamiliar and the ultimate results were untested.[244] Rathindranath Tagore describes the trials and the pain that his father had to court for his dream:

> Very few knew or realized the struggle which Father had to carry on his educational experiment at Santiniketan. When the school was established, he had difficulty in getting pupils and those that came were mostly of the difficult type. People looked down upon the institution and ridiculed Father's attempt to introduce new ideas in education. It took years before people began to recognize the Santiniketan school *as anything else but a reformatory*. To this was added the suspicion of the British Government, and the secret circulars that were issued to warn officials from sending their children to Santiniketan. Considered from a worldly point of view, it was indeed *foolhardy* of Father to have launched into this misadventure, at a time when he hardly had enough to support himself and his family and was actually in debt on account of the failure of the Kushtia business. He had to dispose of everything he possessed including the ornaments belonging to my mother, in order to start the school. Among other things he had to sell his gold watch and chain – a wedding gift – to a friend.[245]

Yet he braved 'alien entanglements' (in the words of Robert Frost) and delightfully submitted to the life of an idea where education came to be seen in the hands of fools whom God needs.[246] He had the romance and obduracy of a fool. Such a fool is always God's chosen child. His ultimate hope, divorced from false optimism and fatalism, conquered the shame of immediate penury with which the ashram-school was tortuously afflicted – a hope that made Tagore and his students refigure the dynamic conjugation between suffering and creativity. This is a hope that had the power to translate cynicism into fortitude and prudence.

Tagore threw all his weight behind 'aesthetic education'. Like Tolstoy he knew that the 'real knowledge is how to live your life' where a few things cannot be taught, where self-education is often intuitive and where 'wisdom could not flow from one man who is full of it to another who has none, in the same way that in two connected vessels water flows from one to the other until the level is the same in both of them . . . to achieve wisdom you have to make an independent, serious effort on your own'.[247] Tagore made such an effort and tried to ensure that most of his pupils and teachers took similar steps in that direction. George Eliot points out that 'aesthetic teaching is the highest of all teaching because it deals with life in its highest complexity. But if it ceases to be purely aesthetic – if it lapses anywhere from the picture to the diagram – it becomes the most offensive of all teaching'.[248] Denying himself the role of a schoolmaster by conceiving and executing a project like a poet, Tagore sought a 'picture' and not a 'diagram' in his ashram. Confessed to having a highly expressive nature, Tagore pointed out repeatedly how he held a 'picture' in his mind about the school for long. The 'picture' in him grew not out of an altruistic urge or ecumenical charity but emerged out of a devotion inscribed in anxiety, angst and agility.[249] His aesthetic education, without the diagrammatic stringency, combined a freedom of thought with a well-carved plan, a system with a lack of system and knowledge with an ignorance of knowledge. Teaching was not technology to him and Tagore alongside the teachers in his school never wanted to diagrammatize pedagogy, preventing, education, thus, from losing out to the arid curriculum of mere skill and 'explicit' learning conducive only to the enhancement of qualifications and the security of employment. Acknowledging aesthetic education as a 'picture', Tagore, like a poet with a dream, had set sail on a journey – in risk, adventure and romance – whose educative mission was not just the 'transfer of skills' and formal prescriptive vocabulary of learning but a commitment to an 'art' that did not reduce life to mere 'maps' and 'boxes' but fostered the consciousness of personal growth inscribed in feelings, instinct, spontaneity, desires, moods, drives and affect. This was the poet's 'butterfly', the aesthetic and ethics of which lie in the creation of spaces between the teacher and the taught – the spaces that were created through a consciousness of location, personalities, surroundings and fraternity. Teaching in the ashram then was not disseminative learning, not didactic modes of instruction only, but ways of exceeding oneself: learning was about how to learn more, about falling blithely into the enticement of surplus.[250]

However, the pregnant sacrality of the ashram built over a period of seventeen years teased out more spaces than it could accommodate, leading to the glocal aspirations of forming Visva Bharati in 1918. Salvaging a university from an ashram, as we shall see in the next chapter, required producing deeper investments in values, communication, politics of knowledge formation, contestation of ideals and ethics within the premises of a new project that Tagore termed the East–West dialogue. The growth of a school into a university required fresh negotiations among institutional structures, greater demands of money and resources, more infrastructural facilities and many other endowments and benefits of Tagore's travels (in Europe and America) across continents. The butterfly needed a separate vein of training to fly merrily again. It fluttered in a fresh preparedness to be his Visva Bharati.[251]

Notes

1. See Tagore, 'Siksha', in *Rabindra Rachanabali* Vol. 14, (Govt. of West Bengal, 1992), 477 (Tagore 1992). Tagore arrived at Santiniketan in 1901. He writes: 'Fortunately for me I had a place ready to my hand where I could begin my work. My father, in one of his numerous travels, had selected this lonely spot as the one suitable for his life of communion with God. This place, with a permanent endowment, he dedicated to the use of those who seek penance and seclusion for their meditation and prayer. I had about ten boys with me when I came here and started my new life with no previous experience whatsoever'. Tagore, 'My School', in *Personality*, (Calcutta: Rupa, 2002), 141 (Tagore 2002b). 'It is against the nature of a genius to be content', writes, Rathindranath Tagore, eldest son of the poet, 'with a monotonous existence or be satisfied with a single purpose in life. Father was no exception. Throughout his life he would constantly want to change his living quarters, his surroundings, his food and his clothes and, what mattered most, he needed fresh fields to give scope to his active and a creative mind. It was no wonder that Shilaidaha could not hold him for very long. His next move was to Santiniketan. He had become restless and was eager to find a congenial place where he could experiment with his ideas about education'. *On the Edges of Time* (Visva Bharati, 1958), 41 (Tagore 1958). The formal opening ceremony was performed on 23 December 1901.
2. Rabindranath Tagore's 'A Poet's School' in *Towards Universal Man* (London: Asia Publishing House, 1961), 285 (Tagore 1961a). This essay was written in 1926. Italics are mine.
3. Tagore revolted at the thought of education being strangulated for material 'use' and ulterior furtherance: commodification of education coupled with an economy of knowledge (*vidya*) whose efficacy is far removed from joy and self-liberation. See *Rabindra Rachanabali*, 470.
4. 'A Poet's School', 285, 286 (Tagore 1961a). One can also see ashram-schools like the Ranchi school founded by Paramhansa Yogananda and Gurukul Kangri Vishvavidyalaya at Hardwar founded by the Arya Pratinidhi Sabha. For more on ashram-schools see Gita Wijesinghe, 'Indian Philosophy as a Means for Understanding Modern Ashram Schools', *Comparative Education*, Vol. 23, No. 2, 1987, 237–43 (Wijesinghe 1987) and

A. S. Altekar, *Education in Ancient India* (Varanasi: Nand Kishore, 1965). (Altekar 1965)

5. Uma Das Gupta, *Rabindranath Tagore: A Biography*, (New Delhi: Oxford University Press, 2004), 15. (Das Gupta 2004)
6. Rabindranath Tagore, 'The Problem of Education', in *Towards Universal Man* (London: Asia Publishing House, 1961), 75. (Tagore 1961a)
7. Tagore, 'A Poet's School', 289 (Tagore 1961a). Italics are mine.
8. *Discourse on Thinking*, (trans.) John M. Anderson and E. Hans Freund (New York: Harper & Row, 1966), 51/19. (Heidegger 1966)
9. L. Mumford, *The Myth of the Machine: The Pentagon of Power* (New York: Harcourt Brace Jovanovich, 1970), 322 (Mumford 1970). Italics are mine. Being alive for Mumford is to act holistically as humans which is about trying to 'exercise all their organs without officious interference, to see through their own eyes, hear with their own ears, to work with their own hands, to move on their own legs, to think with their own minds, to experience erotic gratification and to beget children in direct sexual intercourse – in short, reacting as whole human beings to other whole human beings, in constant engagement with both the visible environment and the immense heritage of historic culture, whereof technology is only a part'. (322)
10. Tagore writes, 'When we know the world as alien to us, then its mechanical aspect takes prominence in our mind; and then we set up machines and our methods to deal with it and make as much profit as our knowledge of its mechanism allows us to do. This view of things does not play us false, for the machine has its place in this world . . . This aspect of truth cannot be ignored: it has to be known and mastered'. *Creative Unity* (London: Macmillan, 1962), 312. (Tagore 1962)
11. Tagore, 'Tapovan', in *Rabindra Rachanabali*, Vol. 14, (Govt. of West Bengal, 1992), 384 (Tagore 1992). Tapovan cult or forest schools had its modern day manifestations in the West namely through Ernest Westlake who through the Order of Woodcraft Chivalry wanted to introduce a new form of learning: a radical movement which saw religion, ritual, tradition, discipline, earth contact and joyful closeness to nature all coming together through a powerful inhabitation of the world. Citing Westlake, van der Eyken and Turner note: 'the child who has been rooted and grounded in Woodcraft will be able to use the higher crafts without injury, and books without pedantry. In this way traditional learning and social culture will have full opportunity to complete the wisdom and refinement necessary to his highest functioning'. W. van der Eyken and B. Turner, *Adventures in Education*. (Harmondsworth: Penguin Press Ltd., 1969), 134. (Eyken and Turner 1969)
12. Tagore, 'A Poet's School', 290–91 (Tagore 1961a). Italics are mine.
13. See 'Ashramer Siksha', in *Rabindra Rachanabali*, Vol. 14, 431 (Tagore 1992). Translation by the poet himself.

14. *Rabindra Rachanabali*, 463.
15. See Bashabi Fraser (ed.) *The Tagore-Geddes Correspondence* (Kolkata: Visva Bharati, 2004), 63–4 (Fraser 2004). The emphases are mine.
16. Tagore, 'A Poet's School', 299. (Tagore 1961a)
17. *Rabindra Rachanabali*, Vol. 14, 470. (Tagore 1992)
18. Tagore writes, 'An atmosphere was created, and what was important, this atmosphere provided the students with a natural impulse to live in harmony with it'. See 'Conversations in Russia', *English Writings of Rabindranath Tagore*, Vol. III (Delhi: Sahitya Akademi, 1996), 933. (Das 1996)
19. *Rabindra-Rachanabali*, 300.
20. See Pierre Mabille, *Egregores ou la vie des civilisations* (Paris: Sagittaire, 1977). (Mabille 1977)
21. C. F. Andrews writes, 'We have no classrooms. The boys sit with their teachers, in the open air, under the trees. There are no large classes. A group of eight or ten boys will be seated round the teacher, asking him questions.... Like the open air education which Plato loved in Athens, the greater part is carried on through conversation. The boys soon learn to bring all their difficulties to their teachers; and the teachers get keenly interested in the boys' questions and answers. Such living education can never be dull'. 'An Open-Air School', *Visva Bharati News*, Silver Jubilee Number, 1957, 2.
22. Himanshu Mukherjee, *Education for Fullness* (London: Asia Publishing House, 1962), 296. (Mukherjee 1962)
23. Bernadette Wegenstein, *Getting Under the Skin, The Body and Media Theory* (Cambridge, MA: MIT Press, 2006), 7. (Wegenstein 2006)
24. Yasuo Yuasa, *The Body: Toward an Eastern Mind-Body Theory* (ed.) Thomas P. Kasulis & (trans.) Nagatomo Shigenori (Albany: State University of New York Press, 1987), 2 (Yuasa 1987). Metapsychics is not metaphysics in the traditional Western sense. Yuasa looks into 'non-dualism' which is central to many Asian traditions undercutting 'such Western dichotomies as spirit-matter, subjectivity-objectivity, and theory-praxis'.
25. Hans Ulrich Gumbrecht, *Production of Presence: What Meaning Cannot Convey* (Stanford: Stanford University Press, 2004), 128. (Gumbrecht 2004)
26. See Johann Wolfgang von Goethe, *The Sorrows of Young Werther and Selected Writings* (trans.) Catherine Hutter (New York: New American Library, Inc., 1962), 62. (Goethe 1962)
27. Tagore, 'Schooling' Rabindranath Tagore to Victoria Ocampo, *The Visva Bharati Quarterly*, 29, 4, 1963–1964, 274, 275, 278. (Tagore 1963–1964)
28. Gumbrecht, *Production of Presence*, 106. (Gumbrecht 2004)
29. A. Dworkin, *Intercourse* (London: Arrow Books, 1988), 25–6. (Dworkin 1988)
30. Gumbrecht, *Production of Presence*, 118. (Gumbrecht 2004)

31. Quoted in Maurice Merleau-Ponty, *The Primacy of Perception*, (ed.) James M. Edie (Evanston: Northwestern University Press, 1964), 169. (Merleau-Ponty 1964b)
32. Enchantment (*zauber*) is being destroyed by the advance of rationality in a process of 'Entzauberung der Welt'. See Max Weber, *Political Writings* (ed.) Peter Lassman & Ronald Speirs (Cambridge University Press, 1994) (Weber 1994); also see Lawrence Scaff, *Fleeing the Iron Cage: Culture, Politics and Modernity in the Thought of Max Weber* (Berkeley: University of California Press, 1989) (Scaff 1989); Nicholas Gane, *Max Weber and Postmodernism: Rationalization vs Disenchantment* (Basingstoke: Palgrave, 2002) (Gane 2002). On Simmel see *The Sociology of Georg Simmel* (ed. & trans.) Kurt H. Wolff (Free Press, 1950) (Wolff 1950); Duk-Yung Kim, *Georg Simmel und Max Weber: Über zwei Entwicklungswege der Soziologie* (VS Verlag für Sozialwissenschaften, 2002). (Kim 2002)
33. Tagore, 'Thoughts on Education', *The Visva Bharati Quarterly*, Vol. XIII, Parts I & II, May-Oct 1947, 4 (Tagore 1947). Amita Gupta notes that 'rational constructivists, led by Piaget, consider the child as an egocentric self and the construction of knowledge as an individual and cognitive process. The focus of Piaget's research has been on genetic epistemology and its scientific discourse has described the human being in such clinical terms as individual, organism, and biological. Piaget's theory explains cognitive development and learning in the human being in terms of the physical interactions between a biological organism and a physical environment through a process of assimilation and accommodation. This precludes the influence that social, cultural, and historical factors – by way of interactions with people, language, traditions, and rituals – have on children's learning and cognitive development. Piaget's emphasis on logicomathematical reasoning denies the multiple realities of children's worlds and the powerful role that fantasy plays in these realities'. See *Early Childhood Education, Postcolonial Theory, And Teaching Practices in India* (New York: Palgrave Macmillan, 2006), 7–8 (Gupta 2006). Also, see J. Piaget, *The Moral Judgement of the Child* (New York: Free Press, 1965). (Piaget 1965)
34. D. H. Lawrence, *Fantasia of the Unconscious* (Rockville: Serenity Publishers, 2008), 43. (Lawrence 2008)
35. John Ruskin, *Fors Clavigera*, (1871–1884), Letter LI. See Judith Hicks, 'The Educational Theories of John Ruskin: A Reappraisal', *British Journal of Educational Studies*, Vol. 22, No. 1, (1974), 71 (Hicks 1974). Jnanendranath Chattopadhyay observes that 'science, particularly experimental science, was not a school subject in North East India under the Calcutta University till very lately. But his [Tagore] school had a laboratory fitted with apparatus gifted by the Maharaja Tippera, and the students had lessons in science. Object lessons and nature-study received due care. There was a large

Reflecting Telescope through which the students peeped at the heavenly bodies, and came to know a good deal about them. He gave the boys a sewing machine and various tools. Book-binding interested many students'. 'Rabindranth and his Asrama School' *The Visva Bharati Quarterly*, Vol. XIII, May–October 1947, 14.

36. Supriyo Thakur, *Chelebelar Santiniketan* (Santiniketan of My Boyhood Years) (Kolkata: Ananda Publishers, 2012), 50–1 (Thakur 2012).
37. H. Owen and I. Bell, *Wilfred Owen: Collected Letters* (London: Oxford University Press, 1967), 179. (Owen and Bell 1967)
38. See K. C. Mukherjee, 'Tagore-Pioneer in Education' *British Journal of Educational Studies*, Vol. 18, No. 1, (Feb., 1970), 77 (Mukherjee 1970). Italics are mine.
39. David Kennedy & Walter Kohan, 'Aion, Kairos and Chronos: Fragments of an Endless Conversation on Childhood, Philosophy and Education', *Childhood and Philosophy*, Vol. 4, No. 8, jul./dex (2008), 7. (Kennedy and Kohan 2008)
40. Ibid., 8. (David and Kohan jul./dex 2008)
41. The 'boy,... just because he more than any other has a fount of intelligence in him which has not yet run clear,... is the craftiest, most mischievous, and unruliest of brutes. So the creature must be held in check...' See E. Hamilton & H. Cairns (eds.). *The Collected Dialogues of Plato* (Princeton: Princeton University Press, 1961), 1379. (Hamilton and Cairns 1961)
42. Erasmus, 'On Education for Children' in E. Rummel (ed.) *The Erasmus Reader* (Toronto: University of Toronto Press, 1990), 67, 69, 65–102. (Erasmus 1990)
43. Tagore's concerns about the isolation of the child within an adult-centric world – the misjudged and misconceptualized alien awaiting to be mastered – find a meaningful wavelength with Norbert Elias's views on this subject: '... The more "natural" the standard of delicacy and shame appears to adults and the more civilized restraint of instinctual urges is taken for granted, the more incomprehensible it becomes to adults that children do not have this delicacy and shame by "nature."... The children necessarily touch again and again on the adult threshold of delicacy, and – since they are not yet adapted – they infringe the taboos of society, cross the adult shame frontier, and penetrate emotional danger zones which the adult himself can only control with difficulty.... In this situation the adult does not explain the demand he makes on behavior. He is unable to do so adequately. He is so conditioned that he conforms to the social standard more or less automatically.... Anxiety is aroused in adults when the structure of their own instinctual life as defined by the social order is threatened. Any other behavior means danger. This leads

to the emotional undertone associated with moral demands and the aggressive and threatening severity of upholding them, because the breach of prohibitions places in an unstable balance of repression all those for whom the standard of society has become "second nature" '. See N. Elias, *The Civilizing Process: The History of Manners* (trans.) E. Jephcott (New York: Urizen Books, 1978), 167. (Elias 1978)

44. Rabindranath Tagore, 'The Schoolmaster', *Visva Bharati News*, May–June, 1980, 253 (reprinted from *The Modern Review*, October, 1924). (Tagore 1980)
45. Ibid., 254. (Tagore May–June, 1980)
46. See David Kennedy, *The Well of Being* (Albany: State University of New York Press, 2006), 167 (Kennedy 2006).
47. William Godwin, 'Essay 1' in *The Enquirer: Reflections on Education, Manners, and Literature: In a Series of Essays* (London: G.G. & J. Robinson, 1797), 1. (Godwin 1797)
48. William Godwin, *Enquiry Concerning Political Justice*, 3rd ed. (1798), facsimile ed. in 3 Vols (ed.) F. E. L. Priestley (Toronto: University of Toronto Press, 1946), Vol. I, ch. IV. (Godwin 1798/1946)
49. Godwin, *The Enquirer*, Essay I, 5–6. (Godwin 1797)
50. Bob Blaisdell, (ed.) *Tolstoy as Teacher: Leo Tolstoy's Writings on Education*, (New York: Teachers & Writers Collaborative, 2000), 177–78. (Blaisdell 2000)
51. See Immanuel Kant, *Anthropology, History and Education* (ed. & trans.) Robert B. Louden (Cambridge: Cambridge University Press, 2007) (Kant 2007).
52. Maria Montessori, *The Absorbent Mind* (New York: Holt, Rinehart and Winston, 1967), 246–47. (Montessori 1967)
53. Montessori, *Dr. Montessori's Own Handbook* (New York: F. A. Stokes, 1914), 77. (Montessori 1914)
54. *Rabindra Rachanabali*, 469.
55. Writing about Satish Roy, Tagore observes, 'He was not like other teachers, a mere vehicle of textbooks. He made his teaching personal, he himself was the source of it, and therefore, it was made of life stuff easily assimilable by the living human nature. The real reason of his successes was his intense interest in life, in ideas, in everything around him, in the boys who came in contact with him. He had his inspiration not through the medium of books but through the direct communication of his sensitive mind with the world. The seasons had upon him the same effect as they had upon the plants. He seemed to feel in his blood the unseen messages of nature that are always travelling through space, floating in the air, shimmering in the leaves, tingling in the roots of the grass under the earth'. See Tagore, 'Introduction' *Shantiniketan* (London: Macmillan, 1916), 22–4. (Tagore 1916)

56. Mukherjee, 'Tagore-Pioneer in Education', 76. (Mukherjee Feb., 1970)
57. See 'Siksha and Sanskriti', 416. My translations.
58. See 'Sikshar Swabanghikoron', 419. My translations.
59. J. L. Axtell, *The Educational Writings of John Locke* (Cambridge University Press, 1968). See section 216. (Axtell 1968)
60. *Hard Times*, chap. II, 254.
61. Ibid., Bk. I, chap. XV, 357.
62. J. A. Green (ed.), *Pestalozzi's Educational Writings* (London: Edward Arnold, 1912), 18. (Green 1912)
63. F. Froebel, [1826] *The Education of Man* (New York: Dover Publications Inc., 2009), 8. (Froebel 2009)
64. J. J. Rousseau, *Emile* (trans.) B. Foxley (London: Dent, 1911), 58. (Rousseau 1911)
65. For more on this subject one may see *Emile* and *The New Héloïse*. Even in his *The Government of Poland* Rousseau exhorts the cultivation of natural disposition of children.
66. Rousseau makes the distinction most clearly here, in the *Lettres morales*: 'The art of reasoning [*L'art de raisonner*] is not reason. It is often the abuse of reason. Reason is the faculty of ordering all the faculties of our soul in conformity with the nature of things, and in conformity with the relation of things to us. Reasoning [*Le raisonnement*] is the art of comparing known truths in order to construct on their basis other truths of which we were previously ignorant and which this art [of reasoning] enables us to discover. But it does not teach us to discover those basic truths [*ces vérités primitives*] which serve as the core of other truths. And when in the place of truths we put our opinions, our passions and our prejudices, far from illuminating us, it blinds us. It then does not elevate the soul, but enervates and corrupts our judgment which it ought to perfect'. See Timothy O'Hagan, *Rousseau* (London: Routledge, 1999), 68. (O'Hagan 1999)
67. See Tagore's letter to Prashanta Mahalanobis (13 September 1928) where he emphasizes the need to cultivate the 'desire' in the child's mind, a 'curiosity' to know the world around them. Physical and mental hungers are of different characters. Curiosity, Tagore felt, is the key to fullness of education. See *Chitipatreh Vidyalaya Prosongoh*, 107–08. (Saha 2001)
68. Bertrand Russell 1903. 'A Free Man's Worship', Accessed 21 September 2015, http://www3.nd.edu/afreddos/courses/264/fmw.htm. (Russell 1903)
69. See C. S. Lewis, *The Abolition of Man* (New York, Macmillan, 1947), 74–86 (Lewis 1947). John Stuart Mill experienced the need of a similar kind of 'solitude' at the age of 20 when he suffered a 'mental crisis'. This search for solitude led him to explore the deeper recesses of the heart. Mill discovered the deficiencies of his 'bookish' education, which, as he says, 'was more fitted for training me to know than to do' (100). The solitude taught him

how his education had failed him by neglecting the artistic-aesthetic side of his life – the habits of sensibility. 'I needed to be made to feel', Mill writes, 'that there was real, permanent happiness in tranquil contemplation' (130). It was Wordsworth's poetry that gave Mill what he lacked so far – 'they expressed, not mere outward beauty, but states of feeling, and of thought coloured by feeling, under the excitement of beauty. They seemed to be the very culture of the feelings, which I was in quest of' (129–130). In short, what Mill learned from Wordsworth's poems was the very 'sources of happiness, when all the greater evils of life shall have been removed. And I felt myself at once better and happier as I came under their influence' (130). See *James and John Stuart Mill on Education* (ed.) F. A. Cavenagh (Westport: Greenwood Press, 1979) (Cavenagh 1979). Tagore, the poet-master, could only have thought about the power of poetry – the solitude and joy – changing the life of his ashram; it was a power and movement which very few people could understand – some members of his family were also not welcoming of the idea – resulting in criticism that he had to defend against all through his life. He believed that the work he began in Santiniketan had been God's vast field for poetry. See Ms. Accession no. 190 (in Bengali), 12–13.

70. *Rabindra Rachanabali*, Vol. 14, 463. (Tagore 1992)
71. See Martin Heidegger, 'Homeland', (trans.) Thomas F. O'Meara, in *Listening* 6 (1971), 231–38. (Heidegger 1971)
72. Tom Colwell, 'The Ecological Perspective in John Dewey's Philosophy of Education,' *Educational Theory*, Vol. 35, No. 3, (1985), 255–66. (Colwell 1985)
73. John Dewey, *Democracy and Education* (New York: The Free Press, 1916), 211. (Dewey 1916)
74. Thomas B. Colwell, 'The Ecological Basis of Human Community,' *Educational Theory*, Vol. 21, No. 4, (1971), 427. (Colwell 1971)
75. Neil Evernden, *The Social Creation of Nature* (Baltimore: The Johns Hopkins University Press, 1992), 55. (Evernden 1992)
76. Tagore observes that 'a boy should live in the midst of nature. Towns are not our natural abodes, and have been built to supply our material needs. That we should be born in towns and be brought up in the lap of stone and brick was never intended by Providence . . . people who live in them, and are absorbed by work, hardly feel that anything is missing from their lives, even though they have already strayed from nature and are daily getting further and further away from the great universe. But nature's help is indispensable when we are still growing up, and still learning, and before we are drawn neck and crop into the whirlpool of affairs. Trees and rivers, and blue skies and beautiful views are just as necessary as benches and blackboards, books and examinations'. See 'The Problem of Education', 72.

77. J. Seed, 'Anthropocentrism' in B. Devall and G. Sessions, *Deep Ecology* (Salt Lake City: Peregrine Smith, 1985), 243. (Devall and Sessions 1985)
78. For more on this see Doris LaChapelle, *Earth Wisdom* (San Diego: Guild of Tudors Press, 1978). (LaChapelle 1978)
79. *Rabindra Rachanabali*, 484. (Tagore 1992)
80. See B. Devall and G. Sessions, *Deep Ecology: Living as if Nature Mattered* (Salt Lake City: Peregrine Smith, 1985), 66. (Devall and Sessions 1985)
81. Aldo Leopold, *A Sand County Almanac, with Essays on Conservation from Round River* (New York: Ballantine Books, 1966), 190. (Leopold 1966)
82. Morris Berman, *The Reenchantment of the World* (Ithaca: Cornell University Press, 1981), 147 (Berman 1981). Also see Warwick Fox, *Toward a Transpersonal Ecology: Developing New Foundations for Environmentalism* (Boston: Shambhala, 1990). (Fox 1990)
83. See Devall and Sessions, *Deep Ecology*, 97. (Devall and Sessions 1985)
84. Ibid., 3.
85. J. Habermas 'A Reply to my Critics', in J. Thompson and D. Held (eds.) *Habermas: Critical Debates* (London: Macmillan, 1982), 247. (Thompson and Held 1982)
86. See Michel Foucault, *Discipline and Punish: The Birth of the Prison* (New York: Vintage, 1979). (Foucault 1979)
87. See F. Trainer, *Abandon Affluence* (London: Zed Books, 1985), 176–78. (Trainer 1985)
88. Tagore 'Ashramer Siksha', 431. (Tagore 1992)
89. Rathindranath Tagore writes, 'The ideal of brahmacharya was the keynote of everything. The yellow uniform, which covered up the poverty of clothes; a pair of blankets, which served as our only bedding; the vegetarian meals comparable to jail diet in their dull monotony – these were the standards laid down. Nobody wore shoes or even sandals and such luxuries as toothpaste or hair oil were taboo'. *On the Edges of Time*, 45. (Tagore 1958)
90. Tagore, 'A Poet's School', 298–99. (Tagore 1961a)
91. Ibid., 295 (Tagore 1961a). Italics are mine.
92. Tagore, 'The Problem of Education', 71. (Tagore 1961a)
93. A. D. Synder, *Coleridge on Logic and Learning* (New Haven: Yale University Press, 1929), 12. (Synder 1929)
94. See Herbert Marcuse, *Counterrevolution and Revolt* (London: Allen Lane, 1972), 59–60. (Marcuse 1972)
95. E. F. Schumacher, *Small is Beautiful* (London: Abacus, 1974), 11. (Schumacher 1974)
96. M. Horkheimer, *Eclipse of Reason* (New York: Oxford University Press, 1946), 103. (Horkheimer 1946)
97. Friedrich Nietzsche, *Ecce Homo,* (trans.) Walter Kaufmann (New York: Random House, 1967), II:1, 240. (Nietzsche 1967)

98. Richard Shusterman, *Performing Live: Aesthetic Alternatives for the Ends of Art* (New York: Cornell University Press, 2000), 203. (Shusterman 2000)
99. Plato notes: '[W]hen the soul uses the instrumentality of the body for any inquiry, whether through sight or hearing or any other sense – because using the body implies using the senses – it is drawn away by the body into the realm of the variable, and loses its way and becomes confused and dizzy, as though it were fuddled, through contact with things of a similar nature'. Plato, *Phaedo* in *The Collected Dialogues of Plato*, (ed.) E. Hamilton and H. Cairns (Princeton: Princeton University Press, 1963), 62. (Plato 1963)
100. See Raymond D. Boisvert, *John Dewey: Rethinking Our Time* (Albany: State University of New York Press, 1998), 97. (Boisvert 1998)
101. E. Durkheim, *Moral Education: A Study in the Theory and Application of the Sociology of Education* (New York: Free Press, 1961), 150. (Durkheim 1961b)
102. Durkheim, *The Evolution of Educational Thought: Lectures on the Formation and Development of Secondary Education in France* (London: Routledge, 1977 [1938]), 150. (Durkheim 1977 [1938])
103. See Bernard Andrieu, *Le corps disperse: Histoire du corps au XXe siecle* (Paris: L'Harmattan,1993). (Andrieu 1993)
104. Maurice Merleau-Ponty, *The Visible and the Invisible* (Evanston, IL: Northwestern University Press, 1968), 141. (Merleau-Ponty 1968)
105. Bernadette Wegenstein, *Getting Under the Skin, The Body and Media Theory* (Cambridge, MA: MIT Press, 2006), 2. (Wegenstein 2006)
106. See Shusterman, *Performing Live*, 138. (Shusterman 2000)
107. Quoted in Sherry B Shapiro, *Pedagogy and the Politics of the Body* (New York: Garland Publishing, 1999), 25. (Shapiro 1999)
108. Martin Heidegger, *Being and Time* (trans.) J. Macquarrier, & E. Robinson (New York: Harper & Row, 1962), 177. (Heidegger 1962)
109. Tagore, 'The Problem of Education', 73–4 (Tagore 1961a). Apart from the word 'Bhuma' all italics are mine.
110. Tagore, 'Abaran', 383. Tagore laments how we ignore the beautiful unclad body of ours. Our face is uncovered in both the summer and the winter and so our facial skin is the most cultivated. It knows the art to balance itself with the outer world, complete in itself, and does not require any artificial refuge like other parts of the body. See 'Abaran', 381.
111. Emerson writes, '.... Books are good only as far as a boy is ready for them. He sometimes gets ready very slowly. You send your boy to the schoolmaster, but 'tis the schoolboys who educate him. You send him *to* the Latin class, but much of his tuition comes, on his way to school, from the shop windows'. *The Complete Works of Ralph Waldo Emerson* (ed.) Edward Waldo Emerson (Vol. X; Boston: Houghton, Mifflin and Company, 1903–1904), Vol. VI, 142. (Emerson 1903–1904)

112. 'Education', *The Complete Works of Emerson*, Vol. X, 135. (Emerson 1903–1904)
113. Emerson, Vol. 111, 257. (Emerson 1903–1904)
114. 'The Oversoul', Vol. X, 131.
115. Tagore, 'A Poet's School', 291–92 (Tagore 1961a). Italics are mine.
116. Tagore, 'Abaran' 343.
117. Ibid., 344.
118. M. Merleau-Ponty, *Phenomenology of Perception* (London: Routledge & Kegan Paul, 2003), 354–55. (Merleau-Ponty 2003)
119. I am tempted to look into the life of the ashram as a totality which Mencius (371–289 BCE) has argued as a developmental continuum and an interpenetration of the sociopolitical and the cosmic – a deep understanding of self and subjectivity, the I-Me dialectic. The ashram-school looked in its own way into what Mencius calls *qi* (氣, vital energies), the allowance for subjectivities and a consequent release of imaginative cohabitation with the natural and the objective world – a mind–body conjugation. Tagore's school ensured that a culture was built across an embodied existence in personal cultivation and psycho-spiritual transformation. See A. K. L. Chan (ed.), *Mencius: Contexts and Interpretations* (Honolulu: University of Hawai'i Press, 2002). (Chan 2002)
120. Tagore, 'A Poet's School', 292. (Tagore 1961a)
121. P. Bunyard & F. Morgan-Grenville (eds.) *The Green Alternative* (London: Methuen, 1987), 71. (Bunyard and Morgan-Grenville 1987)
122. Tagore, 'Problem of Education', 75.
123. Didier Anzieu, *The Skin Ego* (New Haven: Yale University Press, 1989), 12–13. (Anzieu 1989)
124. Merleau-Ponty, *The Phenomenology of Perception*, 234. (Merleau-Ponty 2003)
125. Tagore, 'Thoughts on Education', 3. (Tagore May-Oct 1947)
126. Tagore, 'Problem of Education', 80–1.
127. Aristotle's main exposition on the relationship between education, work and leisure is to be found in his *Ethics* (Penguin, 1973) and *Politics* (Penguin, 1962).
128. Tagore delivered a talk 'The Philosophy of Leisure' on 6 April 1929, at Vancouver on his first visit to Canada. Deeply sceptical of the 'spirit of progress' which was obsessive and frenetic, he saw leisure as the 'wealth which is a creation of human spirit whose material may be money'. The perfection of personality does not come merely through 'cleverness or deftness or even accuracy of observation or the rationality that analyses and forms generalizations'. Creativity needs 'quiet time' and leisure is the way to access it. See P. C. Mahalanobis, *Rabindranath Tagore's Visit to Canada* (New York: Haskell House Publishers Ltd., 1977), 56–9. (Mahalanobis 1977)

129. S. Curtis, *History of Education in Great Britain* (London: University Tutorial Press, 1963), 333–4. (Curtis 1963)
130. M. McMillan, *The Nursery School.* (London: Dent, 1930), 2 (McMillan 1930). Also see her *Education Through the Imagination* (London: Sonnenschein, 1923 [1904]) (McMillan 1923 [1904]) which highlights the importance of imagination in the child helping her to nourish her being. This free play to imagination is also closely connected, in my view to the idea of the open spaces, the freedom that bare and no-bar activity provide. Tagore's ideas come close to these views.
131. See Annie Dillard, 'Teaching a Stone to Talk', in *Teaching a Stone to Talk* (New York: Harper Perennial, 1992), 87, 88. (Dillard 1992)
132. Ibid., 90, 94. (Dillard 1992)
133. 'If a man would be alone, let him look at the stars.... If the stars should appear one night in a thousand years, how would men believe and adore; and preserve for many generations the remembrance of the city of God which had been shown! But every night come out these envoys of beauty, and light the universe with their admonishing smile'. See Emerson, 'Nature', 9.
134. See Tagore, 'Ashontosher Karon', 383 in *Rabindra Rachanabali*, Vol. 14. (Tagore 1992)
135. Tagore wanted his Santiniketan school to be an indigenous attempt in adapting modern methods of education in a truly Indian cultural environment (See his pamphlet *Visva Bharati*, Santiniketan, 1929). On a similar spirit Sri Aurobindo laments, 'We in India have become so barbarous that we send our children to school with the grossest utilitarian motive unmixed with any disinterested desire for knowledge; but the education we receive is itself responsible for this' (*The Harmony of Virtue* 125–26). Education for Tagore is about growing humanity's latent oneness and not what forming what Aurobindo terms as 'economic barbarian' who is a soulless product of a well-honed system. Education for children cannot only be for utility, success in a competitive socialized industrialized existence and merely for comforts and conveniences. (See Aurobindo's *The Human Cycle*, 87). (Ghosh 1998)
136. Lawrence writes, 'we are hopelessly uneducated in ourselves. [...] We wear our education just as externally as we wear our boots, and to far less profit. It's all external education, anyhow'. See his *Phoenix: The Posthumous Papers of D. H. Lawrence* (ed.) Edward D. Macdonald (Viking Press, 1972), 755. (Lawrence 1972)
137. Writing to C. F Andrews, Tagore notes, 'In India the range of our lives is narrow and discontinuous. This is the reason why our minds are often beset with provincialism. In our Ashram at Santiniketan we must have the widest possible outlook for our boys, and universal human interest. This must come spontaneously – not merely through the reading of books, but through

dealing with the wide world'. Kathleen Connell, *Rabindranath Tagore: The Poet as Educator*, 162. (O'Connell 2002)

138. 'Self Reliance', 131. See *Ralph Waldo Emerson* (ed.) Richard Poirier (Oxford: Oxford University Press, 1990). (Poirier 1990)
139. See D. H. Lawrence, *Fantasia of the Unconscious* (Rockville: Serenity Publishers, 2008), 76–7. (Lawrence 2008)
140. See Sri Aurobindo, 'On Education', Accessed 22 October 2015, http://ddceadipur.org/ebooks/sriaurobindoeducation.pdf
141. John Dewey, *Individualism Old and New, in The Later Works of John Dewey*, Vol. 5, (ed.) Jo Ann Boydston (Carbondale: Southern Illinois University, 1977), 81. (Boydston 1977)
142. Dewey, 'Construction and Criticism,' in *The Later Works of John Dewey*, Vol. 5, 136, 133. (Boydston 1977)
143. Friedrich Nietzsche, 'Schopenhauer as Educator,' in *Untimely Meditations*, (ed.) Daniel Breazeale, (trans.) R.J. Hollingdale (Cambridge: Cambridge University Press, 1983), 144. (Nietzsche 1983)
144. Lawrence describes the modern school as a very elaborate railway system: School is a very elaborate railway system where good little boys are taught to run upon good lines till they are shunted off into life, at the age of 14 or 16 or whatever it is. And by that age the running-on-lines habit is absolutely fixed. The good big boy merely turns off one set of rails on to another. And it is so easy, running on rails; he never realizes that he is a slave to the rails he runs on. Good boy! (*Phoenix* II 579) (Lawrence 1972)
145. D. J. Siegel, *The Mindful Brain: Reflection and Attunement in the Cultivation of Well-Being* (New York: W.W. North., 2007), 3–28. (Siegel 2007)
146. Emerson, 'Self Reliance', 131.
147. Lawrence, like Tagore, sees the failure of this parrot compulsion of forcing extraneous ideas on children. This kills all capacity for real feeling, original thinking and spontaneous action – a perception poetically enacted in Lawrence's poem 'Snake'. The poem demonstrates how instinct and spontaneity are drowned out in the high formal pitch of education. There is the need to kill the golden snakes, however beautiful and harmless, because they are dangerous. The triumphant overpowering voice of education has decimated all capacities for feeling and subtler ranges of emotion are treated with revulsion and disdain.
148. Albert Schweitzer, 'The Ethic of Reverence for Life' [1923], in Tom Regan and Peter Singer (eds.) *Animal Rights and Human Obligations* (Englewood Cliffs: Prentice Hall, 1976), 133–38. (Schweitzer 1976)
149. Paul W. Taylor, *Respect for Nature: A Theory of Environmental Ethics* (Princeton: Princeton University Press, 1986), 122. (Taylor 1986)
150. Emerson, 'Self- Reliance', 141. Ashram-school sought to discover the 'gleam of light' in its children which is the sense of one's being, a self-reliance, an

'iron string' contributing to the integrity of the mind. Tagore's school was not built to promote a cosy system, a convenient scheme of things; but with a motive to unsettle all things – the hardened values, emotionless instructions and templated pedagogy. The 'gleam' in his pupils was a combination of both the good and the bad, the benign and the wicked: it was not a school in the sense of a rehabilitation centre. In their closeness to nature, children learnt self-reliance and trust to engage with the world of uncertainty. The poet-master made them know that education for fullness is about believing in the surplus that it provides – 'there is always a residuum unknown, unanalysable', in the words of Emerson. ('Circles', 168).

151. Tagore, 'Tapovan', 357.
152. Tagore, 'A Poet's School', 291. (Tagore 1961a)
153. See Augustin Berque, 'Some traits of Japanese *fūdosei*', in *The Japan Foundation Newsletter* 14 (5) 1987, 1–7 (Berque 1987).
154. Augustin Berque, 'Identification of the Self in relation to the Environment' in Nancy Ross Rosenberger, (ed.) *Japanese Sense of Self* (Cambridge University Press), 94. (Rosenberger 1992)
155. Ibid., 94.
156. Tagore, 'Tapovan', 358.
157. For greater elaboration see Tu Wei-ming, *Confucian Thought: Selfhood as Creative Transformation* (Albany: State University of New York Press), 1985. (Wei-ming 1985)
158. Wing-tsit Chan, *A Source Book in Chinese Philosophy* (Princeton: Princeton University Press, 1963), 698–99. (Chan 1963)
159. Tagore, 'Tapovan', 360.
160. GiambattistaVico, *On the Study Methods of Our Time*, (trans.) Elio Gianturco (Indianapolis: Bobbs Merrill Co., 1965), xxvn. (Vico 1965)
161. Vico, *The New Science* (trans.) Max H. Fisch and Thomas G. Bergin (Ithaca: Cornell University Press, 1944), 4. (Vico 1944)
162. See Georg Kerschensteiner, *Theorie der Bildung* (Leipzig: B. G. Teubner, 1926). (Kerschensteiner 1926)
163. See H. Gaudig, *The Idea of Personality and their Relevance for Education.* Reprograf. Reprograf. Nachdr. d. Ausg. Leipzig 1923. Nachdr. d ed Leipzig 1923 (Heidelberg: Quelle & Meyer, 1965); also see Gaudig, *Schools and School Life* (Leipzig: Quelle & Meyer, 1923). (Gaudig 1923)
164. Adir Cohen, 'Martin Buber and Changes in Modern Education', *Oxford Review of Education*, Vol. 5, No. 1, 1979, 84. (Cohen 1979)
165. Hartmut Sgharfe makes us note that the word guru originally meant 'heavy, weighty', bringing with it the Latin expression of a *vir gravis*, 'a weighty man'. The guru through knowledge provides the junction and through teaching the connection with his students (cf. *Taittiriya-Upanishad*). See *Education in Ancient India* (Leiden: Brill, 2002), 277, 283. (Scharfe 2002)

166. Tagore, 'The Problem of Education', 79 (Tagore 1961a). Tolstoy writes in 'On Popular Education', 'A mother teaches her child to speak only so that they can understand each other. She instinctively tries to come down to the child's view of things, to his language yet the law of educational progress does not permit her to descend down to the child, but compels the child to rise to her knowledge. The same relation exists between the author and the reader, the same between the schools and the pupils, the same between the state and the society – the people. The activity of the person who educates has one and the same purpose. The problems of educational science are only the study of the conditions under which a confluence of these two tendencies for one common end takes place, and the recognition of those conditions that impede this confluence' (181).
167. See *Tolstoy as Teacher: Leo Tolstoy's Writings on Education* (ed.) Bob Blaisdell (New York: Teachers and Writers Collaborative, 2000), 1. (Bob 2000)
168. *The Complete Works of Count Tolstoy* (trans. and ed.) L. Weiner (London: J.M. Dent & Co. 1904), 284–85 (Weiner 1904). Quoted in Dan Moulin, 'Leo Tolstoy the Spiritual Educator', *International Journal of Children's Spirituality*, Vol. 13, No. 4, (November 2008), 349. (Moulin 2008)
169. Tolstoy writes, 'The tutor is the first person very close to them on whom they make observations and draw conclusions which they then apply to all mankind. And the more a person is endowed with human passions, the richer and more fruitful these observations'. *Tolstoy's Letters* (selected, trans. & ed.) R. F. Christian (London: Athlone Press, 1978), 202. (Christian 1978)
170. A. Maude, *The Life of Tolstoy*. Vol. 1: *First Fifty Years*. (London: Constable & Co.1908), 231–2. (Maude 1908)
171. Maude, *The Life of Tolstoy*, 194. (Maude 1908)
172. See *Tolstoy on Education*, (trans.) L. Wiener, with intro. R.D. Archambault (Chicago/London: University of Chicago Press. 1967), 31. (Weiner 1967)
173. *The Complete Works of Count Tolstoy*, 12, 293. (Weiner 1904)
174. There is the 'striving after perfection in love'. See Tolstoy's 'Thoughts on Education and Instruction' (1887–1901) in *The Complete Works of Count Tolstoy* trans. & edited. L Wiener (London: J. M. Dent & Co., 1904), 364. (Weiner 1904)
175. 'The School at Yasnaya Polyana' in *Tolstoy on Education* trans. L. Wiener (Chicago: University of Chicago Press, 1967), 299 (Weiner 1967). Quoted in Dan Moulin, *Leo Tolstoy* (London: Continuum, 2011), 77. (Moulin 2011)
176. See S. Rodríguez, *Obra Completa Tomos* I–II (Caracas: Presidencia de la República, 2001). (Rodríguez 2001)

177. Walter Kohan, *Childhood, Education and Philosophy* (London: Routledge, 2015), 31. (Kohan 2015)
178. Ibid., 32.
179. J. J. Rousseau, *The Social Contract* (New York: Washington Square Press Pocket Books, 1971), 6, 15. (Rousseau 1971)
180. Rousseau, *Emile* (trans.) Barbara Foxley (London and New York: Everyman's Library, 1966), 444. (Rousseau 1966)
181. *Emile* II.362–3/ 120. See Timothy O'Hagan, *Rousseau* (London: Routledge, 1999), 80. (O'Hagan 1999)
182. *Emile* II.364/121.
183. Adir Cohen, *The Educational Philosophy of Martin Buber* (Madison: Farleigh Dickinson University Press, 1983), 33. (Cohen 1983)
184. See Martin Buber, *Between Man and Man* (trans.) Ronald Gregor Smith (New York: Macmillan, 1948), 83 (Buber 1948). See Adir Cohen, 'Martin Buber and Changes in Modern Education', *Oxford Review of Education*, Vol. 5, No. 1, (1979), 87. (Cohen 1979)
185. Buber, *Between Man and Man*, 90. (Buber 1948)
186. The guru cannot be a police inspector or drill sergeant; he has to be one who knows how to respect people younger than him, feebler in strength and less wise than he is. The power of expression never stops in the heart of children and people who tie them up with strict laws of regimentation start the downslide of the educational system. The life force of education is expunged. See 'Chatrasashontantra' in *Rabindra Rachanabali*, 375–76. (Tagore 1992)
187. B. S. Auerbach, *Neues Leben* (Stuttgart: Cotta'scher Verlag, 1871), 139 (Auerbach 1871). Quoted in Dan Moulin, *Leo Tolstoy* (London: Continuum, 2011), 23. (Moulin 2011)
188. *Neues Leben*, 14, quoted in Moulin, 22. (Auerbach 1871)
189. Martin Buber, *I and Thou*, (trans.) Walter Kaufmann (New York: Charles Scribner's Sons, 1970), 6. (Buber 1970)
190. Buber, *Between Man and Man*, 124–25. (Buber 1948)
191. John Dewey, *Democracy and Education* (New York, 1916), 161. (Dewey 1916)
192. See Grete Schaeder, *The Hebrew Humanism of Martin Buber* (trans.) Noah Jacobs (Detroit: Wayne State University Press, 1973), 195. (Schaeder 1973)
193. Buber, *I and Thou*, 67. (Buber 1970)
194. See Emerson, 'Education' (1864), Accessed 24 November 2015, http://aboq.org/emerson/essays/education.htm. (Emerson 1864)
195. Rathindranath Tagore writes, 'We were essentially a happy lot and life was very rich and interesting in spite of our outward poverty. Whenever Father [Rabindranath himself] was present, he poured his soul into the institution and made it lively by singing songs which he never tired of composing,

reciting his poems, telling stories from the *Mahabharata*, playing indoor games with the boys, rehearsing plays, and even taking classes. All the teachers lived with us in the same dormitory, and we shared joys and sorrows equally amongst us. There was a wonderful feeling of genuine camarederie'. *On the Edges of Time*, 46. (Tagore 1958)

196. G. W. F. Hegel, *Phenomenology of Spirit* (trans.) A. V. Miller (Oxford: Oxford University Press, 1977), 22. (Hegel 1977)
197. Hegel, *Hegel's Logic. Part One of the Encyclopaedia of The Philosophical Sciences* (trans.) W. Wallace. (Oxford University Press, 1975), 36 (Hegel 1975). See Nigel Tubbs, 'Hegel's Educational Theory and Practice', *British Journal of Educational Studies*, Vol. 44, No. 2, (Jun., 1996), 181–99. (Tubbs 1996)
198. Hegel, *Hegel: The Letters* (trans.) C. Butler and C. Seiler (Bloomington: Indiana University Press, 1984), 280 (Hegel 1984). The *sishya* (pupil) by touching the feet of the *guru* is giving him his remuneration but the *guru* is not giving back what he owes to his pupil; the *guru* is giving his pupil lessons in abstraction and in an archaic language which hardly inspires the students to learn. They are neither interested nor respectful. The truth in our pedagogic system is indisputably under threat. See 'Sikshabidhi', 364.
199. Kathleen Connell, *Rabindranath Tagore: The Poet as Educator*, 164. (O'Connell 2002)
200. See Tagore, 'The Place for Discipline', *The Visva Bharati Quarterly*, Vol. 27, No. 2, (1961), 93 (Tagore 1961b). He notes, 'Civilization today is in love with too many forms of organization and of discipline which are dead; organized education, organized amusement, organized religion, and organized ways of living, so that we adopt a perpetual hotel-kind of existence' (96).
201. Tagore was keen on seeing a proper implementation of the codes of discipline in his school. In a letter to Mohitchandra Sen (2 July 1904) he betrays his concern over certain areas of laxity and requests discipline and order to be restored. (See Gourchandra Saha ed. *Chitipatreh Vidyalaya Prosongoh*, The context of the School in letters of Tagore, Visva Bharati: Rabindrabhavan, 2001, 39) (Saha 2001). A section of the constitution reads, 'I wish the students to be devoted to their teachers with no reservation. Even the injustices they commit should be politely tolerated without revolt. One cannot join in criticism or rebuke of them in any way'. See Kathleen M O' Connell, *Rabindranath Tagore: The Poet as Educator*, 130 (O'Connell 2002). This is surprising to me for Tagore revised this one-sided position in pedagogic twinhood later when he spoke more about the freedom and articulation of the students and discounted slavish subservience to the dictates of the teachers. In the constitution I find several anomalies in Tagorean anthroposophy and the notion of the guru that he developed later contradicts the image of the teacher that one finds here. Pedagogy like

school can never be neutral: 'it takes sides, it participates in deep and vital ways in the definition of this project whose central theme is not mankind, but his relations with the world, his being in the world, his feeling of interdependence with what is other than himself'. Pedagogy is implied in choices and choices involve 'having the courage of our doubts, of our uncertainties, it means participating in something for which we take responsibility'. See Carlina Rinaldi, *In Dialogue with Reggio Emilia Listening, Researching and Learning* (New York: Routledge, 2006), 8 (Rinaldi 2006). Tagore's politics, aesthetics and pedagogy are, no doubt, problematically entangled.

202. *On Education and Rabindranath* (Calcutta: Subarnarekha, 2000), 131–32. (Chattopadhyay 2000)
203. Michael Oakeshott, *On Human Conduct* (Oxford: Clarendon, 1975). (Oakeshott 1975)
204. See T.V. Sathyamurthy, 'Relationship between Teacher and Pupil in Ancient India: An Upanishadic View', *Educational Theory*, Vol. 15, No. 1, (1965), 26–34. (Sathyamurthy 1965)
205. See S. Radhakrishnan (ed.), *The Principal Upanishads, Taittriya Upanishad* (London: George Allen & Unwin Ltd, 1953). (Radhakrishnan 1953)
206. Emerson, *Journal* (1841), 43.
207. Emerson, 'American Scholar', 56.
208. Emerson, 'Education', 56. Italics are mine.
209. Emerson, 'Divinity School Address', 74.
210. Emerson, 'Education', 61. See Thomas E. Spencer, 'Emerson on Education', *Educational Theory*, Vol. 18, No. 1, (1968), 77–86 (Spencer 1968) & Lawrence H. Maddock, 'Emerson on Education', *Educational Theory*, Vol. 7, No. 1, (1957), 56–8. (Maddock 1957)
211. William Godwin, *The Enquirer* (London: Robinson, 1797), Essay I, 1. (Godwin 1797)
212. *The Enquirer*, Essay XV, 142–3. (Godwin 1797)
213. Edward Baldwin (i.e. William Godwin), *Fables Ancient and Modern* (London, Thomas Hodgkins at the Juvenile Library, [1805]), iii–iv (Baldwin 1805). See Margaret Fearn, 'William Godwin and the Wilds of Literature' *British Journal of Educational Studies*, Vol. 29, No. 3, (1981), 247–57. (Fearn 1981)
214. See Edward Baldwin (i.e. William Godwin) *The History of England for the use of Schools and Young Persons* (London: M. J. Godwin at the Juvenile Library, 1812), v. (Baldwin 1812)
215. See *Crown of Wild Olive* (I866)-II, 'Traffic', 14. Also, see for more details *Sesame and Lilies*, Preface to the 1865 edition. (Ruskin 1866)
216. Quoted from William Boyd, *The Educational Theory of Jean Jacques Rousseau* (New York: Russell & Russell, 1963), 118–19. (Boyd 1963)

217. Ibid., 136.
218. J. J. Rousseau, *Reveries of the Solitary Walker* (translated with an introduction) P. France, (London: Penguin, 1979), 88–9. (Rousseau 1979)
219. Rousseau, *Confessions, I,* (Random House, 1992), 156. (Rousseau 1992)
220. See Jessie White, *The Educational Ideas of Froebel* (New Delhi: Cosmo Publications 2007). (White 2007)
221. See S. Millar, *The Psychology of Play* (Harmondsworth: Penguin Books, 1968). (Millar 1968)
222. Learning outdoors was given as much importance as learning indoors. See T. Bruce, 'Froebel today' in L. Miller and L. Pound (eds) *Theories and Approaches to Learning in the Early Years* (London: Sage, 2011). (Bruce 2011)
223. Friedrich Froebel, *The Education of Man* (New York: D. Appleton and Company, 1887), 73, 75–6. (Froebel 1887)
224. Froebel writes that 'we grant space and time to young plants and animals because we know that, in accordance with the laws that live in them, they will develop properly and grow well; young animals and plants are given rest, and arbitrary interference with their growth is avoided, because it is known that the opposite practice would disturb their pure unfolding and sound development; but the young human being is looked upon as a piece of wax, a lump of clay, which man can mould into what he pleases'. If the plant model here is contrasted with the image of the potter clay, John Stuart Mill contrasts it with the manufacture of machinery. Mill points out that 'human nature is not a machine to be built after a model and set to do exactly the work prescribed for it, but a tree which requires to grow and develop itself on all sides according to the tendency of the inward forces which make it a living thing'. See John Darling, 'Education as Horticulture: Some Growth theorists and their Critics', *Philosophy of Education*, Vol. 16, No. 2, (1982), 173–85 (Darling 1982). Tagore, Froebel and Mill were all opposed to any mechanical 'monitorial' system of teaching but, perhaps, it was always difficult for all to overrule what we generally understand by 'çonditioning'.
225. A. N. Whitehead, *The Aims of Education and Other Essays* (New York: The Free Press, 1967), 39. (Whitehead 1967)
226. Yi-Fu Tuan, *Space and Place: The Perspective of Experience* (Minneapolis: University of Minnesota Press), 1977. (Tuan 1977)
227. E. D. Casey, 'Between Geography and Philosophy: What does it mean to be in the place-world?' *Annals of the Association of American Geographers*, Vol. 91, No. 4, (2001), 683–93. (Casey 2001)
228. See Yi-Fu Tuan, *Cosmos and Hearth: A Cosmopolite's Viewpoint* (Minneapolis: University of Minneapolis Press, 1996). (Tuan 1996)
229. Anne Stenros, 'Orientation, identification, representation: space perception in architecture', in I. Alavalkama, S. Aura and H. Palmquist (eds), *Endoscopy*

as a Tool in Architecture (Tampere: Tampere University Press, 1993), 76. (Alavalkama et al. 1993)

230. See Tagore, 'My School' in *Personality* (London: Macmillan and Co. Limited, 1970), 131. (Tagore 1970)
231. Quoted in Edward S. Casey, *The Fate of Place: A Philosophical History* (Berkeley: University of California Press, 1997), ix. (Casey 1997)
232. See Indra Kargis McEwen, *Socrates' Ancestor: An Essay on Architectural Beginnings* (MIT Press, 1993), 83. (McEwen 1993)
233. See Gaston Bachelard, *The Poetics of Space*, (trans.) Maria Jolas (Boston: Beacon Press, 1969), xxxii. (Bachelard 1969)
234. K. Dovey, 'Putting Geometry in its Place: Toward a phenomenology of the design process', in D. Seamon (ed.), *Dwelling, Seeing, and Designing: Toward a Phenomenological Ecology* (Albany: State University of New York Press, 1993), 250. (Dovey 1993)
235. See Bhupendranath Seal, 'Santiniketan: The Innisfree of C. F. Andrews', *Visva-Bharati News*, (February-March 1971), 218 (Seal 1971). Here are a few lines from Andrews's poem 'The Palms at Santiniketan':

    Peace in the deep mid-air surrounding,
    Peace in the sky from pole to pole,
    Peace to the far horizon bounding,
    Peace in the universal soul. (220)

236. See G. Matoré, *L'Espace humain* (Paris: La Columbe, 1962), 22–3 (Matoré 1962). Quoted in E. Relph, *Place and Placelessness*, (London: Pion, 1976), 10. (Relph 1976)
237. Tagore, 'Personality', 136. (Tagore 1970)
238. See P.T. Karjalainen, 'Real pace images', in A. Haapala (ed.), *The City as Cultural Metaphor* (Lahti: International Institute of Applied Aesthetics, 1998), 101. (Haapala 1998)
239. Tagore, 'Lokkhyo o Siksha' [Aim and Education] in *Rabindra Rachanabali*, Vol. 14, 367. However, Tagore knew that hope cannot be limitless; no country can ever claim a system that fulfils the energy of the mind and body, renders an impeccable nourishment of the soul. No system, however noble and wise it might be, can deliver unbounded freedom which would turn a failure otherwise. Fate, Tagore admits, portions out our share with the mix of gainful satisfaction and deficit. So education needs an intense combination of hope and aims, desire and energy of a telos (369). This hope and target for me brings into play what Friedrich Schiller points out as a conjugation of form drive and sensuous drive in that Tagore looked for gestaltic stability and acknowledged the movements in time and consciousness bespeaking the quiddity of life. Perhaps, achieving the point of

poise – the ludic drive as against categorical imperatives – has baffled Tagore the most. The realities outside and inside us determine our thinking and, hence, our feelings. Tagore for me imagined a unity of all forces contributing to the growth of his desire and dream but not without the stabbing anxiety of an under-accomplishment, a conflicted soul who knew that birds have the right to fly and are not trained to fly but the quotient of education needs to be factored into our development and whose limits and execution have always existed as a contentious issue. See Schiller, *On the Aesthetic Education of Man* (trans. with an introduction) Reginald Snell (New York: Dover Publications, 2004) (Schiller 2004); also see, *Aesthetical and Philosophical Essays* (ed.) Nathan Haskell Dole (Boston: Francis A Niccolls & Company, 1902). (Dole 1902)

240. See J.J. Godfrey, *A Philosophy of Human Hope* (Dordrecht: Martinus Nijhoff, 1987). (Godfrey 1987)
241. See E. Bloch, *The Principle of Hope* (Oxford: Basil Blackwell, 1986). (Bloch 1986)
242. J. Moltmann, *Hope and Planning* (London: SCM Press, 1971), 178. (Moltmann 1971)
243. See his second essay in 'Praktoni' in *Rabindra Rachanabali*, Vol. 14, 464. Tagore talks about the kind of difficulties he faced in giving his dream a reality of life. He candidly admits though that it had its own faults and blemishes. It emerged out of his suffering in the heat of which he found the right note of expression. Failed assignations with the 'possible' (in his later writings on the ashram in the 1930s he repeatedly mentioned about the anguish resulting from the failure of some of his dreams and ideals with which he began the ashram) have sometimes resulted in frustrations to which he could not but helplessly submit.
244. *Rabindra Rachanabali*, 484.
245. Rathindranath Tagore, *On the Edges of Time* (Kolkata: Visva-Bharati, 1958), 154 (Tagore 1958). Italics are mine. He writes, 'Father enjoyed taking risks where others would hesitate' (37). Speaking of courage, Parker Palmer, in his work *The Courage to Teach: Exploring the Inner Landscape of a Teacher's Life* observes: 'The courage to teach is the courage to keep one's heart open in those very moments when the heart is asked to hold more than it is able so that teacher and students and subject can be woven into the fabric of community that learning, and living, require'. P. J. Palmer, *The Courage to Teach: Exploring the Inner Landscape of a Teacher's Life* (San Francisco: Jossey-Bass, 1998), 11. (Palmer 1998)
246. I have tried to see a critical connection between Tagore's emotional investments and Tolstoy's ideas on wisdom of learning and teaching. See his 'Wisdom of Children' (1910) in *Recollections and Essays*, (trans. & ed.) A. Maude (Oxford University Press, 1937), 491, 446–93. (Tolstoy 1937)

247. Tolstoy, *A Calendar of Wisdom*, (trans.) P. Sekirin, (London: Hodder and Stoughton, 1998), 209, 17. (Tolstoy 1998)
248. George Eliot, in a letter to her friend Frederic Harrison, 1866. See George Eliot, 'Letter to Frederic Harrison,' in F.R. Leavis, *Introduction to Silas Marner* (Harmondsworth: Penguin, 1967), 9–10. (Eliot 1967)
249. See *Rabindra Rachanabali*, 463.
250. Tagore while writing about the initial days of the ashram mentions how difficult it was for the headmaster to control his students most of whom were a bundle of chaotic energy: one running after snakes whenever he spotted one, the other reading his lessons atop a tree, some writing their papers sitting on a tree branch. The headmaster's commitment to disciplinize was responded with laughter as the school became of chamber of untamed energy and alacrity. See *Rabindra Rachanabali*, 465. However, such release and relish of experiences came to be non-violently harnessed as the school wore on and added more life to it.
251. In dominant contemporary discourses on child education children are 'officially' treated as similar which, by extension, demands an uniformization of practices of learning and study. Under the pressure of technology, the materialist matrices of existence, the high tide of globalization and new liberal economy, child education today is predominantly about providing consistency with the clear message to implement a system that will leave no child behind in the race to literacy. Both 'conservative and more liberal governments', Nicola Yelland argues, 'want to keep education quantifiable and accountable. This avoids complex discussions and consideration of the long-term goals for an education system that exists in new times that are radically different from those many politicians have experienced' [Yelland, (ed.) *Contemporary Practices in Early Childhood Education* (Maidenhead: Open University Press, 2012), 6, italics are mine.] (Yelland 2012). What kind of a 'difference' then does child education engage with? This difference is generated through the work of a community of thinkers who have brought several wonderfully intriguing segments of critical thinking into the current debates on child education. What is of even more interest is the fact that these experiments in thinking and practice can be considered to have a closely (in)fusionist correspondence with Tagore's ideas on child education as enumerated in the preceding pages. So within the constructivist theories of learning and developmentally appropriate practices (DAPs), learning goals for children need not always be fixated like talismanic truths waiting to be realized. There is a need, as Lenz Taguchi notes, for the 'emergence of strategies and thinking' which might enable us to 'make ourselves aware of what happens now and what might be possible, what emerges, and what can become' [H. L. Taguchi, 'Rethinking Pedagogical Practices in Early Childhood Education: A Multidimensional Approach to

Learning and Inclusion', in *Contemporary Practices in Early Childhood Education* (ed.) Nicola Yelland (Maidenhead: Open University Press. 2012), 30] (Nicola 2012). Tagore had subscribed to both the preset and non-teleological dimensions of education emphasizing the necessity of being aware of the specificities that each educational system brought through its inscription in a particular culture, tradition and ideology (like the idea of the *tapovan* or forest education in ancient Indian school system). He demonstrates how such individualities do not come in the way of imparting liberal and humanist education because particularities or localities are eventually meant to form a pluralist solidarity (his very own ways of creating diffractive transcultural negotiations). Children are better equipped to learn within such a system than be initiated to what we have come to accept as an educational module which formulates 'preset goals' and takes 'universal values as well as normalized practices for granted' (Ibid, 16). In this shift in our thinking of the ethics and justice in education today, Tagore's experiments and principles of aesthetic education achieve their own relevance. Tagore's contribution to contemporary discourses on education lies in intensifying the movement of seeing aesthetic education grow as 'free learning' beyond the mere systematic conveniences of instruction to generate more spaces for imagination, individuality, play and proximity to nature. So within recent developments of paedo-centric cognitive studies where emotion and matter are fused into complex patterns in the integral growth of the child, Tagore's ideas, albeit not undergirded by a strictly scientific support structure, can, however, prove to be useful.

Taghuci's innovative research into 'intra-active pedagogy' is another interesting development in this field – the philosophy of 'intra-actions' can transform our teaching practices by making a productive network between children, teachers and everything that surrounds them [Taguchi, *Going beyond Theory/Practice Divide in Early Childhood Education* (London: Routledge, 2010), 6] (Taguchi 2010). Taguchi emphasizes intra-active relationship that experiments a pedagogy which is 'inclusive of the material as a strong performative agent in learning' (Ibid, 10). Intra-activism is integral to Tagore's ideas of inclusive education. By situating Tagore's project of 'fullness of education' within intra-active pedagogy we can also consider its potential relevance to our recent thinking on 'immanence' (the strong impact of Gilles Deleuze in recent studies in education) and the 'pedagogy of affect' [See C. Albrecht-Crane and J. Daryl Slack, 'Towards a Pedagogy of Affect', in *Deleuzian Encounters: Studies in Contemporary Social Issues* (ed.) A. Hickey-Moody and P. Malins (New York: Palgrave Macmillan, 2007)] (Albrecht-Crane and Slack 2007). This is a part of the strategies of relational understanding of a child learner – the entanglements that learning through nature, the situatedness of the learner, his/her immediate culture and ethos bring. It is the kind of 'spacetimematterings' that comparative educational studies should make more use of. Working outside representational epistemology which does not take the materiality and everydayness of the learner in mind, Tagore can surely be seen in relation to the ideas of 'transcendence' and embeddedness in learning – the constructivist and cognitive pedagogy that subsumes both the spirituality and mentalization of learning with the child's 'inter-activity' with matter and things around him/her. Tagore's child and the pupil-guru relationship are not sundered from the materiality of life and environing forces of existence/performance in the ashram. Tagore never suggested that a child can grow on its own as a 'superior being', as 'free objects' who can mend their development by transcending the entanglements that the child's growing intrinsically has with natural objects, artefacts, ordinary things surrounding him (Yelland 2012, 17). Tagore was for intra-activity pedagogy which just did not involve the teacher and the taught but also a dynamic and formative relationship with the biotic and the non-biotic elements surrounding the children – 'active' materialization. The immanence in Tagore's educational philosophy is thus constructivist, descriptive, transformative, performative, relational and certainly intra-active. Tagore's views are closely connected with the whole material-discursive movement in educational psychology and pedagogy today which sees the children and their learning as a closely connected equation between being and knowledge – the onto-epistemology. As part of the recent theory-practice developments in 'immanence' and 'relationality' in educational psychology, Tagore's experiments in the field of child education then point to the alternative discourse that agential growth of the child and guru can open in our understanding of 'cross traffic' as a significant paradigm in child research.

CHAPTER 3

The Politics of Counter: Critical Education and the Encounters with Difference

In the fall of 1872–1873, Matthew Arnold wrote a letter to Sir Roper Lethbridge who 'during his career served as principal of Krishnagur College in Bengal, fellow of Calcutta University, and political agent of the India Office':

> Dear Sir,
> Pray hold yourself at full liberty to make what use you please of my writings for your excellent design. The progress of native education in India, particularly in all that relates to the higher education, interests me exceedingly.
> Believe me, dear Sir, very faithfully yours,
> Matthew Arnold.[1]

What Roper Lethbridge made out of it is not as much a serious question as Arnold's views on comparative education that can be, clearly, put to some meaningful correspondence with Tagore in his open-ended and comparatist views on educational philosophy and culture. Since Jullien de Paris, comparative education came to be an important source of investigation and both Matthew Arnold and Michael Sadler are prominent 'English' bearers of the baton. Arnold had deep faith in the merits of comparative education and believed that the subject of popular education 'can no more be known without being treated comparatively, than anatomy can be known without being treated comparatively'.[2] Political contexts, rather the national character, vary and so do social and cultural situations from

R. Ghosh, *Aesthetics, Politics, Pedagogy and Tagore*,
Palgrave Studies in Education and Transculturalism,
DOI 10.1057/978-1-137-48026-2_3

one country to another; but, keeping thoughts and ideals in comparison is what Arnold feels can add distinct merit to the existing belief and practice of education in a particular country. He observes that 'one may save one-self from much idle terror at names and shadows, if one will be at the pains to remember what different conditions the different character of two nations must necessarily impose on the operation of any principle'.[3] This is not simply about trying to study foreign educational systems – what the Germans call the *Auslandspädagogik*. Comparison in education is not anatomical co-correspondence, certainly not about co-position; it is the driving force towards gainful appropriation and further extrapolation of virtue and values – self-critical and self-revisionary ways of reformation, redoing of extant beliefs and systems. Such comparatist tendencies open windows on other cultures, thoughts and traditions, weaving webs of cross-cultural intersubjectivities. Sadler's remarks have significant pertinence:

> In studying foreign systems of education we should not forget that the things outside the schools matter even more than the things inside the schools, and govern and interpret the things inside. We cannot wander at pleasure among the educational systems of the world, like a child strolling through a garden, and pick off a flower from one bush and some leaves from another, and then expect that if we stick what we have gathered into the soil at home, we shall have a living plant. A national system of education is a living thing, the outcome of forgotten struggles and difficulties and 'of battles long ago'.[4]

He was conscious that his ideas were in advance of his time, and he appealed to future generations: 'I have attempted', he writes,

> to sketch in outline the plan of reorganization for English instruction which is suggested almost irresistibly by a study of public instruction in other European countries, and of the actual condition and prospects of the modern world.... I have a profound conviction that if our country is destined, as I trust it is destined, still to live and prosper, the next quarter of a century will see a reconstruction of English education as entire as that which I have recommended in these remarks, however impossible such a reconstruction may to many now seem.[5]

Both Arnold and Tagore sought a reconstructionist canvas, endorsing a universalized liberal education that had a lot to offer in a Socratic way of dialogic education. They were very keen on knowing about other nations, cultures and civilizations, undertook several meaningful peregrinations outside their countries, surveyed the promise of a fulfilment in human potential and through humanistic education sought to find an answer to the spectre of 'culture wars'. As strong believers in border-crossings in pedagogy, literature and culture, Arnold and Tagore tried to execute a reformation through 'connection' and self-commitment: 'To know how others stand, that we may know how we ourselves stand; and to know how we ourselves stand, that we may correct our mistakes and achieve our deliverance – that is our problem'.[6] Such a belief made them remain open to the delight and instruction of the 'other'. Arnold sought to learn from his European counterparts by breaking away from parochial British smugness and Tagore, in spite of his sapient endorsement of India's cultural tradition, never failed to manifest his eagerness to connect with what the Europeans were qualified to deliver. Hence, both believed in moving out of their countries on tours which they knew would eventually help them to frame, in particular, their ideas on education and literature and, generally, their vision and practice of life and times (Arnold's reports on France, Germany, Holland and Switzerland are works of an educational prophet) – the 'connect' between the home and the world. India and England, for Tagore and Arnold respectively, were not domains distinctly self-contained and insular: 'the best that is known and thought in the world' could not simply have been British or Indian in origin and growth. Arnold writes:

> In short, it is expedient for the satisfactory resolution of these educational questions, which are at length beginning seriously to occupy us, both that we should attend to the experience of the Continent and that we should know precisely what it is which this experience says. Having long held that nothing was to be learned by us from the foreigners, we are at last beginning to see, that on a matter like the institution of schools, for instance, much light is thrown by a comparative study of their institution among other civilized states and nations. To treat this comparative study with proper respect, not to wrest it to the requirements of our inclinations or prejudices, but to try simply and seriously to find what it teaches us, is perhaps the lesson which we have most need to inculcate upon ourselves at present.[7]

Critical comparative negotiations between the self and the other, the native and the foreign, the insider and the outsider, are what forms 'culture' and Visva Bharati was no stranger to such formations. This made both the educationists experiment their ideas with 'imports' which might speak disfavourably to them – adaptability and appropriation will always have their own limits within certain sociocultural conditions. Yet excursions into different cultures, real-life understanding of situation and values of different communities made them extrapolate spaces for cross-cultural interventions. Despite efforts to deprovincialize their own politico-cultural spaces, Tagore's envisaged arrangement that operated through comparison, contrariety and conflation was larger in scope than his British counterpart. While Arnold looked into Europe becoming a unified community having a European voice instead of bristling nationalist affiliations,[8] Tagore was into seeing his Asia meeting Europe syndrome in a more profoundly capacious and latitudinous way.

Arnold's extensive studies – *A French Eton*, a study of French secondary education and the General Conclusion to *Schools and Universities on the Continent* – were not meant simply to investigate how the education system worked in a foreign land but about the manner in which it stood undergirded with the disciplined intent to evaluate their efficacy on a comparative scale involving his own system of education in Britain. Whatever worked in France might not work in Britain but comparative interest generates the possibility of some profitable appropriations.[9] Arnold is similar to Tagore here in being indigenous without a nativist opacity. Comparative education ought to execute a global awareness, a curiosity to break past the borders of a nation, its cultures and traditions. The scale enlargement in the consciousness of education contributes to the development of the personality of the people in question, resulting in the formation of a cosmopolitan culture. This spirit, as Arnold presciently pointed out, will be European and not nationalist – a European voice ('a common European level of thought') more in line with a confederacy caught in a transcultural traffic whose borders will be porous. Such tendencies will reblood clogged veins of religious inflexibilities, making our spirit more in tune with the encompassive democracy of modernist temper. Modernity for Arnold did not mean 'railroads and the penny post' but 'intellectual deliverance'. In his 1857 lecture 'On the Modern Element in Literature' Arnold wrote:

> An intellectual deliverance is the peculiar demand of those ages which are called modern; and those nations are said to be imbued with the modern spirit most eminently in which the demand for such a deliverance has been made with most zeal, and satisfied with most completeness. Such a

> deliverance is emphatically, whether we will or no, the demand of the age in which we ourselves live. All intellectual pursuits our age judges according to their power of helping to satisfy this demand; of all studies it asks, above all, the question, how far they can contribute to this deliverance.[10]

So the intellectual maturity of man decided to observe facts 'with critical spirit'; it ensured that his maturity enabled him not to wander at random but search for the law of the facts – judged by 'the rule of reason' and not by 'the impulse of prejudice or caprice'.[11] Brendan Rapple rightly interprets Arnold's immaterial aspect of modernity through the poet's belief in 'free and heightened spiritual and intellectual activity', explaining 'modern' as 'a state of mind', the appropriate intellectual leanings, culture or light, together with the requisite social virtues. And it was according to this immaterial understanding of the 'modern', modern as connoting an 'intellectual deliverance', rather than in any sense of material progress, that England, and more specifically the members of the middle class, in Arnold's view, had been little touched by the modern spirit.[12]

Both Tagore and Arnold believed in compulsory and universal education. A strong sense of dissatisfaction with the prevalent modes of education disturbed both of them. Arnold wanted an organized system of education that would bring the disorderly collection of schools – invested in various religious denominations – into a state-controlled coherence. Tagore, unlike Arnold, was functioning under the British colonial regime and it was difficult for him to agree with all the principles of statist ways of nationalist education and sectarian communal modes of education. In fact, as a school inspector, Arnold believed that his job was not 'simply to check the lighting and ventilation or to calculate the exact levels of reading, writing and arithmetic achieved, but "to test and quicken the intellectual life of the school," a phrase which to Arnold meant intellectual curiosity, a spirit of inquiry, and a genuine interest, respect and desire for intellectual achievement on the part of both students and staff'.[13] This is quite close to Tagore's educational experiments that were informed by a high level of curiosity and aesthetic-intellectual engagement; it also addressed a character of 'thinking' which brought the poet-master in intense alliance with the pragmatic educationist.

Like Tagore, what Arnold decidedly aimed for was an inner reconstruction that suffered mercilessly under man's trenchant 'faith in the machinery'; this faith needed the antidote of 'culture' which did not believe in mere puritanical rituals of external perfection but sought a harmonious perfection of the inner life. As Bruce Novak argues:

> For Arnold, culture was not alien to politics, but the key to its true success. In contrast to the qualities of 'common sense,' 'resolution,' and 'enthusiasm' assumed by pretty much everyone – in our own time just as much as in his – to be central to democratic power politics, Arnold thought the qualities of 'experience,' 'reflection,' and 'renouncement' would lend *true* power to democratic life. He saw a system of education based *only* on 'common sense' 'performance standards,' inward 'resolutions' of 'diligence,' and outward 'enthusiastic' competition for 'excellence' to be fit only for a narrow-minded, unpluralistic and unfree 'Progress through Puritanism.' A democratic system of education based on 'Progress through Culture,' on the other hand, might serve as the midwife for a new birth of freedom.[14]

Tagore's educational ideals were obligated to a culture that sought harmonious development of one's personality through education conducted with method, sense and sensibility. Culture lends a freedom which is transformative and sustaining in that it connects different cultures across social and historical boundaries. This freedom is dialogic and pins its faith in conversation that is far from pretence and compulsion. The culture that such a freedom promotes renounces prejudices and announces a traffic into the heart of others promoting the communal will and the life spirit; and, 'as more and more of us learn to do this, we collectively create the phenomenon of "social spirit" – a general feeling of equanimity and *creative* community'.[15] Tagore's Visva Bharati was conceived and eventually performed as a non-anarchic space well opposed to cultural predilections, ideological monologism and cultural immurement. Tagore proposed an exit from complexities that colonial education and strategies of pedagogy threw upon the Indians. If the French suffered from looseness of morals and the Germans wrestled with pedantry, England, for Arnold, needed 'lucidity' (one can see his 1882 'A Liverpool Address') and must avoid 'nonsense' (the crassness of the middle class). But rationality, lucidity and 'intellectual deliverance' come healthily together to produce a system to Arnold's liking. Tagore, like Arnold, threw his weight behind a system that displayed accessibility to diverse ideas and sought rational conjugation of traditions and cultures. He needed a fresh line of thinking, a different philosophy of schooling and higher studies to exit on a pervasive ignorance that the middle class and the greater community considered as 'knowledge'. The meeting of minds was a meeting of cultures, as Tagore's university saw a host of international scholars spending productive time on the campus at different periods of its growth and establishment – true to the demands of an intellectual and modern *zeitgeist*.

This 'meeting' is also about the Hebraic finding correspondences with the Hellenic. Arnold's understanding of Hellenism and Hebraism explains, to an extent, the functional dynamics of Tagore's school. Donald Stone argues that 'whereas Hebraism, with its concern for inward rectitude, requires an obedience on the part of the individual that might lead to an unquestioning acceptance of the status quo, Hellenism prompts a counter impulse: the desire to have an objective grasp of reality that might very well lead to a questioning of the status quo'.[16] Tagore, hellenistically, challenged several dimensions of the regnant colonial structures of education and, hebraically, through some strictness, obligated a respect for norms by which he ran his school and university – both the 'strictness of conscience' and 'spontaneity of consciousness'. This was not a kind of prejudiced dismissiveness; but, with the intent to dissolve the 'bad' things to enable the surfacing of the good, Arnold and Tagore set up a structure of educational ideas that was progressive and liberal without being dehumanisingly hermetic. Both subscribed to the credo of 'returning upon oneself' and the principle of 'imaginative reason'. Arnold had identified a Hellenic infusion in certain forms of educational system in France. This bespoke an ethics of free play of the mind, trying to know the best that is known and thought in the world – an absorption of experiences around oneself without permanent ascetic injunctions and also not without some forms of rectitude and discipline impinging on conduct and conscience.[17]

The poet-educationists had a distaste and committed abhorrence for religion that was 'narrow, unintelligent, repulsive'; they disfavoured any repressive forms of faith and practice. If Arnold was disgruntled with the English for not being able to 'see objects as they really are' and failing to rise above their own narrowness, Tagore saw a certain parochialism and myopism among his countrymen – a common disinterest in the 'tastes and habits of our neighbour'. Arnold, like Tagore, saw connection everywhere and believed that no single event or literature could be adequately comprehended without its correspondence with others – thoughts and happenings being an integral and intrinsic part of an ever vibrant and active neighbourhood. Both thinkers agree on knowing others and thinking in comparison with others to know where one stood. Indeed, the English mind arrested Tagore's attention for its intellectual courage.

The British thought that education had its permanent vessel in their own mind: its permanent supply came from their own living spring of culture. This organic triadic unity of the mind, life and culture enabled them to seek knowledge from all lands and all times, conflating them into a position of discernment and appraisal. This spirit of embracement in learning and espousing attitude towards knowledge made for a close fit with Tagore's ideas about transnationality which did not propose to cobble things or ideas together but clearly accented the discovering of one's tradition inflected with creativity and self-awareness. Each tradition, each culture, has its own consciousness, assertiveness and peculiar standard for judging identities. European culture, Tagore wrote, has its 'truth and strength' in its 'fluid mobility' for nothing comes as fixed.[18] Uncritical drawing upon other cultures does not speak for cultural progress; progressive dialogue thrives in reinventing oneself, in investments in newer things, in lessons learnt through the 'traffic' among cultures. Tagore observed that 'culture which is the life of the mind, can only be imparted through man to man. Book learning, or scriptural texts, may merely make us pedants. They are static and quantitative; they accumulate and are hoarded up under strict guards. Culture grows and moves and multiplies itself in life'.[19] He believed that an adjustment of knowledge through comparative study and the progress effectuated through cross-intellectual solidarity could be the 'keynote of the coming age'.

Ro(u)oted Rootlessness

With a profound consciousness of the other, Visva Bharati fledged and flourished as an institution where the West and the East took close measure of each other in a cultural and intellectual 'traffic' of varied scope and potential—*Yatra Visvam Bhavatyekanidam*—'where the whole world finds one nest'. Ascribing to a belief that he who confined himself to his own self lies lost and, he who realized himself in *all* attains self-expression, Tagore proposed to survive at the centre of things.[20] Civilization for him meant a life among many; barbarism was 'isolation'. The derivative meaning of the Sanskrit *sabhyata*, is 'civilization'; *sabhyata* is derived from the word 'company' which, again, derivatively means 'where there is light'. Visva Bharati symbolized *sabhyata* for him. Peter Cox writes:

> At one end of the scale is the home or the nest, to use his phraseology – the single community or village or the small institution where essential

> relationships can be created, where the issues and the needs are particular and specific, where action can be initiated and taken. At the other end of the scale there is the world at large – the sky where he could take his flight – with its many diverse elements and different peoples with their own religions, cultures and languages, all to be taken into account, none to be imposed on others, none to be exploited at the expense of others.[21]

This introduces a 'cross-traffic' in a non-impositional and non-hegemonic space that fights against 'moral alienation'. Traffic of this nature creates opportunities 'for revealing the different peoples to one another' and engenders a 'great federation of men' which is not 'a meeting of individuals, but of various human races'.[22] Indeed, Visva Bharati's defining element was its commitment to the constructive work of knowledge. Emphasizing the need for cross-traffic, Tagore writes that 'it is the task of Visva Bharati to invite all the ages and all the peoples to that India which belongs to all ages and all people'.[23] He proposed that people should be brought together and full scope must be given to them for their work of intellectual exploration and creation. Teaching, he asserted, should be like the overflowing water of this explorative spring of culture – spontaneous and inevitable. Education can only become natural and wholesome when it is the direct fruit of a living and growing knowledge.[24] He could grasp the profound historic significance of the 'awakening of the East' and the coming together of the East and the West in the physical sense.[25] And he alone was powerfully actuated by the mission to convert that physical closeness into a truly spiritual union. In 'Vidyasomobyay' he points out that isolation can come through two ways – one through indifference, ignorance and sovereign pride. He argues that the result is the same because energy is lost in both. Mikado used to remain translucent within the regal décor and dominance, concealed from popular attention and aspirations. But when sovereignty was thrusted on Mikado, the dominant veil cutting him off from the populace was removed and he became more available than ever before, increasing prospects of public intercourse. Tagore animadverted the xenophobic wrap that most Indians were caught in – a self-incarceration under the consternation of external contamination. He saw the foolishness of the Indians who tried to sever themselves from the nourishment that the potency of 'worlding' could provide; instead, he desired to see India 'branch out' of its anxious immurement into a space where knowledge was formed through an enfranchisement made possible by diverse communities of power, tradition, culture and values.[26] Tagore writes:

> At first, I had founded the school in Santiniketan and invited children here with the purpose of liberating them in the wide field of Nature. But gradually it occurred to me that the formidable gulf that existed between man and man had to be removed and all men had to be released in the vast Universe of Man. This inner aspiration found expression in the history of the evolution of my institution. For, the institution that bore the name of Visva-Bharati was founded with this call that *man had to be set free not only in the field of Nature but also among mankind.*[27]

However, this particular venture to 'free man among mankind' was not to be gained by a complete loss of one's identity and individuality because Tagore believed that only those who possessed real individuality could truly unite: true union was based upon genuine individuality. So the nations of the world must stir to attain true individuality, to achieve what Tagore termed as a 'true unification of mankind'. Tagore observes that 'when the great European countries found their individual languages, then only the true federation of cultures became possible in the West, and the very differences of the channels made the commerce of ideas in Europe so richly copious and so variedly active. We can well imagine what the loss to European civilization would be if France, Italy and Germany, and England herself, had not through their separate agencies contributed to the common coffer their individual earnings'.[28] Organistically, he looked into the significance of one's 'own separate history and their own life-growth', 'indigenous growth of culture' and 'individuality of judgment, and perfect freedom of self-expression'.[29] The cross-traffic need not make one lose focus of his cultural and social epicentres. In trying to communicate within the format of a mutually enriching milieu, the intermeshing 'cultures' required engagements born out of the pride of their individuality and a complement of values which made them desirous of knowing the 'other'.

Tagore's immediate contemporaries, philosophers Karl Jaspers and Gabriel Marcel for instance, betrayed serious anxieties over the submission to the domination of objective knowledge, scientific technologicalization and the loss of 'mystery' from our lives. Truth for them, as it was for Tagore, never manifested as a 'whole truth' – the corruscative holity of scientific truth. Order and understanding at a purely objective level might leave the self in an act of 'slipping away', forever withdrawing from its inmost potential. Represented knowledge could not do without limits and it would know how principles of unpresentability contributed to its formation. So knowing the other completely was an impossibility and Tagore knew that the best way of knowing was to build on the capacities of communication, developing a perception of human situation based on endotelic listening, a trial for and by the other. 'There was,' says Jaspers, 'almost until the present time a cohesion among men which rarely permitted communication to become a special problem. People could content themselves with the saying: we can pray together, but not talk together. Today, when we cannot even pray together, we are at length becoming fully aware that humanity implies unreserved communication among men'.[30] Visva Bharati was Tagore's one big and wide space for 'talking' – a call for greater depth in living that granted the other, in a Buberian way, a speaking personality.[31] With the emphasis on a close connection between existence and education and what could be considered as 'educable', Tagore, like Jaspers, argued against the 'interminable pedagogic experiment' that could never cultivate real values and purpose. Teaching was not about inculcating 'facts' alone but was pronouncedly about experiencing their 'reverberatory power'. Visva Bharati was a 'free act' because it was not intransigently teleological, but experimental without being prohibitively indulgent; it was not a global abstraction which Marcel pointed out as a 'final high terrace' climbing on which human condition became unchanging and a project turned into a rarefied sanctuary.[32] Tagore, like both Marcel and Jaspers, believed that education was mostly for the inner being – how man contemplated his world and grew aware of it – less about memory and intellection than it was about assimilation and refinement.

The entire *project* on education encouraged correspondences between the 'aesthetic' and the 'ethical': a moral rationality caught in a mix with the concern for a meaningful and full life. Tagore aspired for a project of 'fullness' and organicity underpinned by 'respect'. Stephen Darwall provides us with a dual notion of respect: recognition respect and appraisal respect.[33] Without making any distinction among people based on merit and achievements, recognition respect offers to show respect for all approximating the Kantian universals of mutual respectful recognition. Appraisal respect is centred on individuality, the ends of human action and fall-outs. Tagore, in his pursuit of 'fullness', sought to combine both forms of respect that Darwall mentions – *what* the man is is bound with *where* he is coming from. Charles Taylor argues that in order to have 'a sense of who we are, we have to have a notion of how we have become, and of where we are going. . . . My life always has this degree of narrative understanding, that I understand my present action in the form of an "and then": there was A (what I am), and then I do B (what I *project* to become)'.[34] This has bred informed tolerance. However, this 'thick' notion of respect need come in the form of recognition and not mere eulogies sung in the name of the distinctness of the other.

Tagore's project of 'fullness' then was predominantly about widening and encompassing 'horizons'. His universal man was not an undifferentiated category armed with the Kantian wholeness; rather, it promoted 'horizoning' where the particularity of being a man and the force of universality were brought together. The identification of the universal man supervened on locating the power of 'specificities', the locality and locationality of man in relation to his universal appeal. Taylor emphasizes an 'acknowledgement of specificity' by which he means our conscious avoidance of cultural misrecognition of individual identity.[35] Cultural dialogue is then about forming what Richard Rorty calls 'solidarity' which is the 'imaginative ability to see strange people as fellow sufferers'.[36] The strangeness is recognized and respected to form a solidarity and this comes diffractively close to Hannah Arendt's notion of 'visiting,' in which you 'see with your own eyes from a position that is not your own'.[37]

How can then the regime of self-cultivation come? What would be the new meaning of *swaraj*, emancipated selfhood and redesigned livelihood? How can university education prevent the clash of civilization and the conflict of knowledge systems? Citing the cohabitative spaces and the regulative ideal – among scholars, traditions, knowledge systems – generated in universities like Nalanda and Vikramshila from ancient India, Tagore envisioned a similar growth in his Visva Bharati: àn effort to understand how the Indian genius expressed itself, the need for integration of diverse streams of thought and the production of knowledge in the universities that made dissemination a secondary task. Thriving on borrowed knowledge, Indian universities under the colonial rule were 'like a lighted railway compartment in a train passing through the countryside which is enveloped in darkness'. By the time Tagore was born (1861), a colonial system of education had already found its own permanent settlement – a system that declared the support and proliferation of English language and English studies as against the consequent denudation of importance and interest in Sanskrit and Persian language and studies. Vernacular means of education were ignored for colonial educational ideals and patterns of execution. This strategic segregation effected under impositional colonial structures of education brought home a backlash – a rebound energy for the restitution of one's cultural past, making education combative when it ought to have been synergic and osmotic. Dispirited by such ideological warfare and institutional superintendency, Tagore wanted a university with a different culture inscribed in individuality, indigeneity, otherness, curiosity and desire hitherto unavailable in contemporary universities during his time. The exemplarity in education was in knowing the art of 'negotiation' – both a vertical negotiation with one's tradition, languages and cultures and a horizontal dialogic familiarity with a corpus of knowledge that indigeneity would not be able to deliver but could surely have profited from.

Tagore's observes that 'had the deep water fishes happened to produce a scientist who chose the jumping of a monkey for his research work, I am sure he would give most of the credit to the branches of the trees and very little to the monkey itself'.[38] This act of missing the 'monkey' was a 'category error' that Tagore's Visva Bharati refused to commit. The responsibility to effect this healthy and prudent 'traffic' between the self and the other, the consciousness of individuality and the values beyond the perils of self-immurement were possible with modern education only. This education was ensured to have been left unaffected by 'symbolic violence' – the system of cultural arbitraries that expressed the 'objective interests (material and symbolic) of the dominant groups' – the symbolic order of a particular cabal of interests that reproduced socially and culturally mediated structures of power.[39] Within the rationale of Tagorean cross-traffic we find an exception being taken to the dominant cultural arbitrary which is usually misrecognized as the only cultural capital in need of transmission and reproduction. This is not the Parsonian notion of a shared normative system but an understanding of 'distinction' among cultures and the fields of power and sites of contestation that go with it. Tagore did not have a definitive idea as to the 'integration' that he was aiming at for clearly his mission and mechanism to see a 'meeting place' of the East and West could not appraise the conditions of legitimation that distinctions brought through accreditation, selection and hierarchy.

However, he had a committed declaration to make:

> the education of the present epoch, should be in harmony with the ideals and endeavours of the epoch. The most important education today is the education of mankind to give up national pride. For the history of tomorrow

> shall begin with the chapter of international co-operation. That is why the educational institutions of our country should become the *meeting place* of the East and the West – this is my heart's desire.[40]

Tagore was committed to execute a space which was in no fear of being foreshadowed by a European knowledge economy; rather, the thrust was to establish a 'knowledge society'. Visva Bharati, in trying to establish its knowledge society, vouchsafed at once for the production of knowledge and reflection on knowledge. It was not templated on the Humboldtian notion of the university where institutions were envisaged to have a role service to the nation state. Visva Bharati, unlike modern universities formed during the classical times, never had an organically unified culture with a single set of values and ideals as its founding and functional agenda. The modern university, as Hillis Miller points out, 'was to serve the nation-state in two ways: (1) as the place of critical thinking and research, of finding out the truth about everything, of giving everything its rationality, according to the Leibnizian formula that says nothing is without its reason; (2) as the place of education, formation, or *Bildung*, where male citizens (they were all male then in the university) are inculcated, one might almost say "inoculated," with the basic values of a unified national culture. It was the business of the university to produce subjects of the state, in both senses of the word subject: as subjectivities and as citizens accountable to state power and capable of promulgating it'.[41] Tagore's educational *bildung* had its *Auseinandersetzung* and epigenetic aims of development (a sort of *perfectibilité*) – an emancipatory progress without being seamless to the point of anarchy. Unlike what *bildung* spelt in its conceptual and operative emergence at the end of the eighteenth and nineteenth century, Tagore's educational vision was more about connecting the human with environing processes of learning – a learning society (also in the sense of *sich-bilden*, self-education, the autopoeisis)[42] that was deeply aesthetic and humanistic.

If John Henry Newman's idea of the university was mostly subordinated to the demands of a protestant state, Kant's advocation for division of the faculties into lower and higher types was seen within a harmonic reason of knowledge related to life, its experiences and also the interests of the state. He writes, 'for a faculty is considered higher only if its teachings – both as to their content and the way they are expounded to the public – interest the government itself, while the faculty whose function is only to look after the interests of science is called lower because it may use its own judgment about what it teaches.... Accordingly, the government reserves the right itself to sanction the teachings of the higher faculties, but those of the lower faculty it leaves up to the scholar reason'.[43] But both Kant and Newman did not believe in totalitarian statist control in that Newman desired a space for reflection 'in which truth is discoverable by the human intellect, that the investigator should be free, independent, unshackled in his movements'[44] and Kant insisted on a faculty 'that is independent of government's command with regard to its teachings' and is hence 'free to evaluate everything'.[45] But, again, this is at variance with Tagore's notion of academic freedom invested in a non-obsessiveness with the diffusion of enlightenment knowledge regimes and responsible limits to social utility and anti-elitism. Clearly, the traffic that Tagore conceived within the formations of his Visva Bharati was not strictly bound by a regulative idea of a social contract and the ethical lineaments of a cultivated Catholic society. Informed with a critical innovative spirit to resist things that are established, Visva Bharati, pressing on illative sense, was much more than simply Newmanian. Humanistic studies in Visva Bharati sought an integration of domains of thinking and harmonization of disciplines of thoughts and study – not a quiescent co-existence. However, like Newman, Tagore's liberal education believed in training to discern things in perspective, to generate 'good sense, sobriety of thought, reasonableness' and steadiness of view.[46] Newman saw liberal education as not strictly confined to rationalization alone – 'we require an organon more delicate, versatile, and elastic than verbal argumentation'.[47] Laws and concreteness matter as much as personal peculiarities informed one's statements of understanding and existence. Talking of a logic beyond concrete reasoning, Mulcahy explains how Newman is confident

> that we do possess such an alternative means of proof, what might be referred to as phronesis in the Aristotelian sense of the word. The inadequacy of logic can be compensated for by one's 'own living personal reasoning', by one's 'good sense', he maintains. Such good sense is the healthy condition of such personal reasoning even if it cannot properly express itself in words. It is the means by which one is 'possessed with the most precise, absolute, masterful certitude' of his dying sometime, a conclusion to which logic alone could never bring one. Many of one's most strenuously held yet 'reasonable' convictions or certitudes, he continues, are similarly dependent

> upon proofs that are 'informal and personal, which baffle our powers of analysis, and cannot be brought under logical rule.[48]

Formal logic was not always at Tagore's rescue for he believed in judging circumstances, often, by his own lights. This welcomed a reasoning that was delicate and personal and, at times, intricate, opposed to any subordination to a greater or master reason.

As *Project*

We need not be teased out to submit to the argument that Tagore was looking into a simple Habermasian communicative discourse that could engineer all diversity into a consensus. Communities are projected to have an intersubjectively shared life through a communicative rationality and dialogism resulting in a mutual recognition of claims on culture, heritage and tradition. This makes for a discourse ethics where diverse cultures and communities contend with certain exclusive judgements – evaluative, expressive and elective. Tagore looked into a traffic that was not an endorsement of radical cultural relativism; rather, it was an investment in a procedure of participation that respected norms of valid transcultural import and responsibility for a universality that made the understanding of *difference* an acceptable way of progress. Widely different from other intellectuals of his day, Tagore explored the possibilities of extrapolating a geo-cultural place that could only be embedded in differences ('we must know that the great mind of man is one, working through the many differences which are needed to ensure the full result of its fundamental unity. When we understand this truth in a disinterested spirit, it teaches us to respect all the differences in man that are real, yet remain conscious of our oneness; and to know that *perfection of unity is not in uniformity, but in harmony*'.[49]). This 'unity' without 'uniformity' – a pluralist solidarity – does not have a 'dogmatic rigoristic temper' (in the words of William James), but, in its combination of individuality and collectivity, it leaves us with the 'common sense world, in which we find things partly joined and partly disjoined'.[50] Visva Bharati formed itself around an agonistic solidarity in a multiverse traffic. Mary Parker Follet arguing about unity in diversity seeks unity, and not uniformity, as her aim. She observes that 'differences must be integrated, not annihilated, nor absorbed'. The university is embedded in 'intricate reciprocities', an equilibrium which is not quiescent but shifting, varying and yet compounding, coordinating and harmonizing.[51] Visualizing an ideal commonwealth Tagore went on to reveal different people to one another, exploring the 'meeting ground' where there could be – albeit ideally – no question of intractable conflicting interests. He pointed out that 'some of us belong to the Brahma Samaj sect and some to other sects of Hinduism; and some of us are Christians. Because we do not deal with creeds and dogmas of sectarianism, therefore this heterogeneity of our religious beliefs does not present us with any difficulty whatever'.[52] Visva Bharati, with its harmonious heterogeneity, was one such territory – a multiversity – where people could work together in a common pursuit of truth, share their common 'human' heritage and realize that artists in all parts of the world have created forms of beauty, scientists have discovered secrets of the universe, philosophers the problems of existence, saints made the truth of the spiritual organic in their own lives, not merely for some particular race to which they belonged but for all mankind. Visva Bharati became a site for struggle where 'local knowledge' was made to meet 'global knowledge' in a cultural pluralization that would represent different worlds in different ways.[53] The indigenous and exogenous were pragmatized into a 'knowledge society' which renegotiated self-definition with self-othering. Visva Bharati, thus, produced 'human knowledge' which did not have the cussedness of 'local' and the imperious recalcitrance of the 'global'; it considered 'conversation' as one of its major paradigms of unfoldment. Michael Oakeshott writes:

> The world of learning needs no extraneous cement to hold it together; its part moves in a single magnetic field, and the need for go-betweens arises only when the current is gratuitously cut off. The pursuit of learning is not a race in which the competitors jockey for the best place, it is not even an argument or a symposium; it is a conversation. And the peculiar virtue of a university (as a place of many studies) is to exhibit it in this character, each study appearing as a voice whose tone is neither tyrannous nor plangent, but humble and conversable. A conversation does not need a chairman, it has no predetermined course, we do not ask what it is 'for', and we do not judge its excellence by its conclusion; it has no conclusion, but is always put by for another day. *Its integration is not superimposed but springs from the quality of the voices which speak*, and its value lies in the relics it leaves behind in the minds of those who participate.[54]

Oakeshott points out that the tradition of liberal education gets started with Socrates and whether or not it is institutionalized in democratic political life, constitutes *in itself* a kind of democracy of the spirit, being 'above all else, . . . an initiation into the art of . . . conversational relationship' necessary for the individual human person to make his or her 'debut into [the drama or adventure of] human life'.[55] So Tagore could not have allowed Visva Bharati to simply grow into a Hindu university which would have resulted in the occlusion of the conversation paradigm, the obfuscation of values and the 'quality of the voices' under the weight of an invidious presuppositiveness. He, hence, authoritatively maintains:

> religious sects are formed in every country and every age owing to adversity of historical causes. There will always be many, who, by tradition and temperament, find special solace in belonging to a particular sect; and also there will be others who think that the finding of such solace can only be allowed as legitimate within the pale of their own . . . making ample provision for such inevitable and interminable squabbles, can there be no wide meeting place, where all sects may gather together and forget their differences?[56]

By substituting wisdom for knowledge, practical experience for theoretical abstraction and fostering a harmonious interplay of mind and body, Tagore dreamt something into existence that – however, imperfect, to an extent, in reality – aspired towards a unity from which neither the concerns of everyday life nor human attempts at creative endeavour were excluded. In fact, Tagore's intuitive comprehension of world problems convinced him that national interests the world over were interrelated. He believed that the nature of our problem was 'worldwide' and salvation would never fructify through any recourse to detachment. But he urged on the need to ensure 'nurture' in comparative seclusion – a fact necessary for the growth and consequent consolidation of the universal element in each civilization. This seclusion in the event of a 'cultural dialogue' could be a kind of strategic initial retreat. Tagore's Visva Bharati was, in its initial years, on a retreat, nurturing its position by basing its structure on a synthesis of all the different cultures that it had promoted and nested with, working continually and productively within its protective 'sheath of individuality'. Tagore, by being an intellectual legislator and interpreter, ensured that Visva Bharati took time to enter into a dialogue with the West, grew its own views of truth, formed its vantage ground of argument and became confident of exuding a 'sense of mental freedom'. Consequential and meaningful conversation could not have begun from a platform between non-equals, not when one is heavily loaded against the other, a phenomenon which Tagore observed in Asia's exaggerated intellectual dependence on the West. As a prophet of 'free inquiry' he called for sympathy, a connection, a mutuality, which would successfully contribute to a consortium of cultures and constitutions of knowledge. The knowledge inherited at birth is not the gift of any one nation. Knowledge makes us powerful but sympathy helps us to attain fullness. Tagore's transnationalism was a natural and logical manifestation of his humanistic philosophy, his philosophy of 'secular humanism', generated from his distinct and nuanced understanding of the *Upanishad*. Shocked by the horrors of the world wars, he realized that calamities in history have always sprung from the 'nonavailability' for the other – the 'traffic-deficit'. Tagore's speculative philosophy was committed to a moral dynamics that brought elements of reverence and order into our structures of existence. The university as a space did not qualify as a universal category but was an affirmation in relationality and experience – complex and interdependent. In the words of Whitehead, the ethical dimension of education cannot be 'morally neutral'. Visva Bharati, at some point in its inception, became a 'duty' which ascertained a belief in changing prevalent forms of experience with 'attainable knowledge'.[57] In its trials of exfoliation, Visva Bharati spoke at once of a rootedness and rootlessness, working outside the preparedness and value-neutral schematization of a modernist institution and yet not entirely processual in its value radicality. It worked towards an enhancement of value, a humanization of learning and interactive practices, without ethical absolutism or ethical nihilism. However, the affirmative traffic was more postmodernist in nature where its organismic growth, falling out of modernist Eurocentric models, refused to subscribe to a single universal cultural hegemony but, promoted instead, an advancement of diverse human systems and affiliations.

Working on Dewey's two aims of education – socialization and individuation – it can be said that the reasonably instructive mode in the ashram where the children were familiarized with truths and long-held beliefs (the *brahmacharya*, for instance) came to mean differently in the space that Visva Bharati offered. This was the space where Tagore, in a kind of openness, welcomed 'interrogation' of certain truism, providing moral and cultural inquiry. Was Tagore, in all his efforts to establish something irreverently outside the conventional frameworks of institution, Harold Bloom's 'strong poet' and arguably Richard Rorty's 'liberal ironist'? In the unfolding praxiality of his institution as a *project*, Tagore indulged in 'unconditional commandment' which brought him to commit to his own 'poetic', construct his own moral content and fix his own principles of right and wrong.[58] Tagore's moral thinking, as dominantly prevalent in the institutional space, evinced a liberal, passionate and yet 'ironical' commitment to his project of life. Interestingly, the socialization that he clearly monitored in the ashram paired up with an individuation in the university: his moral thinking which operated from within his private understanding of pedagogic ways integrated with the solidarity of the liberal society that the university was envisaged to provide. The 'irony' in Tagore was the struggle that a life-project of 'hypergoods' (in the words of Charles Taylor[59]) brought, compounded by balancing forces of 'self-creation' with allegiances, rather, filiations to community or greater good – the enormous 'ironic' pain to conjugate the two. Tagore's educational projects were witness to this pain.

Was learning about *others* meant to be pedagogic and, hence, as both Derrida and Levinas would say, violent? Was the other made to speak to Tagore within a certain orientation or was the other left in its own autonomy to decide its ways of speaking? It may be argued that the openness that Tagore proposed and perpetuated was a performance conditioned to determine the difference existing between what is external to the space and what lies outside the space. Perhaps, again, Tagore's determining ways about the 'outside' and the 'external' clearly failed to rule out a certain form of violence. The other refusing to be an 'infinitely unknowable' category became a construct of Tagore's own ideas about its construction – the 'imperialism of consciousness open upon the world'[60]– the possibilities of the other and the potential that he thought the other was capable of generating. The uncritical dialectic of the East and the West was clearly a pointer to that 'violence'. This could not have qualified as Levinasian 'ethicity' in the sense that Tagore's other did not come through in its irreducibility and its unknowable alterity and non-reciprocity; thus, his ethical education did not derive comfort from the knowledge of the other as unassimilable and the exposedness that the subject in its 'passivity' could produce. For him, knowing the other was educating oneself as much as proliferation of knowledge through relationality and reciprocation. Tagore's intersubjectivity, the agency of the 'responsible' subject, was non-Levinasian.[61]

Visva Bharati emerged from the construction of an outside-external problematic through Tagore's own discoursal and 'egoist' ways of understanding the other. What was at stake was the self-reconstruction conducted on the strength of its conversations with and mapping of the other. So Visva Bharati, Tagore ensured, had its 'fore-meanings' or 'fore-having' of understanding: certain set of fore-conceptions because Visva Bharati remained open without losing on its agenda, an openness not without its politics. Tagore had his prejudices (*vorurteil*) and this awareness evinced no submission to any kind of neutrality because understanding of localism determined how communication without aggression – key to his communicative and liberal rationality – could be conducted. So listening to others was no self-abnegation but keeping one's prejudice as part of a judgement on the hermeneutics of intersubjectivity. Otherness was in realizing one's individuality and not impartiality because impartial objectivity was an impossibility. Going with Gadamer it may be argued how we belong to history to constitute our identity – the self-evident way in which we conduct ourselves in the family, society, class, race, nation, state – without giving us much leverage on self-examination or self-conscious processing.[62] So our historical reality is the handmaid of prejudice. Tagore sponsored a prejudice in Visva Bharati – a historical reality constituted through the foremeaning of a tradition, custom and cultural inheritance – but there were many other hardened prejudices let loose through colonial education and consciousness, social stratification and hierarchical longings that he chose to oppose through another set of prejudices. Visva Bharati as the dynamic space cultivated 'prejudice against prejudice'; it became communicative through conversations built on multiple levels of prejudices – the power of the 'in-between'.[63] Being in a tradition was also freedom – the 'highest type of hermeneutical experience: the openness to tradition characteristic of historically effected consciousness'.[64] Democratic listening of Visva Bharati would know that 'when two people understand each other, this does not mean that one person "understands" the other'.[65] Difference, not similarity, determines us.

An arresting question confronts us here: was the space that Visva Bharati provided pluralist or multicultural in nature? Without being assimilationist it had more to do with the ontologics of multiculturalism than pluralism. Pluralism by giving more credence to individual choices does not promote any remarkable societal commitment to keep certain cultural structures in place. It vouchsafes for individual conditions enabling 'choices' to hold sway. But Visva Bharati was multicultural because of the importance that Tagore credited certain 'agreed' cultural principles with. The space was not culturally neutral for deep traditions of India's cultural past made certain structures of thought and execution irreplaceable – a 'multicultural' opening whose affiliations and recognitions were distinguished from a deeply pluralist society. It just did not work on the differences that different communities of culture have; but, Tagore evinced the underlying points of correspondences which made for greater 'talking' spaces.

With such notions of the *other*, Tagore's idea of hybridity was probably deeper than what he could express and envisage as a poet-thinker. He admittedly looked into the space where self-essentializing was not self-ghettoization but, rather, a moving out in acts of recognition of the other for greater ways of self-definition. The Hindus needed the Buddhist and the Christians to 'define' themselves. And Tagore clearly maintained that in such articulations of hybridity the historical locations were as important as a sense of belonging to a place and community was. The consciousness of *difference* was the inspiration to negotiation – his unique ways of conjugating the aesthetics with politics. Jeremy Waldron notes pertinently that 'though we may drape ourselves in the distinctive costumes of our ethnic heritage and immure ourselves in an environment designed to minimize our sense of relation with the outside world, no honest account of our being will be complete without an account of our dependence on larger social and political structures that goes far beyond the particular community with which we pretend to identify'.[66] The man is superstructured to meet the universal man. Waldron notes further that 'we need to understand our choices in the contexts in which they make sense, but we do not need any single context to structure our choices. To put it crudely, we need culture, but we do not need cultural integrity'.[67] Tagore's Visva Bharati – interestingly, as time wore on Visva Bharati struggled in a coeval mutation, becoming an extension of Tagore's utopic ideal and an un-Tagorean organism whose evolutionary reality conflicted with the poet's sublimic aspirations – defended the minority, the ignored, and, their rights were allowed to surface and circulate in a kind of culture which was proposed to be adaptive and co-optative. He advocated the necessity to feel entitled to one's community, the vernacular identity, but the 'potential' which such entitlements and particular ethnic habitus generated prepared the grounds for what he envisaged as the communal *sanmilan*. Specificities of this nature were not obdurate determinants of communal behaviour; but they oriented the community to make choices out of the power and confidence that the community felt for transborder openness – vernacularism and nativism were no hindrance to Tagore's universalism. The interest in hybridity can easily submit to 'parity' where acknowledging difference is not about engagement with the 'differential' but cultivating a certain compulsive indifference to it. Coco Fusco is right to note that too often 'the postcolonial celebration of hybridity has been interpreted as the sign that no further concern about the politics of representation and cultural exchange is needed. With ease, we lapse back into the integrationist rhetoric of the 1960's, and conflate hybridity with parity'.[68] Tagore's search for hybridity had an identitarian character to it, was invested in subjectivities, which, however, did not disable a submission to finding a legitimate political and cultural identity, a constituency that forbade deracination. Gómez Pena captures the concept of postcolonial hybridity through what he calls the New World Border, 'a great trans- and intercontinental border zone, a place in which no centres remain. It's all margins, meaning there are no "others," or better said, the only true "others" are those who resist fusion, mestizaje, and cross-cultural dialogue. In this utopian cartography, hybridity is the dominant culture: Spanish, Frangle and Gingonol are *linguas francas*; and monoculture is a culture of resistance practiced by a stubborn or scared minority'.[69] Tagore was in support of an enactment – a critical responsiveness – that introduced a new logic of justice built on multicultural education and understanding. This concept of diversity was fluid and transitive working on the contingent and the relational, rendering a broad side to the frigidity that ontological and transcendental proclamations generated. Tagore saw identity as constellative and coalitional inscribed in strife and freedom. His critical pedagogy bespoke historical agency, self-transcendence and invention.

Ethnic and cultural specificities in Visva Bharati then were not allowed to impede on the tactical and productive solidarity that syncretism was allowed to build. Becquer and Gatti point out that 'syncretism designates articulation as a politicized and discontinuous mode of becoming. It entails the "formal" coexistence of components whose precarious (i.e., partial as opposed to impartial) identities are mutually modified in their encounter, yet whose distinguishing differences, as such, are not dissolved or elided in these modifications, but strategically reconstituted in an ongoing war of position'.[70] Syncretism, thus, 'signals, not the preordained telos of a redemptive higher unity contained within a diachronic self-unfolding, but the historicized interchange between elements based on the complex play of differences and affinities in a collective will to hegemonize'.[71] Tagore's massive and yet vastly intriguing project to syncretize was certainly aware of the ambiguity and participatory complexity of such enactments. The respect for difference made such an enactment dialectical where pluralization was not merely about coercing submission to certain universals. It acknowledged the absence of justice that was denied to certain communities and cultural practices. Visva

Bharati, thus, became a site of restive democracy where interdependence and integration owed to an unease of cultural communication and resurgent modes of mutual toleration amidst continual rancour of misjudged injuries. Tagore believed that we were destined to live with our differences that called for living outside any 'superior totality'; this enabled the demythologizing of our sociocultural enactments for a social world that awaited denaturalization and defatalization.

Crossing Over

Tagore did not see culture in Visva Bharati as a 'tensionless whole' uncritically overarched by a principle or spirit.[72] It submitted to the reality of accepting people as belonging to certain ethnic, religious and class background and, acknowledging identities with judgement, sense and life experiences. This was a culture that vindicated solidarity, exemplarity, critical thinking and liberatory action – a culture that did not believe in community-specific cultural practices and conditions as being solely responsible for the growth of an individual. Individual, for Tagore, responsibilized himself by 'being-for-others' and so the culture brought over from one's conditioning into a particular community of power became less important in relation to the culture that was generated through the eros for the other. Tagore's engagement with difference was intriguing in that his non-denominational attitude to education, on closer inspection, had its own deep moorings in Vedantic learning. This pronounced leaning did not turn Visva Bharati into a workshop of Vedantic culture though. But this certainly problematized the cosmopolitanization of the space within which Tagore conducted his educational experiments and rode his dream. If the local and the global find their home and the world in each other, we need not compulsively, somewhat uncritically, at times, overarch Tagore as a cosmopolitan, bringing, thus, his ideas within a bounded frame of understanding. I refuse to admit that Tagore, in spite of his professed idealization of educational mission, wanted something close to, for instance, Johann Bernhard Basedow's (1724–1790) Philanthropinum Institute where a system was sought to promote moral perfection and pedagogy had its own strict premises of execution.[73] Basedow, who later influenced Kant, with his cosmopolitan thinking advocated natural religion and religious tolerance with the aim to produce (another version of the *bildung*) world-citizens, 'friends of humanity' (*Menschenfreunde*). Tagore could not have been as authoritative in his choices as Kant was when he desired the realization of a 'cosmopolitan whole'[74] inscribed in the highest moral and political good. Within bounded rationality where one produces a fixed centre of one's principles and monitor the redrawing of concentric circles towards the formation of world citizenry, the 'crossing over' (*Übergang*) phenomenon comes with its own disposition and discourse. Tagore's 'crossing over' does not proceed from such normative strictness and regulative reason and clearly stands distinguished from Kantian moralization and statist structuration both at the level of cosmopolitan disposition (*Gesinnung*) and the conduct of thought (*Denkungsart*). Poulomi Saha appropriately observes that 'the notion cosmopolitanism, in Nussbaum's account, that distanced Tagore from baser and more chauvinistic loyalties to nation and creed appears incongruous with Tagore's own explicit repudiation of both nationalism and cosmopolitanism as inadequate affective and communitarian ideals. Instead, in his writing and in his own relationships, he sought to negotiate local attachment with global engagement. The emancipatory conception of the cosmopolitan intellectual, though alluring, ignores a crucial historical and hermeneutic question of whether the colonial subject be can in fact be cosmopolitan. Empire's specter haunted not only the body politic and its conditions of possibility in the colonial moment, but also the intimacies and legacies produced therewith'.[75] A widely travelled tourist or a *flaneur* is not a cosmopolitan; drawing on Diogenes's cynicism when he characterized him as *kosmo politês* one can see a deeply vexed antithetical space in efforts to integrate *cosmos* and *polites*, world and citizen. Visva Bharati to be cosmopolitanically different could not just have generously imbibed the Stoic and the Kantian tradition because the realities of its complicated affiliation to a colonial India, the difficulties of crossing 'borders' both culturally and politically, the implacable tangle between Tagore's cultural past and his political 'British' subjecthood and the vexatious habitation in the liminality of patriotism and nationalism could not be set out of focus. So Tagore's politics of inclusiveness – the cosmopolitan capaciousness – was more of an aesthetic judgement than certain determinate and teleological judgements on ethical conduct and norms of living. The global soul in Visva Bharati is not so much 'a citizen (a *polites*) of the world (*cosmos*) as an itinerant inhabitant of many disparate worlds, able to move comfortably among them (the globe is not an ordered cosmos, and the soul is not a citizen). Without these residual anchors, the global soul ceaselessly transposes the world into the self and finds its orientation in the vector of values and attachments internal to the self'.[76]

The metaphor of cosmopolitanism, as Torill Strand rightly explains, should be conceived as a verb, a process, an activity, a discourse, or simply something happening. Premised in Aristotle's term *meta-phora* which literally means 'between-motion', we connect with change (*phora*) or 'meta-change', namely the transposition of meaning from one location to another. Much in the spirit of the meta-change, Visva Bharati verbalized as 'a surprising *shift* between scenes, a *movement* from one realm of language to another, a *transposition* from one outlook to another'.[77] It operated as a deviation, a stranger in the circle of ordinary and established patterns of belief and values. Visva Bharati's 'discourse ethics' then was a happy obligation to communication built on certain principles of reason, ideals and thought. Tagore, deeply committed through his life to expression and communication, realized how Visva Bharati's communicative ethics needed both imagination and the strong principles of reason to become responsible and productive. Tagore, to whom cosmopolitanism was *sahit*, the idea of 'stranger' became an interesting negotiatory quotient. In the back of a colonial regime and the soul-shattering scenario of the First World War *strangerhood* became a dominant wrestling point in Tagore's institution. Kwame Appiah argues that since there is a considerable difficulty in reaching a final consensus over the ranking and order of local and universal values, the productive role of conversation becomes particularly significant.[78] This conversation is not for moral reconciliation or cultural conformism as much as it is not simply for facetious agreement or coercive compromise. It is about acknowledging the stranger in language and culture, in race and class, in education and background which, then, leads to the conversation that brings about negotiation of ideas without forsaking the strange otherity of the other – the irreducible individuality required to 'live together as global tribe'.[79] Negotiating strangerhood – neighbouring the stranger – is the new vocabulary of Tagore's discourse ethics.[80]

Working on the notion of the 'border' Visva Bharati raised the problematic of cosmopolitanism as against patriotism. Tagore was less interested in the narrowness of patriotism than he was with the spirit of openness and inclusiveness that cosmopolitanism promised and promoted. Cosmopolitanism was not about achieving perfectablity in exchanges and cross-flow and Visva Bharati was not simply about hurrahing for a globalist discourse. Marianna Papastephanou writes:

> When cosmopolitanism is understood only in terms of encountering diversity, enriching one's existential opportunity through diversity and

> setting laws for protecting diversity from illiberal infringement, it becomes a political ideal of an individualist freedom that is restricted solely by negative duties. What is left out is the whole set of positive duties that restores global and interstate relations and comprises contrite apologies and reparations for caused harm up to supererogatory ethics of material aid. In silencing all this, contemporary conceptions of cosmopolitanism seem no longer drastically separated from the standard account of patriotism in the following sense: what was supposed to divide them, i.e. the treatment of insiders and outsiders, now appears to be what unites them, in the doubleness that is most eloquently expressed by the French verb *partager*, where division coincides with sharing. Both converge on treating the other, local or global, in a politically correct way.[81]

Was Tagore under some kind of obligation to prove his political correctness? Tagore's ideals were heavily invested in the intricacies of the self-other programme keeping ideas of 'limits' in play. Historical (nativist or indigenous) and political (colonial or hegemonic) 'entanglements' were hard to evade and critical inclusivism or relational politics pointed to the apparently stridulous enterprise of sharing and division. This brings us to talk about the weighty relationship that tolerance and recognition share with each other. Visva Bharati was more keen on 'recognition' because tolerance carried with it an indifference and precluded, most often, the urge to explore and discover the features of the other.[82] However, toleration led to recognition also. Did Visva Bharati leave any alternative other than toleration? Toleration in Visva Bharati was never a 'paternalistic' phenomenon where the majority had what Rainer Forst calls 'the permission conception' of toleration.[83] The social imaginary of Visva Bharati then was both a product of a non-hegemonic and intersubjective commitment and also a space that did not succumb to the 'ontology of determinism'.[84] This projected a contested site where socio-historical worlds involved and interacted with each other.

What becomes interesting to observe is that Tagore's project began with a philosophical humility. This humility came from the acceptance of not knowing everything, the denial of sovereignty of knowledge and a submission to the other to endow and refurbish whatever knowledge the project needed for its competent and complementary fulfilment. Such Socratic humility identified the aporia as a necessary condition to question, to dissemble parts in order to rearrange towards the project's search for fructification. But humility is not what comes out of rational consensus; rather, it springs out of agonistic pluralism where identity is built on uncovering forms of difference and complications – a prudent dialectic between 'certainty' (the formed, entrenched, convinced) and clarity (the forming, the questions and perceptive) – without overbearing efforts to domesticate possible hostilities.[85] Tagore's humility, rather than pride, lay in the vulnerability of choosing this project of Visva Bharati – the risk, the entailments, the challenges and seductions.

Counter-Institution?

'Neither in its medieval nor in its modern form,' observes Jacques Derrida, 'has the university disposed freely of its own absolute autonomy and of the rigorous conditions of its own unity. During more than eight centuries, "university" has been the name given by a society to a sort of supplementary body that at one and the same time it wanted to project outside itself and keep jealously to itself, to emancipate and to control. And in a certain way it has done so: it has produced society's scenography, its views, conflicts, contradictions, its plays and its differences, and also its desire for organic union in a total body'.[86] Perhaps, aware of these imprisoning projections that have constituted universities in its medieval and its modern form, Tagore decided to call his university just 'Visva Bharati' and *not* 'Visva Bharati University', a preference that made allowance for deconstructive claims on spaces and notions that a classical university was expected to celebrate and establish. By naming it 'Visva Bharati', Tagore intended more meaning, sense and 'traffic' into his idea of the university as a site for contestation, conflation and construction; for me, it is '. . . That creative supplement. . . . '[87]

The university, with its space distinct from what we usually get in society and other areas of our daily existence, was a world built around certain principles of normativity and isolation. Even within the encompassive traffic, Visva Bharati, as was the case with ashram-school, had a disciplinizing machine which exacted conformity, a network that made claims on power and knowledge. However, this was not a feudalistic hierarchy; rather, a place, as Derrida has argued, where 'people know how to learn and learn how to know'.[88] This space reconfigurates our notions of 'tradition' and questions the rationality and raison d'être of university as a modern-day institution. Its pupils look both ways: 'inside' and 'outside' and like the Derridean ship our focus changes once we are on board at the port and then again when on board at mid sea. Visva Bharati was envisaged as a space for 'reflection' and 'analytic thinking', a site for Socratic dialecticism, without any collapse into undifferentiated syncretism. This secular agonistic space was not without foundations because Tagore laid deep faith in India's cultural past; but he questioned the 'problematic of responsibility' which attended a vocation or call, non-aporetically – a 'setting-to-work'. This certainly changed the ethical dimension of the idea of the university. Tagore was not aware of any rules about establishing a 'modern' university because he had never been to any institution of such order and had reservations as to its ideology, philosophy and functional principles. Interestingly, he had to invent a rule which comes, in a certain sense, from 'no-responsibility' (from the perspective of a non-affiliation to a stable and established centre of knowledge and authority); this no-responsibility was a responsibility demanding response of a different order, as Derrida argues, to two injunctions, 'different' and 'incompatible'. Derrida points out:

> That's where responsibility starts, when I don't know what to do. If I knew what to do, well, I would apply the rule, and teach my students to apply the rule. But would that be ethical? Ethics start when you don't know what to do, when there is a gap between knowledge and action, and you have to take responsibility for inventing the new rule which doesn't exist.[89]

Within such premises of 'wilderness', Tagore started with a responsibility to invent a rule that was born out of an uncanny gap between knowledge and action – a notional uniqueness which became his Visva Bharati as against the claims of pragmatism that the imperium of a modern university rigorously imposed. This was the pregnant 'abyss' that inspired an invention of a rule, a space, a rationality, a judgement and a reason different from the accredited, well-funded, reified principles of institutionalization. The poet finds his true inspiration, writes Tagore, 'only when he forgets that he is a schoolmaster'.[90] Visva Bharati was conceived with the responsibility of a poet who 'invents' and 'supplements' and certainly not with the dour intent of a schoolmaster who instructs and, bound within rules, validates. Tagore had the philosopher's crisis in that he was unable to resolve the tension between theory and practice, his ideals and prospective enactments, in the face of the mounting paradigm conflict generated from 'outside'. This required getting responsible towards the responsibility that others had for this space. Responsibility and risk conjugated in the dynamics of this well-trafficked space that tried to hold on to the troublous, at times inscrutable, subtlety of this conjugation – the actional aporeticism in conflation with oneiric inexorability.

Tagore spelt out the aims of the university and what he set out to achieve. But this 'doing' spelt out rules and yet unmade many as it progressed, setting off a life-long angst. The ethics of the university worked itself out on 'showing' and 'performing' which in a Wittgensteinian sense can be qualified as 'practice', the performative ability. The 'conduct' of the reality and the ideal within the institutional space never went for a conscious rule following but, instead, kept learning in contexts through observation, communication, emulation, trials and experiments. Tagorean practices were not aberrative and idiosyncratic because he ensured that enactments in his moral-aesthetic education were both a part of the pedagogical heritage and derivations external to the relentless lockstep certainty of authoritative programmes.

Tagore's Visva Bharati was the 'everyday' by which Derrida means a phenomenon that does not stop. It was 'everyday traffic' – inauguration of departments, politics of institutional governance, concourse of people from various places in India, international visitors programme, fund-raising trips and ventures, the ineluctable anxiety of staying afloat amidst ideological worries about collapsing into colonial educational machinery and the pragmatic impulsion to avoid being anachronistic. Tagore did not believe in the erasure of hierarchy but had a kind of Derridean opposition to 'a certain stabilizing or stabilized coding of a hierarchy'.[91] This was not anarchism or a provocation to remain stranded between tradition and the neglected and phobic other. It was a way of interrogating the *arche*, the commandment, without being irreverent to certain hierarchical codes required to continue 'negotiations'. Derrida notes:

> in the knot of negotiation there are different rhythms, different forces, different differential vibrations of time and rhythm. The word knot came to me and the image of a rope. A rope with entanglement, a rope made up of several strands knotted together. The rope exists. One imagines computers with little wires, wires where things pass very quickly, wires where things pass very slowly: negotiation is played along all of these wires. . . . Also, cables that pass under the sea and thousands of voices with intonations, that is, with different and entangled tensions. Negotiation is like a rope and an interminable number of wires moving or quivering with different speeds and intensities.[92]

Tagore's negotiations – quivering and radiant with different intensities – were not uncritical assimilations but a process in 'entangled tensions' that was underwritten by a conflictual syncretism; it was a complex and uninterrupted engagement, a continual countering, 'with-against'. By seeking such a purchase on the concept of the university, Tagore left rigid-framed institutionalists in a state of discomfiture. Visva Bharati was a constellative space of 'counter' – redemptive and yet non-inimical – to the totalizing ways of institutionalization. It was a 'problem' and Tagore knew the vexed harvest of a 'counter'. Derrida writes:

> In abstract and general terms, what remains constant in my thinking . . . is indeed a critique of institutions, but one that sets out not from a wild and spontaneous pre – or non-institution, but rather from counter institutions. I do not think there is, or should be, the 'non-institutional'. I am always torn between the critique of institutions and the dream of an other institution that, in an interminable process, will come to replace institutions that are oppressive, violent and inoperative.[93]

Tagore chose a 'counterpath' within which the university did not merely include its own institution but had susceptible trajectories involving the 'sidepaths', 'off the highway' and into the 'with-against' mode of appropriation and acknowledgement of the 'other'. Counter here is to encounter, to meet and to engage, to be in contact with an intent to reciprocate – the complicated intimations of hospitality. Visva Bharati's 'inside' was mediated by the 'outside', and also by something outside the normative teaching machine – institutionalized in counterpoint, in the 'dream of an *other*' (in the words of Derrida). The other manifested as the presence of a variety of cultures and discourses from across the world was like a dream which, was, at once, irreducibly attached to the other and existed also as a hunger for the other, an aspiration to think 'counter'. Visva Bharati was a 'dream for an other', enfolding institutions within institutions and, like a dream, did not necessarily promote closure, balance and resolution. It was the deterritorialization of the familiar space that a university 'institutionally' projected and perpetuated, morphing, thus, into an extra-territorial standpoint which Derrida would like to see as keeping the institutionality of institution open and having a future (*avenir*). One must note that Tagore's celebration of one's tradition was conditioned upon its openness to other traditions, a promissory structure that could not do without the dream and the breath of the 'other'. Acknowledging one's roots is not about forgetting the profit that comes from the 'counter' which is a form of negotiation and not condescension – a solidarity that comes through a sense of the *avenir* and activism across borders. This speaks of a 'sovereignty' that is, however, not in consonance with the notions of a timeless independence of traditional universities. Rather, Visva Bharati's sovereignty as a counter-institution had the logic of an informed and fecund traffic.

The exceptionality of this space, distinct from the unified community that the German Idealists proposed, anticipated dereferentialization of culture and, in a certain sense, a post-historical position which had a separate logic of cultural syncretism and performativity. Tagore combined a consciousness of past, the impress of inheritance and also a critique of a future. Understanding culture was an acknowledgement which did not fail to mark out the 'exchange', the note of 'traffic' hidden in it. The traffic was not mere economism but an economy of exchange within notions of reciprocity, deference, deferment, debt and obligation. This entailed both the notions of response and responsibility. Visva Bharati as a space was meant to be generative – actively produced and, in being produced, produced itself further. However, true to Henri Lefebvre's anxiety about the blurring of distinction between the object and the activity that produced it, Visva Bharati was a site under permanent construction, where spaces produced are akin to the writer's rough draft tossed away for another redaction. Tagore kept committed to the 'process of its genesis and the development of its meaning'.[94] In fact, in conceiving 'things in space' responsibly, this process resulted in the actual 'production of space'. Tagore's philosophy of finding a 'religion of man', connecting 'man with man', could not have been done by thinking of objects as 'things in isolation' or' things in themselves'; rather, man in his relation to man, trying to imbibe the ideals of 'universal man' produced spaces and the unfolding drama of humanity worked within the productionist dynamics of such ever-proliferating spaces. Tagore's ideals of education were about begetting spaces, courageously fought for and courteously incorporated.

Deeply aware of nativist identity and informed by a refusal to be 'eternal rag pickers in other people's dustbins'[95] and yet alertly conscious of the contributory and complementary 'other', Tagore understood Visva Bharati as a discourse at the cross-roads of power and exchange. He knew, in a Levinasian way, that possessing or seizing the other was extinguishing the other. So discourses of one's identity were important to the extent that it did not become imperialist and, hence, violent. Discourses were there to be negated and contaminated and the fermenting space across such discursive crossroads could not avoid being conflictual and confounding. The university space was bound to be 'smooth' in its inexorable transculturality. Tagore, to my mind, was aware of the difficulty that such a space might generate. Visva Bharati, in its inception and subsequent ramification produced this confusion in its engagements with the 'other' which only an 'unconditioned' smooth space was capable of generating.

So Tagore's trial with his idea of the university made him 'dwell' on the notions of confinement, *finis*, border and the margin of discourse, ideology and power. Tagore looked into the logic of the 'margin' and the 'centre' in a new reckoning which identified the ferment on the borders as a way to negotiate 'traffic' at the centre, sponsoring new formations that appreciated locations, instances and structures. Tagore worked on deconstructing reified notions of inheritance of knowledge through an astute intertwining that acknowledged a centrality of cultural emission (Tagore writes, 'it is this which makes me urge that all the elements in our own culture have to be strengthened, not to resist the western culture, but truly to accept and assimilate it; to use it for our sustenance, not as our burden; to get mastery over this culture, and not to live on its outskirts as the hewers of texts and drawers of book-learning'.[96]) and *espacement*. So the planetary site of the university offered the opportunity to investigate the 'relevance of the limit'.[97] For Tagore, then, it was about thinking outside a university to 'frame up' a university, rather, as Derrida has put it, 'how can we not speak of the university?' By *not* speaking about university as it existed – within a discourse that academies usually produce – he *was* speaking of a creative 'anarchy' that refused to flinch before the power of axiomatic institutional locations and reductive ideologies. Visva Bharati, in its intertextual ramifications, redrew boundaries which had a logic outside the prevalent law where walls between students and teachers, between text and teaching, between vernacular and the foreign, between nativism and other cultural discourses should not be misread in their conventional logic of obduracy, permeability and pliancy. Despite harbouring obvious reservations about bounded discourses that neo-humanist institutions were embedded in, Tagore did not think of a modern university as a 'ruined institution' and so Visva Bharati was not reactively projected as a redeeming legitimate model to disestablish it. As a topos of possibilities he tried to work on the notion of 'community' as absence: the 'yet to be achieved' forms of human contact where non-recognition of otherness was a statement of the incompleteness of the self. As I have pointed out, Visva Bharati was envisaged within a separate logic of responsibility and hospitality: 'responsibility' seen as going beyond the academic time-tested version and 'hospitality' as not being envisaged to merely absorb and accept differences – both 'being for' and 'being with'. In fact, Visva Bharati was never designed to become 'responsible before a non-academic instance' which meant that its autonomy contested the superior reason that the state imposed as the founding and functioning principle of an institution. This flexed up the 'academic freedom' and reconcepted the 'self-legitimation and self-affirmation of the university'.[98] As a 'constructum', Visva Bharati, rather, was marked by Derrida's phenomenology of the *finis*[99] that repremised academic topology, investing distinct values into 'academic reason' where 'finitude' was not about drawing up the 'yes' and the 'no's' but was a dialecticism in disclosures and enclosures, bordering the 'inside and the outside' of the reflexive non-cynical habitus of the university. Visva Bharati, thus, becomes for me a deconstructive commentary on the unquestioned 'rational idea' of a university. It addresses to what Derrida qualifies as 'question of man, to a concept of that which is proper to man'[100] through the experience of knowledge and humanization which is both relational and dialogical. Visva Bharati was not about looking into the future of a university but was an experiment to transcend 'conditional university' – not 'as should be' but 'can possibly be'.

Within such formations, what should be the nature of hospitality that Visva Bharati in its counter-institutionality could afford to provide? It is difficult to accept that Visva Bharati offered unconditional hospitality but it allowed a gesture of invitation that provided shelter, recognition and possibilities of value-laden encounters. In a letter to Kshitimohan Sen, Tagore observes, 'I have taken courage to invite Europe to the fields of Bolpur. There will be a meeting of truths here. I feel confident that they shall accept our invitation. What we have to ensure is that their hearts are not starved when they are with us. As a poet I can merely play the flute at the gate'.[101] The music of the flute was not absolute hospitality. The threshold politics involved in Visva Bharati's potential as a counter-institution grids up three issues: the discursive ethics which Tagore established and could not have been happy seeing it violated in the least; an openness which was deeply tied to a conditioned possibility and the compelling pressure of throwing up a non-nomadic hospitality different from the one that we encounter in conventional institutes of power and learning. The hospitable space was problematic for it seduced and yet knew its limits, ambivalent and processual and yet could not be remorselessly transitive. Identities were not questioned but a correspondence with the quintessential character of Visva Bharati became a conditioned token for an entry: passage came with an ideological similarity in passport. In its apparent openendedness and unbounded hospitality Tagore, unlike Derrida, encrypted his own password – a shared space with the violence of limits.

Though not a believer in 'absolute hospitality', Tagore, to an extent, wanted a disquietude in his world by getting people to visit his university – an interval in the lull of repetitive solitude, trials of conceptual accommodation, a 'war embrace' (in the words of Coleridge) with realms of possibility. He was always committed to invent a present and, thus, construct a future, which, in the sense of the not yet, held incalculable dimensions for him. Hospitality cannot just be timely only. Patterns of negotiation, expected structures of exchanges can be intertwined with untimeliness in the form of effacement and renomenclaturing of identities. Tagore's 'foreign' visitors – Indo-Sinologist Sylvain Levi, Moritz Winternitz of the Oriental Institute in Prague, Sten Konow from Norway, British sociologist Arthur Geddes from France, linguist Fernand Benoit of Switzerland, painter Ju Peon from China, historian Stella Kramrisch from Vienna, Irish poet and writer James Cousin, Indologist Guiseppe Tucci and Carlo Formichi of the University of Rome, Dutch musicologist Arnold Bake, Chinese savant Tan Yun-Chan and others[102] – brought with them response ability because foreignness came as a question, with a note of reflexibility, and did not naturalize but left behind further questions – the viable ethics of such moves, efficacies of cultural collusion and aesthetic transgression of borders of thinking and hosting. Here Tagore's conceiving of hospitality transformed the inmates into becoming 'guests' of foreigners – allowing the visitors to extrapolate in the potency of the host a space whether students and teachers inhabited as guests to experience the services of learning and educate themselves through the uniqueness of a homely 'foreignness'.[103] Visva Bharati as utopia in the sense of 'no place' and 'out of place' was inscribed in transcendence – the intriguing dynamics of being transcended by the other, the host transcended by the guests and the hosts staying guests in a perpetual possibility of being transcended. This alludes to 'transcendifferances'[104]: Tagore, in a state of *host*age, looked out for the other as a way to unshackle him and also make the other know his own resources. This is the radical processuality of 'is' – 'is' as both 'has been' and 'not there'. What this does to Tagore's project is that the spectrality of Bharati comes unfailingly to haunt Visva. Visva and Bharati never blurred into each other but transcended one another without discrediting the mutual presence. This problematic of transcendence is interesting because the process subjectivizes Tagore all through his life both as a dwelling host and an indwelling guest.

Counter-Education: Bharati Visva

Listening across discourses and communities of thought and identities makes men relate critically to their world. 'To be human', writes Paulo Freire, 'is to engage in relationships with others and with the world. It is to experience that world as an objective reality, independent of oneself, capable of being known'.[105] Being human also comes with a conscious existence in time: men being both 'inside' and 'outside', they 'incorporate' and 'modify'. Freire notes that 'men are not imprisoned within a permanent "today"; they emerge and become temporalized'.[106] Tagore's growth into a relationship with the world brought with it a host of consequences. His concern for poverty and under development in the villages ('Gradually the sorrow and poverty of the villagers became clear to me, and I began to grow restless to do something about it. It seemed to me a very shameful thing that I should spend my days as a landlord, concerned only with money-making and engrossed with my own profit and loss'[107]) accompanied by the raging requirement to produce the fruits of self-independent education made him restive, always ill-adapted to situations at hand and relentlessly in need for what Freire calls 'integration'. Education annihilates itself when it loses touch with moments of unease and the politics of 'counter' and Tagore, in a near existential authenticity and positive angst, brought about his own ways of integration.

Sriniketan made Tagore participate in an unfinished universe – education is always an unfinished project caught in the passion of reconstruction and imagination. Tagore could not have worked through a dispassionate bureaucratic logic but through a reasonableness stewed in imagination, the eros of a possibility and empathy that brings temporary 'suspension' of loaded self-consciousness to 'glide with one's own feeling into the dynamic structure of an object' and an inclusivism which is 'the extension of one's own concreteness, the fulfilment of the actual situation of life, the complete presence of the reality in which one participates'.[108] Dewey rightly points out that a 'sense of possibilities that are unrealized and that might be realized are, when they are put in contrast with actual conditions, the most penetrating "criticism" of the latter that can be made. It is by a sense of possibilities opening before us that we become aware of the constrictions that hem us in and of burdens that oppress'.[109] Tagore subjected himself to continual criticism and experienced positive abject for not being able to connect proper education with village reconstruction profitably. So Tagore's self-conscious organized intelligence and poetic eros went out to meet the mind of the whole community. Both Tagore and Dewey develop an educational identity based on the dialectical correspondence with the community. Tagore, like Dewey, knew that individuality develops through socialization – 'the dialectics of maximum individuality within maximum community'.[110] Sriniketan then, to an extent, was a Deweyan democracy. Dewey writes:

> A democracy is more than a form of government; it is primarily a mode of associated living, of conjoint communicated experience. The extension in space of the number of individuals who participate in an interest so that each has to refer his own action to that of others, and to consider the action of others to give point and direction to his own, is equivalent to breaking down barriers of class, race, and national territory which kept men from perceiving the full import of their activity.[111]

Sriniketan challenged historical habits of existence – the economy and social reality – to develop a cooperative habitat invested in group attitude. George Mead considers thinking as standing for 'public consideration' which takes into consideration the attitude of others and language. Based on Mead's idea of what constitutes 'thinking', Jürgen Oelkers points out that 'individuality is no longer the "inner" counter-world to "external" society, as in the European tradition of personal self-cultivation. The dualism of individual and society itself comes into question, for society is not a "thing" confronting the individual, but rather complex interactions between individuals and groups'.[112] Tagore re-explored the complexities that inscribed group and individual behaviour – its constitutional and institutional ramifications.

Tagore did not lack ethical imagination, a troubled consciousness and the transformative intent, enabling the revealment of further experiences in humanitarianism, enlightenment and amelioration.[113] Sriniketan could not have been Plato's ideal state, hence, a static state. Tagore intended a reconstructionist evolution – temporal and progressive – penetrative and exposed to possibilities. He points out that 'the education, the desires and the pursuits of those whom we call gentle folks and the opportunities they enjoy belong to the dry cave on one side of the dead river: an impassable distance separates them from those who are on the other side in knowledge and beliefs, customs and habits and the mode of daily life. The villagers have neither education, nor medical care, nor do they posses wealth, food and clothing. On the other side those who read in the college, practise law or medicine or pile up money at the banks find themselves on an island surrounded by bottomless separation'.[114] As feudal *pater familias*,[115] Tagore's pedagogical directivity presupposed a reflective consciousness of the history of the villagers and the system within which they survived. This is Freirian in that Tagore exhibited the intentionality to see a 'becoming-human' project that underwrote the much invested connection humans have with the world. Tagore submitted to a kind of pedagogic performativity as a knowing subject. The reading and experience of a situation came with the acknowledgement of 'oppression' at various levels of understanding. The difficulty in this project was the mediatory subjecthood of a zamindar with the proprietorship of *zamins* (lands) and other telluric parameters. This made allowance for an understanding of a separate epistemology of culture which Friere argues as the 'systematic acquisition of knowledge' requiring an investigation into the history, politics and fraught situatedness of the people and their connection with the world around – the land, economy, settlement, debt, production and ownership. The habitus of a peripheralized community – exception, exploitation and embargo – called for a social normativity against dynamic individual agency. A settled disposition to their state of oppression and ignorance brought forth a structure designating as, Bourdieu has argued, a 'way of being, a habitual state', a 'predisposition, tendency, propensity or inclination'.[116] The habitus of living – material conditions of social practice, however exploited and exiguous – came with the 'field' comprising the disempowered and disenfranchised community. Tagore's critical pedagogy wanted to resurrect the weakened soul of the people, undermining an intellectual laziness that assigned the other a more capable and intelligent status. This was not to simply redefine the monolithic relationship with the landlord and the land but a reunderstanding of the world through scientific developments, methods of modernization that would increase the soil–crop ratio, a libidinal economy that would see the landowner's capital-benefit in conjunction with the tiller's 'encashing' on his physical investments in the land with greater harvest ('A huge capital gathers together the money-making power scattered in many men and starts an all-devouring concern, before the organized strength of which isolated units needs must yield. The only remedy is in voluntary union of those disparate forces in order to ensure the flow of profit to all. The remedy is not in killing the capitalist, but in giving all equal opportunities of becoming capitalists'.[117]), and investigations into the sources that sapped the life-force out of the village life – a 'permanent process of search' and a 'mutual process of liberation'[118] in what turned out as a co-subjective existence *with* the world. Tagore brought a 'new gaze, a sociological eye'. He initiated with a projective vitality a 'genuine conversation, a metanoia, a mental revolution, a transformation of one's whole vision of the social world'.[119] So the Sriniketan centre, as part of Tagore's Bourdieuian reflexivity, came up with 'a number of demonstration units, where economists, agriculturalists, social workers, doctors, midwives and specialists in various fields of rural industry and education worked on the problems brought to them by the villagers. The idea was to put their heads together on different aspects of rural life. Social work for example consisted of holding weekly meetings with the village priest and the *mullah*, where readings from spiritual texts were arranged for adults, festivals were celebrated, community singing with *kirtans* and *bhajans*, as well as performing *jatras* or drama were organised, as well as the repairing of temples and mosques'.[120] These acts – more activities in the form of night school, primary educational units (*pathsalas*) in villages, mobile libraries, philosophy and principles of peripatetic university, *Brati-Balakas*, 4H clubs looking into issues of *health*, employing *head* in relation to collegiality, understanding soil texture and other economic conditions, using *hands* for vocational training of different forms and *heart* to reach out to people in adversity[121] – developed a 'field' where habitus produced a transcending power making an effort to change the 'game' not through a hermeneutic detachment but a participatory consciousness inscribed in 'directly concerned aims of practical understanding'[122]: rules were revised with caution and disposition and practice brought about the distinction between 'rule' and 'regularity'. The emancipatory discourses and reflexivity through Sriniketan changed a few rules and became the locus of certain regularities.[123]

A critical understanding of history comes with a revisionary understanding of the other. Tagore laments that 'there have been many a movement among our people, but that remains unknown to our students. They do not want to know because it does not fetch them pass marks in examinations'.[124] The contemptuous divide between the villagers and conventional *bhadralok* class withered out the 'tactile' in education, the sense of *touch* that can rejuvenate the connection experience has with learning. Here the epistemological curiosity must come with a physical engagement with the object of enquiry. It is an understanding of lived reality, the subjectivities that can scarcely be monologized because they come with their own vagaries and multiple valences. Tagore knew that pedagogization could not be simple on this occasion for learning would mean encountering the starkness of a living reality of oppression, suspicion, opacity, xenophobia and class consciousness. Sriniketan's rural reconstruction pedagogy was both societal and intellectual emancipation, conscious of the politics and socio-economic forces that intertwined its structures. Tagore projected both the visibility of the subject – mostly during the period when he managed the estate and later through his inspection of the settlements around Santiniketan – and hiddeness of the agenda of exploitation and the prevalent administrative machinery. He relied on his own will, in a critical intelligence that refused to see oppression as uniform in degree and kind among villages he surveyed and had knowledge about. So pedagogy could not have had a uniform spread, working its effect on every situation and context with a common assumption and praxis. Emancipatory education fails when the individual issues are decimated over group will; emancipation can work through enactment of opinion and specificities which only reflective consciousness can generate. Tagore was not much interested in 'antidiological acts' – in protest marches, myth making and other forms of cultural intrusions that infuse mistrust among people. Emancipation could not have come with a tried and generic method for Tagore sought his means and mechanism through his own will, imagination and eros.

Tagore's liberatory education looked into the connect existing between economy, *swaraj* and social emancipation – a problem-posing orientation that demanded a critical pedagogy involving the joint cooperative of diverse people and a contesting consortium of values. In a Freirean way, such critical activism did not see the world 'as a static reality but as a reality in process'.[125] Social groups and conditions became keen objects of study and liberatory education sought organized modes of representation. Tagore's *dharma-golas* project (cooperatives) was apprehensive of dialogue where he came to represent the authoritative side of the projective conversation. In such a pedagogy of the oppressed the history and identity of the initiator could not be oversighted. Consequently, consciousness was driven by critical reflection and the manifestations were not innocent. This invited group behaviour and more critical knowledge that decodified the challenging reality of dialogue deficit.

Tagore's aesthetics then was deeply inscribed in his critical pedagogics – both a sociopolitical act and aesthetic event. The emancipatory politics was a kind of enactment in art and knowing. Reconstructive pedagogy at Sriniketan therefore was not mere transfer of knowledge; rather, as Freire points out 'production or construction of knowledge'.[126] The philosophical imaginary of the earth-connect unveiled and problematized at ashram-school refigured its politics at *Siksha-Satra* (the school at Sriniketan) through a remarkable biopolitics in self-expression, *atma-sakti* and sensualization of pedagogy. The tactility and sense-drive (the performative and aesthetic investments through 'garden plots'[127]) in education inserted the existential quotient at the heart of learning and educational maturity. Students were made to undermine the schoolmaster and got exempted from 'banking education' within a politics of transmission that came with a living connect with the earth – freedom and instruction, imagination and *techne* having an integrated manifestation in 'gardening, weaving, sewing their own clothes, constructing their own tables and boxes, cooking, painting, writing Bengali, reciting poems and solving mathematical problems in relation to life situations'.[128] Students and villagers needed the company of the educated – Tagore's sedulous army of workers included Leonard Elmhirst, Santosh Majumdar, Kalimohan Ghosh, C. F. Andrews, Arthur Geddes,[129] Kim-Taro Kashahara, Harry Timbres and others – to find the efficacious direction of culture. The culture of critical education cannot ignore the conatus and contrivance, delight and deliberation in a generative tension with the potential economic and situational constraints of society, something that T. S. Eliot has recommended as the weighing of one's mind and perceiving the moral differences that apply it. Referring to vocational training, Eliot sees the potency in the combination of livelihood, growth as a citizen and self-development: 'the greatest danger of a naive acceptance of this aim is that education may eventually come to mean nothing more than adapting someone to his environment. Naturally, notes Eliot, a person must be adapted to his political environment because without being adapted to it, he cannot play a part in it, he can hardly survive in it. But he must not be completely adapted to it in the form in which he finds it around him; for that would be to train a generation to be completely incapable of any change or improvement, unable to make discoveries or experiments, or to adapt itself to those changes which go on perpetually without anyone's having deliberately intended to bring them about'.[130]

Like Coleridge, Tagore saw the point in injuring understanding by making knowledge the 'prime object'.[131] Knowledge is not attained in a vast labyrinth which only encourages misdirected running. Coleridge notes that the 'happiness of mankind is the end of virtue, and truth is the knowledge of the means; which he will never seriously attempt to discover, who has not habitually interested himself in the welfare of others. The searcher after truth must love and be beloved; for general benevolence is a necessary motive to constancy of pursuit; and this general benevolence is begotten and rendered permanent by social and domestic affections'.[132] Sriniketan, as an injury to regnant understanding, became a production of knowledge about constituting communities and not mere two communities on the master-subject axis – sense experience that worked on assumptions, realities of distribution in values and power, inclusivity and the throb of the inaudible and the invisible. Tagore's critical pedagogy was a project in unveiling, in love, an effort to make a different sense of the forms of the visible – collectives which spoke of a different constitution and distribution of roles, ethics and communitarianism – 'it is food which nourishes, not money; it is fullness of life which makes one happy, not fullness of purse'.[133] Tagore was seeking a utopic politics which was not built on the inane harmony between the empowered and the disprivileged. It turned out to be the theatre of the oppressed – poetics of inequality – where disharmony or rupture was a way to reconstruct further knowledge and reaestheticize what Rancière described as connecting with the unconnected. Tagore's creative humanization – the aesthetic-political counter-education – was affective hope. All of Tagore's projects were 'sublime' resulting in longing, hope, desire and rupture. Hence, much in character with the relationship that disappointment has with the supersensible and the indeterminate, Tagore's experience and experiments bled on the stubs of anxiety – an inconsummation where, significantly, the poetics of creativity resided. His educational experiments could not be niched as 'problem posing, problem shooting' acts because of their inherent sublimic nature which, again, disallowed hardened institutionalization. Ideal is agony, vision is struggle, thinking is power, anxiety is reality, and life a poet's dream. Tagore was unhappy with the ways in which his son and some of his colleagues changed the character of his project at Sriniketan where Rathindranath, his son, was more a practicalist and he, as always, a utopianist; he could not conceal his helplessness before Pearson when he decided to quit Santiniketan because Visva Bharati was struggling to hold on to the ideals that inspired its inception.[134] Tagore knew that 'it is not possible to go too much against the current of the times. If we have an arrangement in one place which has nothing corresponding to it then that is a loss, it cannot survive'.[135] The inevitable tangle inscribing imagination, eros and reality delivered its own ounces of unremitting anxiety – the outbreak of war, depleting financial resources, drying up of external assistance, a deficit of about thirty thousand rupees that the university stood confronted with, the roiling complexities intrinsic to the governance of organizations (Tagore's referring to Sriniketan as a 'complex organization'[136] is surely a loaded ascription) and his seriously failing health.

Tagore's projects possessed an 'Archimedian conceit of the idealist utopian view' of life and education but not without a rationalist and relational pedagogic and performative praxis. What Peter Mclaren said of Freire is true of Tagore: the 'politics of liberation resists subsumption under a codified set of universal principles; rather, it animates a set of ethical imperatives that together serve as a precipitate of our answering the call of the other who is suffering and of a heavy heart. Such imperatives do not mark a naive utopian faith in the future; rather, they presage a form of active, irreverent, and uncompromising hope in the possibilities of the present'.[137] Liberatory pedagogy is meant not to extinguish tension but generate it for the success of a creative experiment. The resultant tension keeps alive the circuit of subjectivity. And it is to these areas of 'becoming human' that pedagogists as cultural educators need to address. Writing to Elmhirst, Tagore pointed out his creative eros which was no mere construction but the expression of his being: 'The ideal which I cherish in my heart for the work I have been struggling to build up through the best portion of mature life does not need qualifications that are divided into compartments. It was not the kingdom of the Expert in the midst of the inept and ignorant which we wanted to establish – although the experts' advices are valuable. The villages are waiting for the living touch of creative.... '[138] This required a new order of desire and wisdom which Dewey qualifies as a 'conviction about moral values, a sense for the better kind of life to be led'. The morality of the project called for choice 'about something to be done, a preference for living this sort of life rather than that. It refers not to accomplished reality but to a desired future which our desires, when translated into articulate conviction, may help bring into existence'.[139] The facts of the life of the dispossessed and the marginal did not make the wisdom productive: the eros generated an aesthetic power that could imagine the possible in the actual situation and disciplinize the eros into meaningful action. Sriniketan redefined Tagore's philosophy of life and man into a new poetics of love subjected to rational discriminations, to a working programme of action, 'a prophecy of the future, but one disciplined by serious thought and knowledge'.[140]

Tagore then is a half ignorant schoolmaster in that he did not see a complete equality-in-intelligence relationship with the people; but certainly envisaged a will to will dialogue through a reflective and emancipatory consciousness. His attention to such projects and schemes of development and rehabilitation involved an enactment of will and belief without a consciousness of superiority. Tagore was intelligent to read into the codification of such conditions and open to learn from the intelligence of the other. So for Tagore this became an act of love: 'we have to keep in mind the fact that love and action are the only mediums through which perfect knowledge can be obtained; for the object of knowledge is not pedantry but wisdom'.[141] In an interview, Freire explained: 'I understand the process of teaching as an act of love. I mean, it is not an act of love in the formal sense, and never in the bureaucratic sense. It is an act of love as an expression of good care, a need to love, first of all, what you do. Can you imagine how painful it is to do anything without passion, to do everything mechanically?'[142] Tagore's relational praxis vouchsafed for a sensualism which connected the 'rigorous acts of knowing the world' with 'the passionate ability to know'.[143] The dialogue that Tagore initiated could not have operated in a politically neutral space for dialogue, as Freire points out, works within a tension, implying responsibility, directiveness, determination, discipline, objectives.[144] This dialogue owes immensely to Tagore's profound love of the world, an education for fullness where the 'lighted lamp' is the desired end and not a 'lump of gold'.[145]

Education, as Alain Badiou maintains, is about arranging the 'forms of knowledge in such a way that some truth may come to pierce a hole in them'.[146] I see Tagore as piercing a hole in all his educational *projec*tions as a marker of his 'new way of being' and revisionary acts in response to changing situations. His life-vital projections of truths are sometimes acts that operate outside the recognizable and established power-relations. Patha Bhavan, Visva Bharati and Sriniketan were new forms of truth in the institutional landscape of colonial India: singularity of events that did not norm its logic of inclusion, problematized the recovery of institutional learning and reclaimed knowledge through continuous punches that produced 'holes' for greater realizations and proleptic endowment. Tagore's Visva Bharati and Sriniketan perhaps never stopped to evolve, and, hence the dream that set them off was always an event in a state of withdrawal where affirmative truths were political and, most often, reflexive. These were not conditioned achievements neither axiomatically conceived nor spurned. They had, conceptually, remained 'insignificant' because as an event of difference they functioned in a network of knowability and ignorance, inconceivable others and the phenomenon of the 'coming to be'. I call it insignificant because their points of inception, the psycho-empirical rationale, the historical moment of deliverance are too unique to install a law, a conformist principle for future emulation and epitomization. Living in the aesthetics of the 'sensible' informed with dissensus and inclusion, their insignificance is their empowering truth, enabling more holes to be punched in their knowledge (de)formations – insignificance as an 'active thought that is both subtle and dogged'.[147] Tagore's Visva Bharati and Sriniketan society then were revisionary but authoritative (*archai*) and yet unfailingly welcoming of the virtues and freedom of good life (*eu zein*) – a totality and yet not an addition of the parts that went into their making because the parts kept on changing their functional unitive force and value with time and changing situations. They functioned like a composite (*sun-theton*) with interdependent parts and also an assemblage of parts whose existence, in the words of Philip Armstrong, was 'not reducible to its teleological anticipation as one part of a *pre*given whole, or to preexisting identities that, taken together, go to make up a given totality'. The *koinonia* of these projects was 'inscribed by the essential possibility of a partitioning or portioning out, at once beyond, in excess, or subtracted from the totalizing arrangement of parts'.[148] Within such restive reticulation, they ensured to establish habits but were built around disrupting habits also for there was the continual privileging of earnest and collateral *listening* across cultures and knowledge and traditions.[149]

All of Tagore's projects then were forms of utopia and, the happy tragedy of utopia is in sustaining its own unfulfilment – a state that is telic and, yet, transitive. He probed the necessity of being human, becoming educated, a state of 'becoming culture', of becoming *homo viator*. More than politico-pedagogical projects they were aesthetic projections: points to reach but reaching as a form of travel. This was the Tagore *agonistes* who is a provocaetuer, an inciter, and in whom 'the sense of the heroic and saintly can be evoked'. As against the self-actualization motif we encounter the self-potentiation dynamic where 'the seed itself is not yet formed, that there is unformedness in each soul, and that we must struggle to add new powers to our spiritual base'.[150] In a complex interplay of horizons of understanding, Tagore, a figure caught in the ideological and ideational dynamics of contra-counter-con, tried to fix truths knowing how *living* every question is consorting incertitude, 'cultivating patience with everything unsolved', as Rainer Rilke argues, 'in your heart': an effort to love the questions themselves, and not searching for the answers 'which could not be given you now, because you would not be able live them. And the point is to live everything'.[151] Having their own *itihasa*, Tagore's projects did not forget to *live* the questions and, on most occasions, without his formally alert consciousness, lived his way into many answers and unanswerable questions. Self-legislative and self-reformatory and, yet, perpetually under trial Tagore fought for moments that stood elected outside the constrictions of the 'herd'. The events of sublimation did not come in a strict Nietzschian way though in that the self-overcoming did not rule out the consciousness of the social: the complicated matrices for 'the being-in-and-for-self' and 'being-for-others'. His projects were always on the move: knowing where they stood and yet vitalized with the possibility to reconsider and revise their movements and formations to keep active the potency to deliver – institutions always at risk where contamination was fecundity, fermentation was life.

Notes

1. Written in the fall after Arnold's long vacation of 1872–73, this letter grants permission for use of Arnold's works to Sir Roper Lethbridge. He wrote a *History of India* and edited the *Calcutta Quarterly Review* 1871–1878. See Forrest D. Burt and Clinton Machann, 'Matthew Arnold and Education: Nine New Letters', *Victorian Poetry*, Vol. 28, No. 1, (Spring, 1990), 83. (Burt and Machann Spring, 1990)
2. *Higher Schools and Universities in Germany*, 215.
3. Ibid, xxx. See N. Hans, 'English Pioneers of Comparative Education' *British Journal of Educational Studies*, Vol. 1, No. 1, (Nov., 1952), 56–59. (Hans 1952)
4. Hans, 'English Pioneers of Comparative Education', 58. (Hans Nov., 1952)
5. *Universities in Germany*, 249. Quoted in Hans, 'English Pioneers of Comparative Education', 57. (Hans Nov., 1952)
6. M. Arnold, 'On the Modern Element in Literature', *The Complete Prose Works of Matthew Arnold* (ed) R. H. Super (Ann Arbor: University of Michigan, 1960–1977), Vol. I, 21. (Super 1960–1977)
7. Quoted in Brendan Rapple, 'Matthew Arnold and Comparative Education' *British Journal of Educational Studies*, Vol. 37, No. 1, (Feb., 1989), 58 (Rapple 1989). Arnold was far more insistent (as evident in *A French Eton* & 1868 *Schools and Universities on the Continent*) than Tagore on the role of the state as the inevitable centre in an educational apparatus.
8. What deserves a complementary mention is that Arnold spent his life time in the 'delicate and inward task of determining racial and national characteristics,

focussing, like Taine, on the dominant trait (*pensée maîtresse*). Frederic Faverty points out that Arnold chose representative features of a particular race or nation to frame this methodology of interpretation. He writes, 'to each of the great nations of Europe he assigned a particular "power" under which the elements of the national life could be classified, as, for example, "the power of knowledge" among the Germans, and "the power of social life and manners" among the French. Objection can be made to the method and has been made to it as it is employed by Taine and his disciple Émile Boutmy. The aspects of the national being are too many, too complex, and too varied to be comprehended in such neat categories. There was justice in the charge of Arnold's English contemporaries that he had fallen victim to the French habit of generalizing. Yet, as an English political scientist has recently insisted, there is a rock on which each nation stands and from which it is hewn. If on occasion Arnold floundered in the quick sands, he not infrequently discovered the solid foundations on which the national life was established'. See Frederic E. Faverty, *Matthew Arnold, the Ethnologist* (Evanston, IL: Northwestern University Press, 1951), 186–87 (Faverty 1951). What kind of a political and cultural rationale one wonders Tagore had when he proposed a meeting of the spirituality of the East with the mechanic kineticism and scientific rigour of the West? Was it a collapse into an ideological and discursive quicksand?

9. See David Phillips, 'Beyond Travellers' Tales: Some Nineteenth-Century British Commentators on Education in Germany', *Oxford Review of Education*, Vol. 26, No. 1, (Mar., 2000), 59. (Phillips 2000) 'I hope with time to convince people,' he wrote in a letter of April 1868, 'that I do not care the least for importing this or that foreign machinery, whether it be French or German, but only for getting certain English deficiencies supplied'. See David Phillips, *Investigating Education in Germany: Historical Studies from a British Perspective* (London: Routledge, 2016), 31.
10. *The Complete Prose Works of Matthew Arnold*, Vol. 1, 19. (Super 1960–1977)
11. Ibid., 24.
12. Brendan A. Rapple, 'Matthew Arnold's Views on Modernity and a State System of Middle – Class Education in England: Some Continental Influences', *The Journal of General Education*, Vol. 39, No. 4, (1988), 214–15. (Rapple 1988)
13. Mary E. Black, 'Matthew Arnold as School Inspector: A Revaluation', *Pacific Coast Philology,* Vol. 22, No. 1/2, (Nov., 1987), 16. (Black Nov., 1987)
14. Novak Bruce, 'National Standards" vs the Free Standards of Culture: Matthew Arnold's *Culture and Anarchy* and Contemporary Educational Philistinism', *Philosophy of Education*, 2003, 380. (Novak 2003)
15. '"National Standards" vs the Free Standards of Culture', 382. (Novak 2003) http://ojs.ed.uiuc.edu/index.php/pes/article/view/1763/480
16. Donald D. Stone, 'Matthew Arnold and the Pragmatics of Hebraism and Hellenism', *Poetics Today*, Vol. 19, No. 2, (Summer, 1998), 180. (Stone 1998)

17. Ibid., 182.
18. Tagore, *The Centre of Indian Culture* (Visva-Bharati: Calcutta, 1921), 12. (Tagore 1921)
19. Ibid., 13.
20. Tagore writes: 'there is a private corner for me in my house with a little table, which has its special fittings of pen and ink stand and paper, and here I can best do my writing and other work. There is no reason to run down, or run away from this corner of mine because in it, I cannot invite and provide seats for all my friends and guests. It may be that this corner is too narrow, or too close, or too untidy, so that my doctor may object, my friends remonstrate, my enemies sneer. . . . My point is that if all the rooms in my house be likewise solely for my own special convenience, if there be no reception room for my friends or accommodation for my guests, then indeed I may be blamed. Then with bowed head I must confess that in my house no great meeting of friends can ever take place'. *The Centre of Indian Culture*, 228–29. (Tagore 1921)
21. Peter Cox, 'A Journey into the World of Rabindrananth Tagore,' in *Rabindranath Tagore and the Challenges of Today* (ed.) Bhudeb Chaudhuri & K. G. Subramanyan (Simla: Indian Institute of Advanced Study, 1988), 180. (Cox 1988)
22. Tagore, 'An Eastern University' in *Creative Unity* (London: Macmillan and Co., 1922), 170–71. (Tagore 1922)
23. Himangshu Bhushan Mukherjee, *Education for Fullness* (London: Asia Publishing House, 1962), 106. (Mukherjee 1962)
24. *The Centre of Indian Culture*, 2. (Tagore 1921)
25. The First Visva-Bharati prospectus (1922) states: To bring into more intimate relation with one another through patient study and research, the different cultures of the East on the basis of their underlying unity: To approach the West from the standpoint of such a unity of the life and thought of Asia: To seek to realize in a common fellowship of study the meeting of East and West and thus ultimately to strengthen the fundamental conditions of world peace through the free communication of ideas between the two hemispheres.
26. See Rabindranath Tagore, 'Vidyasomobyay', *Rabindra Rachanavali*, Vol. 14, 386–87. (Tagore 1992)
27. Mukherjee, *Education for Fullness*, 98. Italics are mine. (Mukherjee 1962)
28. 'An Eastern University', 189–90. (Tagore 1922)
29. Ibid., 190.
30. See Karl Jaspers, *The Perennial Scope of Philosophy* (1949), 172 (Jaspers 1949). See W. R. Niblett, 'On Existentialism and Education', *British Journal of Educational Studies*, Vol. 2, No. 2, (May, 1954), 101–11. (Niblett 1954)

31. 'Everything depends as far as human life is concerned, on whether each thinks of the other as the one he is, whether each, that is, with all his desire to influence the other, nevertheless unreservedly accepts and confirms him in his being this man and in his being made in this particular way'. See Martin Buber, *Knowledge of Men: Selected Essays* (New York: Humanity Books, 1998), 59. (Buber 1998)
32. See Gabriel Marcel, *The Mystery of Being*, Vol I, (London: Regnery Publishing, Inc: 1950), 133. (Marcel 1950)
33. Stephen L. Darwall, 'Two Kinds of Respect,' in *Dignity, Character, and Self-Respect* (ed.) Robin S. Dillon (New York: Routledge, 1995), 183, 192. (Darwall 1995)
34. See Robert Kunzman, *Grappling with the Good: Talking About Religion and Morality in Public Schools* (Albany: SUNY, 2006), 43. (Kunzman 2006)
35. Charles Taylor, *Multiculturalism and the Politics of Recognition* (Princeton: Princeton University Press, 1992), 39. (Taylor 1992)
36. Richard Rorty, *Contingency, Irony and Solidarity* (Cambridge: Cambridge University Press, 1989), xvi. (Rorty 1989)
37. See G. J. J. Biesta, *Beyond learning: Democratic Education for a Human Future* (Boulder: Paradigm Publishers, 2006), 91. (Biesta 2006)
38. 'An Eastern University' in *Creative Unity* (London: Macmillan and Co., 1922), 185. (Tagore 1992)
39. P. Bourdieu and J-C Passeron, *Reproduction in Education, Society and Culture* (London: Sage, 1977), 9. (Bourdieu and Passeron 1977)
40. Mukherjee, *Education for Fulness*, 144 (Mukherjee 1962). Italics are mine. Emphasizing cooperation in thinking and learning, Tagore observes it is the West that has triumphed across the world through the force of education and knowledge and, hence, a whole scale obloquy directed at the West might just prove counterproductive because education is truth. Unlike animals, man has the ability to protest and be a rebel. He is equipped to 'connect' with a variety of thoughts and objects. The East and the West need not stick like a glue or get screwed into a point because meeting of minds cannot happen with an adhesive or a hammer and nail. The union is internal which, again, makes us realize that a portrait is not a metanarratival line but a fraternity of several lines – minor, causal, necessary and fundamental. See 'Sikshar Milon' [Unity in Education] in *Rabindra Rachanavali*, Vol. 14, 387–399. (Tagore 1992)
41. J. Hillis Miller, *Black Holes* (Stanford: Stanford University Press, 1999), 29. (Miller 1999)
42. Jan Masschelein and Norbert Ricken, 'Do We (Still) Need the Concept of Bildung?' *Educational Philosophy and Theory*, Vol. 35, No. 2, 2003, 150 (Masschelein and Ricken 2003). In the course of a long discussion of the term in *Truth and Method*, Gadamer defines *bildung* as follows: '... *Bildung*:

keeping oneself open to what is other – to other, more universal points of view. It embraces a sense of proportion and distance in relation to itself, and hence consists in rising above itself to universality. To distance oneself from oneself and from one's private purposes means to look at these in the way that others see them'. H-G. Gadamer, *Truth and Method* (London, Sheed & Ward Ltd., 1989), 17. (Gadamer 1989)

43. Hans Reiss (ed.) *Political Writings* (Cambridge: Cambridge University Press, 1970), 26–27. (Reiss 1970)
44. John H. Newman, *The Idea of a University* (Oxford: Clarendon Press, 1976), 379. (Newman 1976)
45. Reiss, *Political Writings*, 28–9. (Reiss 1970)
46. See Ian Ker, *The Achievement of John Henry Newman* (London: University of Nortre Dame Press, 1991), 6 (Ker 1991); also see, C. F. Harrold (ed.) *The Idea of a University Defined and Illustrated* (New York: Longmans, Green and Co, 1947). (Harrold 1947)
47. See David Nicholls and Fergus Kerr, *John Henry Newman: Reason, Rhetoric, and Romanticism* (Carbondale: Southern Illinois University Press, 1991), 111 (Nicholls and Kerr 1991). Also, see chapter 'Formal and Informal Inference' in Jay Newman, *The Mental Philosophy of John Henry Newman* (Carbondale: Wilfrid Laurier University Press, 1986), 135–64. (Newman 1986)
48. D. G. Mulcahy, 'Newman's Theory of a Liberal Education: A Reassessment and its Implications', *Journal of the Philosophy of Education*, 2008, 225 (Mulcahy 2008). Also see Mulcahy, *The Educated Person: Toward a New Paradigm for Liberal Education* (Lanham: Rowman and Littlefield, 2008). (Mulcahy 2008)
49. 'An Eastern University', 171–72. (Tagore 1922) Italics are mine.
50. William James, *Pragmatism* (Cambridge, MA: Harvard University Press, 1975), 78–9. (James 1975)
51. Mary Parker Follet, *The New State: Group Organization and the Solution of Popular Government* (New York: Longmans, Green and Co., 1918), 35, 76. (Follet 1918)
52. *Personality* (Bombay/London: Macmillan and Co. Ltd, 1970), 136. (Tagore 1970)
53. Alistair Pennycook, 'English, Universities and Struggles over Culture and Knowledge', in Ruth Hayhoe and Julia Pan (ed.) *East-West Dialogue in Knowledge and Higher Education* (New York: M.E. Sharpe, 1996), 64–82. (Pennycook 1996)
54. Michael Oakeshott, 'The Idea of a University', *Academic Questions* (Winter 2003–2004), 25–6. Italics are mine. (Oakeshott 2003-2004)
55. Michael Oakeshott, 'A Place of Learning,' *The Voice of Liberal Learning: Michael Oakeshott on Education*, (ed.) Timothy Fuller (New Haven: Yale University Press, 1989), 24. (Fuller 1989)

56. *The Centre of Indian Culture* (Visva-Bharati: Calcutta, 1921), 43. (Tagore 1921)
57. Alfred North Whitehead, *The Aims of Education and Other Essays* (New York: Mentor Books, 1929), 26. (Whitehead 1929)
58. Richard Rorty, *Contingency, Irony, Solidarity* (Cambridge: Cambridge University Press, 1989). 37 (Rorty 1989). Also see Richard Rorty, 'Education Without Dogma,' *Dissent* (Spring 1989), 198–204.
59. See Charles Taylor, *Sources of the Self* (Cambridge: Harvard University Press, 1989), 4–5. (Taylor 1989)
60. Emmanuel Levinas, *Otherwise Than Being or Beyond Essence*, (trans.) Alphonso Lingis (Pittsburgh: Duquesne University Press, 1998), 92. (Levinas 1998)
61. Tagore considers the 'other' primarily as the European other, seeking certain forms of knowledge and eventually finding more to learn from them than he thought was possible. For Levinas the experience of responsibility was tied to the susceptibility one had to the Other – the alterity of the other coming unbidden and exceeding the subject's grasp of knowledge. It avoids totalizing the other and subjects the self to keep making itself responsive to the other. This in the Derridean sense calls for challenging the aporetic status of the other, the immobility of thinking that the self can develop about its idea of the other. Here, for Tagore, Derrida and Levinas the other comes through as the 'unthought', the very possibility of thinking and thinking the possibilities that the other can evoke.
62. *Truth and Method*, 276–77. (Gadamer 1989)
63. Ibid., 295.
64. Ibid., 361.
65. Ibid.
66. J. Waldron, 'Minority cultures and the cosmopolitan alternative', in W. Kymlicka (ed.) *The Rights of Minority Cultures* (Oxford: Oxford University Press, 1995), 104. (Kymlicka 1995)
67. Ibid.,108.
68. Coco Fusco, *English Is Broken Here: Notes on Cultural Fusion in the Americas* (New York: New Press, 1995). 76. (Fusco 1995) Quoted in Peter McLaren, *Multiculturalism: Pedagogies of Dissent for the New Millennium* (Boulder: Westview Press, 1997), 10. (McLaren 1997b)
69. See *The New World Border* (San Francisco: City Lights Books, 1996), 7. (Gomez-Pena 1996)
70. Marcos Becquer and Gatti Jose, 'Elements of Vogue' *Third Text* 16/17, 1991, 69. (Becquer and Jose 1991). See Peter McLaren, *Revolutionary Multiculturalism*, 90.
71. Ibid., 70.
72. See B. Parekh, *Rethinking Multiculturalism: Cultural diversity and Political Theory* (Basingstoke: Palgrave, 2000), 73. (Parekh 2000)

73. See Johann Bernhard Basedow, *Für Cosmopoliten Etwas zu lesen, zu denken und zu thun* (Leipzig 1775) (Basedow 1775); also, Basedow, *Ausgewählte pädagogische Schriften* (ed.) Albert Reble (Paderborn: Ferdinand Schöningh, 1965). (Basedow 1965)
74. See Immanuel Kant, *Perpetual Peace* (2000), 300. Also see 'Kant's Right of World Citizens: a historical interpretation' in Georg Cavaller, *Embedded Cosmopolitanism* (Berlin: Walter de Gruyter, 2015), 49–56 (Cavaller 2015); Pauline Kleingeld (ed.) *Toward Perpetual Peace and Other Writings on Politics, Peace and History* (New Haven: Yale University Press, 2006). (Kleingeld 2006)
75. Poulomi Saha, 'Singing Bengal into a Nation: Tagore the Colonial Cosmopolitan?' *Journal of Modern Literature*, Vol. 36, No. 2, (Winter 2013), 4, 1–24. (Saha 2013) Saha observes further: 'The transformative will and power of a cosmopolitan ethics is of dubious efficacy for one not in the position of power, one not on the eve of a successful imperial campaign, one who is indeed subject to and a subject of imperial power. What does it mean to be a cosmopolitan colonial subject? I want to suggest here that for all of the trappings of wealth and celebrity, Tagore, who was not a citizen of any nation, and legally a subject of Britain, could not actually be a citizen of the world. The passport on which he travelled – both literally and figuratively – was a British one, just as the vehicle of his literary fame was the English language. Nussbaum's idyllic notion of cosmopolitanism is blind to the deeply vexed relationship between cosmopolitanism, imperialism, and citizenship rights. The refined statelessness of cosmopolitanism is not simply available to the already stateless'. (16)
76. Emily Zakin, 'Crisscrossing Cosmopolitanism: State-Phobia, World Alienation, and the Global Soul' *Journal of Speculative Philosophy*, Vol. 29, No. 1, (2015), 62. (Zakin 2015)
77. Torill Strand, *Paideusis*, Vol. 19, No. 1, (2010), 55. (Strand 2010)
78. See Kwame Anthony Appiah, *Cosmopolitanism: Ethics in a World of Strangers* (London: Penguin Books, 2007). (Appiah 2007)
79. Ibid., xi.
80. Tagore struggled to find a place to build a nest, a stranger: 'I am afraid the West has lost its foothold of the inner life and has been hopping with one leg, reveling in the very jerkiness of its difficult movement, because that has the appearance of power. Unfortunately, the East has gone to the other extreme, and instead of using the inner life as the source of all harmonious movements, has used it as a retreat for its practice and hibernation. But I, who have the amphibious duality of nature in me, whose food is in the West and breathe air in the East, do not find a place where I can build my nest. I suppose I shall have to be a migratory bird and cross and recross the sea, owning two nests, one on each shore'. Mary Lago, *Imperfect Encounter:*

Letters of William Rothenstein and Rabindranath Tagore (Cam, MA: Harvard University Press, 1972), 136. (Lago 1972)

81. Papastephanou Marianna, *Thinking Differently about Cosmopolitanism: Theory, Eccentricity and the Globalised World* (London: Routledge, 2015), 220. (Papastephanou 2015)
82. Rainer Forst, 'Toleration, justice and reason' in *The Culture of Toleration in Diverse Societies* (eds.) C. McKinnon and D. Castiglion (Manchester: Manchester University Press, 2003), 71–85. (Forst 2003)
83. Ibid., 73. Also see, Wendy Brown, Rainer Forst, *The Power of Tolerance: A Debate* (ed.) Luca Di Blasi & Christoph F. E. Holzhey (New York: Columbia University Press, 2014), 25–28. (Blasi and Holzhey 2014)
84. See the chapter titled 'Magma' in Suzi Adams (ed.) *Cornelius Castoriadis: Key Concepts* (London: Bloomsbury, 2014) (Adams 2014). Also see Marcela Tovar-Restrepo, *Castoriadis, Foucault and Autonomy: New Approaches to Subjectivity, Society and Social Change* (London: Continuum, 2012), 33–64, (Tovar-Restrepo 2012) where the discussion is on the ontology of creation.
85. See Chantal Mouffe, *Politics and Passion: The Stakes of Democracy* (London: Centre for the Study of Democracy, 2002), 5–8. (Mouffe 2002)
86. Jacques Derrida, 'The principle of reason: the university in the eyes of its pupils', *Diacritics* 13, (Fall, 1983), 19. (Derrida 1983)
87. This is in deliberate imitation of the title of the seventh chapter ('. . . That Dangerous Supplement . . .') from Derrida's *Of Grammatology* (trans.) Gayatri Chakravorty Spivak (Baltimore: Johns Hopkins University Press, 1998), 141. (Derrida 1998)
88. Derrida, 'The principle of reason: the university in the eyes of its pupils', 4. (Derrida 1983)
89. M. Paine, M and J. Schad (eds). *Life.After.Theory* (London/New York: Continuum, 2003), 31–32. (Paine and Schad 2003)
90. Tagore, 'An Eastern University' in *Creative Unity* (London: Macmillan and Co., 1922), 179. (Tagore 1922)
91. *Negotiations: Interventions and Interviews 1971–2001* (edited and translated with an introduction) Elizabeth Rottenberg (Stanford: Stanford University Press, 2002), 21. (Derrida 2002b)
92. Ibid., *Negotiations*, 29–30. (Derrida 2002b)
93. Derrida, 'I Have a Taste for the Secret' in Jacques Derrida and Maurizio Ferraris *A Taste for the Secret* (ed.) Giacomo Donis & David Webb, (trans.) Giacomo Donis (London: Polity Press, 2001), 50–51. (Derrida and Ferraris 2001)
94. Henri Lefebvre, *The Production of Space* (Oxford: Basil Blackwell, 1991), 110. (Lefebvre 1991)
95. Tagore, 'An Eastern University', 196. (Tagore 1922)

96. Ibid., 194.
97. Derrida, *Margins of Philosophy* (translation with additional notes) Alan Bass (Chicago: University of Chicago Press, 1982), xi. (Derrida 1982)
98. Derrida, 'Mochlos ou le conflit des facultes', *Du Droit a la philosophie* (Paris: Galilee, 1990), 401, 404. (Derrida 1990)
99. Christian Moraru, 'Fringes, Margins, Diaphragms: The University and Textual Reason after Derrida', *Crossings* 3 (1999), 84. (Moraru 1999)
100. Derrida, 'The future of the profession or the university without condition' in T. Cohen (ed.) *Jacques Derrida and the Humanities. A Critical Reader* (Cambridge: Cambridge University Press, 2001), 25. (Cohen 2001)
101. Letter written on 30 November, 1920. Quoted in Das Gupta, *Rabindranath Tagore*, 81.
102. See Uma Das Gupta, *Rabindranath Tagore: an Illustrated Life* (Delhi: Oxford University Press, 2013), 83. (Das Gupta 2013)
103. In 'Hostipitality,' Derrida claims, 'Hospitality is the deconstruction of the at-home; deconstruction is hospitality to the other'. Jacques Derrida, *Acts of Religion* (trans.) Gil Anidjar (New York: Routledge, 2002), 364 (Derrida 2002b). Also, see *Of Hospitality* (trans.) Rachel Bowlby (Stanford: Stanford University Press, 2000) (Derrida 2000) and *Rogues* (trans.) Pascale-Anne Brault and Michael Naas (Stanford: Stanford University Press, 2005). (Derrida 2005)
104. Thomas Claviez (ed.) *The Conditions of Hospitality* (New York: Fordham University Press, 2013), 32 (Claviez 2013). Claviez writes: 'If the figure of two legs moving alternately and equally toward some telos adequately captures the teleological movement of dialectical sublation, limping toward a radical concept of hospitality that dispenses with a dialectical economy of reciprocity connotes the fact that we acknowledge multiple transcen*dances* moving and tearing left and right, veering us off a fixed track, and maybe making us go in circles – even in our own homes' (40–41).
105. Paulo Freire, *Education for Critical Consciousness* (London: Continuum, 2005), 3. (Freire 2005)
106. Ibid., 4.
107. Tagore, 'The History and Ideals of Sriniketan', *The Modern Review* November 1941, 433. (Tagore 1941)
108. Martin Buber, *Between Man and Man* (trans.) Roger Gregor Smith (New York: Macmillan, 1969), 97. (Buber 1969)
109. John Dewey, *Art as Experience* (London: Penguin Book, 2005), 360. (Dewey 2005)
110. Francis A. Samuel, 'Educational Visions from Two Continents: What Tagore adds to the Deweyan Perspective', *Educational Philosophy and Theory*, Vol. 43, No. 10, 2011, 1162. (Samuel 2011)

111. John Dewey, 'Democracy and Education (Dewey 1916),' in *John Dewey: The Middle Works, 1899–1924*, Vol. 9, (ed.) Joann Boydston (Carbondale: Southern Illinois University Press, 1980), 58. (Boydston 1980)
112. See Jürgen Oelkers 'Some Historical Notes on George Herbert Mead's Theory of Education', www.ife.uzh.ch/dam/jcr:ffffffff-bb47-55f9 . . . / Meadtranslationfirst.pdf
113. Elsewhere Dewey observes, 'Any experience is mis-educative that has the effect of arresting or distorting the growth of further experience,' see John Dewey, 'Logic: The Theory of Inquiry,' in *John Dewey: The Later Works, 1925–1953*, Vol. 12, (ed.) J Ann Boydston (Carbondale: Southern Illinois University Press, 1986), 11. (Dewey 1986)
114. Tagore, 'Education for Rural India', *The Visva-Bharati Quarterly* (May-Oct), 1947, 27–28 (Tagore 1947). This was an address delivered at the anniversary of the Rural Reconstruction Institute, Sriniketan, in February, 1931.
115. See Bhabatosh Dutta, 'Tagore and the Economics of Rural Development' *The Visva-Bharati Quarterly*, Vol. 48, Nos. 1–4, (May 1982-April 1983), 348. (Dutta 1983)
116. Bourdieu, *Outline of a Theory of Practice* (trans.) R. Nice (Cambridge: Cambridge University Press, 1979), 214. (Bourdieu 1979)
117. Tagore, *The Co-operative Principle* (translated from Bengali) A.K. Chanda & Others (Calcutta: 1963), 26 (Tagore 1963). The original text is titled *Samavaya-Niti, Rabindra Rachanavali*, Vol. 13, 415–50 (Tagore 1990).
118. Freire, *Pedagogy of the Oppressed* (New York: Continuum, 1997), 312, 306. (Freire 1997)
119. See P. Bourdieu and L. Wacquant, *An Invitation to Reflexive Sociology* (Cambridge: Polity, 1992), 251. (Bourdieu and Wacquant 1992)
120. 'Tagore's ideas of Social Action and the Sriniketan Experiment of Rural Reconstruction, 1922–41', in *Rabindranath Tagore: Reclaiming a Cultural Icon* (ed.) Kathleen M. O'Connell & Joseph T. O'Connell (Visva Bharati, 2009), 242–43. (Das Gupta 2009)
121. See Dikshit Sinha, *Rabindranather Pallypunargathan Prayas* (Kolkata: Paschimbanga Bangla Academy, 2010), 228–234. (Sinha 2010)
122. P. Bourdieu, *In Other Worlds: Essays Towards a Reflexive Sociology* (trans.) M. Adamson (Cambridge: Polity, 1994), 61. (Bourdieu 1994)
123. See Bourdieu, *The Logic of Practice* (trans.) R. Nice (Cambridge: Polity, 1990), 64. (Bourdieu 1990)
124. Tagore, 'Palli Seva', *Palli Prakriti*, 64.
125. *Pedagogy of the Oppressed*, 66. (Freire 1997)
126. P. Freire, *Pedagogy of Freedom: Ethics, Democracy, and Civic Courage* (Lanham: Rowman & Littlefield, 1998), 30. (Freire 1998)
127. Leonard Elmhirst writes: 'The inclusion of garden within his home compound, properly supervised provides an ample basis for the widest and best

form of education'. See his 'A Home School for Orphans', *Visva Bharati Quarterly*, 1924.

128. Connell, *Rabindranath Tagore: The Poet as Educator*, 298. (O'Connell 2002).
129. Inspired by Tagore's rural reconstructive thinking, Geddes produced his *Bengal Study, Study of Soil and Civilization of Bengal* and then went on to collect his doctoral degree from Edinburgh based on this work under population geography. See Madhu Mitra, *Shikor-er Udaan Swabhimaan o Rabindranath* (Kolkata: Udaar Aashash, 2014), 42. (Mitra 2014)
130. See T. S. Eliot. 'The Aims of Education: Can "Education" be Defined?' in *To Criticize the Critic and Other Writings* (Farrer, Strauss and Giroux, 1965), 73. (Eliot 1965)
131. Kathleen Coburn, *Inquiring Spirit: A New Presentation of Coleridge from His Published and Unpublished Prose Writings* (New York: Pantheon Books, 1951), 81. (Coburn 1951)
132. Ibid., 77. (Coburn 1951)
133. Tagore, 'City and Village', *Visva-Bharati Bulletin*, No. 10, 1928, 24–5. (Tagore 1928)
134. As an instance of the organisational and structural changes that Visva Bharati had to undergo we encounter an advertisement in a leading Bengali daily *Ananda Bazar Patrika* in 1931 where details as to the kind of degrees that Santiniketan provided and the subjects that the institution offered can be found. For more on timely and, often undesired, structural modifications and the concomitant politics see Dikshit Sinha, *Rabindranather Pallypunargathan Prayas*, 41, 31–53. (Sinha 2010)
135. Das Gupta, *Rabindranath Tagore*, 101. In 1930, he wrote to Elmhirst: 'I have come to accept the inevitable limitation of ideas when solidied in an institution'. See Krishna Dutta & Andrew Robinson (ed.) *Purabi: A Miscellany in memory of Rabindranath Tagore* (London: 1991). (Dutta and Robinson 1991)
136. Letter to Elmhirst, 13 December, 1937.
137. Peter McLaren 'Paulo Freire's Pedagogy of Possibility', in *Freirean Pedagogy, Praxis, and Possibilities: Projects for the New Millennium* (ed.) H. Mark Krank, Peter Mclaren, Robert E. Bahruth (New York: Falmer Press, 2000), 14. (McLaren 2000)
138. Letter to L. K. Elmhirst, 3 September 1932. See Leonard Elmhirst, 'Rabindranath Tagore and Sriniketan' *The Visva Bharati Quarterly* 24, no. 2 (Autumn 1958), 132. (Elmhirst 1958)
139. Quoted in Jim Garrison, 'Dewey, Eros and Education', *Education and Culture* Fall 1994, Vol. XI, No. 2, 2. (Garrison 1994)
140. Ibid.
141. Tagore, 'Poet's School' quoted in Alex Aronson, 'Rabindranath's Educational Ideals and the West', *The Visva-Bharati Quarterly* (May–Oct), 1947, 37. (Aronson 1947)

142. See P. Leistyna, *Presence of Mind* (Boulder: Westview, 1999), 57. (Leistyna 1999)
143. *Pedagogy of the City* (New York: Continuum, 1993) 87. (Freire 1993)
144. See I. Shor and P. Freire, *A Pedagogy for Liberation* (Washington, D.C.: Bergin & Garvey, 1987). (Shor and Freire 1987)
145. Letter to Elmhirst, 25 June 1924. See Leonard Elmhirst, 'Rabindranath Tagore and Sriniketan', 137. (Elmhirst Autumn 1958)
146. Alain Badiou, *Being and Event* (trans.) O. Feltham (London: Continuum, 2005), 9. (Badiou 2005)
147. Badiou, *Metapolitics* (trans.) J. Barker (London: Verso, 2005), 77. For more on Rancière see J. Rancière, *The Philosopher and His Poor*, (trans.) J. Drury, C. Ostert & A. Parker (Durham, NC: Duke University Press, 2003); J. Rancière, 'From Politics to Aesthetics?' *Paragraph*, Vol. 28, No. 2, 2005, 12–25. (Rancière 2005)
148. Philip Armstrong, *Reticulations: Jean-Luc Nancy and the Networks of the Political* (Minneapolis: University of Minnesota Press, 2009), xiv. (Armstrong 2009)
149. Bill Readings notes: 'Lyotard's insistence on institutional critique requires of us that we find a way to make our pedagogical activities, as students and teachers, difficult for the system to swallow, hard to insert within the generalized economy of capitalist exchange. The exponential growth in the commodification of information itself, thanks to new technologies, renders this situation even more acute. If pedagogy is to pose a challenge to the ever-increasing bureaucratization of the university as a whole, this will require a decentring of our vision of the educational process. Only in this way can we hope to open up pedagogy, to lend it a temporality that resists commodification, by arguing that listening to Thought is not the spending of time in the production of an autonomous subject or in an autonomous body of knowledge. Rather, to listen to thought, to think beside each other and beside ourselves, is to explore an open network of obligations that keeps the question of meaning open, a locus of debate – doing justice to thought, listening to our interlocutors, means trying to hear what cannot be said, but which tries to make itself heard, a process incompatible with the production of (even relatively) stable and exchangeable knowledge'. See *Education and the Postmodern Condition* (ed.) Michael Peters (Westport, CT: Bergin & Garvey, 1995), 205. (Peters 1995)
150. See Bert P. Helm, 'Emerson Agonistes: Education as Struggle and Process', *Educational Theory*, Vol. 42, No. 2, (1992), 171. (Helm 1992)
151. Rainer Maria Rilke, *Letters to a Young Poet* (trans.) Stephen Mitchell (New York: Random House, 1984), 34–35. (Rilke 1984)

Bibliography

Abrams, M. H. *Natural Supernaturalism: Tradition and Revolution in Romantic Literature*. New York: W.W. Norton, 1971.

Adeyemi, Michael B, and Augustus A. Adeyinka. Some Keys Issues in African Traditional Education. *McGill Journal of Education* 37, no. 2 (Spring 2002): 223–240.

Alavalkama, S., I. Aura, and H. Palmquist (eds.). *Endoscopy as a Tool in Architecture*. Tampere: Tampere University Press, 1993.

Albrecht-Crane, C., and J. Daryl Slack. Towards a Pedagogy of Affect. In *Deleuzian Encounters: Studies in Contemporary Social Issues*, (ed.) A. Hickey-Moody and P. Malins, 99–110. New York: Palgrave Macmillan, 2007.

Altekar, A. S. *Education in Ancient India*. Varanasi: Nand Kishore, 1965.

Andrieu, Bernard. *Le corps disperse: Histoire du corps au XXe siecle*. Paris: L'Harmattan, 1993.

Ankersmit, Frank. *Sublime Historical Experience*. Stanford: Stanford University Press, 2005.

Anzieu, Didier. *The Skin Ego*. New Haven: Yale University Press, 1989.

Appiah, Kwame Anthony. *Cosmopolitanism: Ethics in a World of Strangers*. London: Penguin Books, 2007.

Armstrong, Philip. *Reticulations: Jean-Luc Nancy and the Networks of the Political*. Minneapolis: University of Minnesota Press, 2009.

Aronson, Alex. Rabindranath's Educational Ideals and the West. *The Visva-Bharati Quarterly* (May-Oct, 1947): 32–38.

Assad, Maria L. *Reading with Michel Serres: An Encounter with Time*. Albany: SUNY, 1999.

Auerbach, B. S. *Neues Leben*. Stuttgart: Cotta'scher Verlag, 1871.

R. Ghosh, *Aesthetics, Politics, Pedagogy and Tagore*,
Palgrave Studies in Education and Transculturalism,
DOI 10.1057/978-1-137-48026-2

Axtell, J.L. *The Educational Writings of John Locke*. Cambridge: Cambridge University Press, 1968.

Bachelard, Gaston. *The Poetics of Space*. (trans.) Maria Jolas. Boston: Beacon Press, 1969.

Badiou, Alain. *Ethics: An Essay on the Understanding of Evil*. (trans.) P. Hallward. New York: Verso Press, 2001.

Badiou, Alain. *Being and Event*. (trans.) O. Feltham. London: Continuum, 2005a.

Badiou, Alain. *Metapolitics*. (trans.) J. Barker. London: Verso, 2005b.

Baldwin, Edward (i.e William Godwin). *Fables Ancient and Modern*. London: Thomas Hodgkins at the Juvenile Library, 1805.

Baldwin, Edward (i.e William Godwin). *The History of England for the use of Schools and Young Persons*. London: M. J: Godwin at the Juvenile Library, 1812.

Barad, Karen. Diffracting Diffraction: Cutting Together-Apart. *Parallax* 20, no. 3 (2014): 168–187.

Barron, Jonathan N. (ed.). *Roads Not Taken: Rereading Robert Frost*. Columbia: University of Missouri Press, 2000.

Basedow, Johann Bernhard. *Für Cosmopoliten Etwas zu lesen, zu denken und zu thun*. Leipzig, 1775.

Basedow, Johann Bernhard. 1965. *Ausgewählte pädagogische Schriften*. (ed.) Albert Reble. Paderborn: Ferdinand Schöningh.

Baucher, David. The Creation of the Past: British Idealism and Michael Oakeshott's Philosophy of History. *History and Theory* 23, no. 2 (1984): 193–214.

Becquer, Marcos, and Jose Gatti. Elements of Vogue. *Third Text* 5, no. 16/17 (1991): 65–81.

Beiner, Ronald. Walter Benjamin's Philosophy of History. *Political Theory* 12, no. 3 (1984): 423–434.

Benjamin, Walter. *Selected Writings 1931–34*. Vol. 2. Cambridge, MA: Harvard University Press, 1999a.

Benjamin, Walter. *The Arcades Project* (trans.) Howard Eiland and Kevin McLaughlin. Cambridge, MA: Harvard University Press, 1999b.

Benjamin, Walter. *Selected Writings of Walter Benjamin*. Vol. 4. (eds.) Howard Eiland and Michael W. Jennings. Cambridge, MA: Harvard University Press, 2003.

Berman, Morris. *The Reenchantment of the World*. Ithaca: Cornell University Press, 1981.

Berque, Augustin. Some traits of Japanese fūdosei. *The Japan Foundation Newsletter* 14, no. 5 (1987): 1–7.

Biesta, G. J. J. *Beyond learning: Democratic Education for a Human Future*. Boulder: Paradigm Publishers, 2006.

Black, Mary E. Matthew Arnold as School Inspector: A Revaluation. *Pacific Coast Philology* 22, no. 1/2 (Nov., 1987): 15–21.

Blasi, Luca Di, and Christoph F. E. Holzhey (eds.). *The Power of Tolerance: A Debate*. New York: Columbia University Press, 2014.

Bloch, E. *The Principle of Hope*. Oxford: Basil Blackwell, 1986.

Bob, Blaisdell (ed.). *Tolstoy as Teacher: Leo Tolstoy's Writings on Education*. New York: Teachers & Writers Collaborative, 2000.

Boisvert, Raymond D. *John Dewey: Rethinking Our Time*. Albany: State University of New York Press, 1998.

Bourdieu, P. *Outline of a Theory of Practice*. (trans.) R. Nice. Cambridge: Cambridge University Press, 1979.

Bourdieu, P. *The Logic of Practice*. (trans.) R. Nice. Cambridge: Polity, 1990.

Bourdieu, P. *In Other Worlds: Essays Towards a Reflexive Sociology*. (trans.) M. Adamson. Cambridge: Polity, 1994.

Bourdieu, P., and J-C Passeron. *Reproduction in Education, Society and Culture*. London: Sage, 1977.

Bourdieu, P., and L. Wacquant. *An Invitation to Reflexive Sociology*. Cambridge: Polity, 1992.

Boyd, William. *The Educational Theory of Jean Jacques Rousseau*. New York: Russell & Russell, 1963.

Boydston, Joann. (ed.). *The Later Works of John Dewey*. Vol. 5. Carbondale: Southern Illinois University, 1977.

Boydston, Joann. *John Dewey The Middle Works, 1899–1924*. Vol. 9. Carbondale: Southern Illinois University Press, 1980.

Bruce, T. Froebel today. In *Theories and Approaches to Learning in the Early Years* (eds.) L. Miller and L. Pound, 55–70. London: Sage, 2011.

Buber, Martin. *Between Man and Man*. (trans.) Ronald Gregor Smith. New York: Macmillan, 1948.

Buber, Martin. *I and Thou*. (trans.) Walter Kaufmann. New York: Charles Scribner's Sons, 1970.

Buber, Martin. *Knowledge of Men: Selected Essays*. New York: Humanity Books, 1998.

Bunyard, P., and F. Morgan-Grenville (eds.). *The Green Alternative*. London: Methuen, 1987.

Burch, K. *Eros as the Educational Principle of Democracy*. New York: Peter Lang Publishers, 2000.

Burt, Forrest D., and Clinton Machann. Matthew Arnold and Education: Nine New Letters. *Victorian Poetry* 28, no. 1 (Spring, 1990): 79–88.

Capra, Fritjof. *The Web of Life: A New Scientific Understanding of Living Systems*. New York: Anchor Books Double Day, 1996.

Casey, Edward. *The Fate of Place: A Philosophical History.* Berkeley: University of California Press, 1997.

Casey, Edward. Between Geography and Philosophy: What does it mean to be in the place-world?. *Annals of the Association of American Geographers* 91, no. 4 (2001): 683–693.

Cavaller, Georg. *Embedded Cosmopolitanism.* Berlin: Walter de Gruyter, 2015.

Cavenagh, F. A. (ed.). *James and John Stuart Mill on Education.* Westport: Greenwood Press, 1979.

Chan, A. K. L. (ed.). *Mencius: Contexts and Interpretations.* Honolulu: University of Hawai'i Press, 2002.

Chan, Wing-tsit. *A Source Book in Chinese Philosophy.* Princeton: Princeton University Press, 1963.

Chattopadhyay, Bratin. *On Education and Rabindranath.* Calcutta: Subarnarekha, 2000.

Chattopadhyay, Jnanendranath. Rabindranath and his Asrama School. *The Visva-Bharati Quarterly* (May-October, 1947): 9–16.

Christian, R. F. (trans. & ed.). *Tolstoy's Letters selected.* London: Athlone Press, 1978.

Claviez, Thomas (ed.). *The Conditions of Hospitality.* New York: Fordham University Press, 2013.

Coburn, Kathleen. *Inquiring Spirit: A New Presentation of Coleridge from His Published and Unpublished Prose Writings.* New York: Pantheon Books, 1951.

Cohen, Adir. Martin Buber and Changes in Modern Education. *Oxford Review of Education* 5, no. 1 (1979): 81–103.

Cohen, Adir. *The Educational Philosophy of Martin Buber.* Madison: Farleigh Dickinson University Press, 1983.

Cohen, T. (ed.). *Jacques Derrida and the Humanities. A Critical Reader.* Cambridge: Cambridge University Press, 2001.

Collingwood, R. G. *Speculum Mentis.* Oxford: Clarendon Press, 1924.

Collingwood, R. G. *The Idea of History.* Oxford: Clarendon Press, 1993.

Colwell, Thomas B. The Ecological Basis of Human Community. *Educational Theory* 21, no. 4 (1971): 418–433.

Colwell, Thomas B. The Ecological Perspective in John Dewey's Philosophy of Education. *Educational Theory* 35, no. 3 (1985): 255–66.

Cox, Peter. A Journey into the World of Rabindrananth Tagore. In *Rabindranath Tagore and the Challenges of Today,* (eds.) Bhudeb Chaudhuri and K. G. Subramanyan, 173–184. Simla: Indian Institute of Advanced Study, 1988.

Crilly, A.J., R. A Earnshaw, and H. Jones (eds.). *Fractals and Chaos.* New York: Springer, 1991.

Curtis, S. *History of Education in Great Britain.* London: University Tutorial Press, 1963.

Darling, John. Education as Horticulture: Some Growth theorists and their Critics. *Philosophy of Education* 16, no. 2 (1982): 173–185.

Darwall, Stephen L. Two Kinds of Respect. In *Dignity, Character, and Self-Respect*, (ed.) Robin S. Dillon, 181–197. New York: Routledge, 1995.

Das Gupta, Uma. *Rabindranath Tagore: A Biography*. New Delhi: Oxford University Press, 2004.

Das Gupta, Uma. Tagore's ideas of Social Action and the Sriniketan Experiment of Rural Reconstruction, 1922–41. In *Rabindranath Tagore: Reclaiming a Cultural Icon*, (ed.) M. O'Connell Kathleen and T.O'Connell Joseph, 234–249. Visva Bharati, 2009.

Das Gupta, Uma. *Rabindranath Tagore: An Illustrated Life*. Delhi: Oxford University Press, 2013.

Das, S. K. (ed.). *English Writings of Rabindranath Tagore*. Vol. III. Delhi: Sahitya Akademi, 1996.

David, Kennedy, and Walter Kohan. Aion, Kairos and Chronos: Fragments of an Endless Conversation on Childhood, Philosophy and Education. *Childhood and Philosophy* 4, no. 8 (jul./dex 2008): 5–22.

Davis, Brent. Complexity and Education: Vital Simultaneities. *Educational Philosophy and Theory* 40, no. 1 (2008): 50–65.

Derrida, Jacques. *Acts of Religion*. (trans.) Gil Anidjar. New York: Routledge, 2002a.

Derrida, Jacques. *Negotiations: Interventions and Interviews 1971–2001*. (edited and translated with an introduction) Elizabeth Rottenberg. Stanford: Stanford University Press, 2002b.

Derrida, Jacques. *Rogues*. (trans.) Pascale-Anne Brault and Michael Naas. Stanford: Stanford University Press, 2005.

Derrida, Jacques. *Margins of Philosophy*. (translation with additional notes) Alan Bass. Chicago: University of Chicago Press, 1982.

Derrida, Jacques. The principle of reason: The university in the eyes of its pupils. *Diacritics* 13 (Fall, 1983): 2–20.

Derrida, Jacques. *'Mochlos ou le conflit des facultes', Du Droit a la philosophie*. Paris: Galilee, 1990.

Derrida, Jacques. *Of Grammatology*. (trans.) Gayatri Chakravorty Spivak. Baltimore: Johns Hopkins University Press, 1998.

Derrida, Jacques. *Of Hospitality*. (trans.) Rachel Bowlby. Stanford: Stanford University Press, 2000.

Derrida, Jacques and Maurizio Ferraris. *A Taste for the Secret* (ed.). Giacomo Donis & David Webb, (trans.) Giacomo Donis. London: Polity Press, 2001.

Devall, B., and G. Sessions. *Deep Ecology: Living as if Nature Mattered*. Salt Lake City: Peregrine Smith, 1985.

Dewey, John. *Democracy and Education*. New York: The Free Press, 1916.

Dewey, John. Logic: The Theory of Inquiry. In *John Dewey: The Later Works, 1925–1953* (ed.) J Ann Boydston, Vol. 12, 11. Carbondale: Southern Illinois University Press, 1986.

Dewey, John. *Experience and Education*. West Lafayette: Kappa Delta Pi, 1998.
Dewey, John. *Art as Experience*. London: Penguin Book, 2005.
Dillard, Annie. *Teaching a Stone to Talk*. New York: Harper Perennial, 1992.
Dimock, Wai Chee. Theory of Resonance. *PMLA* 112, no. 5 (1997): 1060–1071.
Dimock, Wai Chee. Deep Time: American Literature and World History. *American Literary History* 13, no. 4 (2001): 755–775.
Dole, Nathan Haskell. (ed.). *Aesthetical and Philosophical Essays*. Boston: Francis A Niccolls & Company, 1902.
Dovey, K. Putting Geometry in its Place: Toward a Phenomenology of the Design Process. In *Dwelling, Seeing, and Designing: Toward a Phenomenological Ecology* (ed.) D. Seamon, 247–269. Albany: State University of New York Press, 1993.
Durkheim, E. *Education and Sociology*. (trans.) S. D. Fox. Glencoe: The Free Press, 1961a.
Durkheim, E. *Moral Education: A Study in the Theory and Application of the Sociology of Education*. New York: Free Press, 1961b.
Durkheim, E. *The Evolution of Educational Thought: Lectures on the Formation and Development of Secondary Education in France*. London: Routledge, 1977 [1938].
Dutta, Bhabatosh. Tagore and the Economics of Rural Development. *The Visva-Bharati Quarterly* 48 Numbers (May 1982–April 1983): 344–358.
Dutta, Krishna, and Andrew Robinson (eds.). *Purabi: A Miscellany in memory of Rabindranath Tagore*. London: The Tagore Centre UK, 1991.
Dworkin, A. *Intercourse*. London: Arrow Books, 1988.
Elias, N. *The Civilizing Process: The History of Manners*. (trans.) E. Jephcott. New York: Urizen Books, 1978.
Eliot, George. Letter to Frederic Harrison. In *Introduction to Silas Marner*, F. R. Leavis. Harmondsworth: Penguin, 1967.
Eliot, T. S. *To Criticize the Critic and Other Writings*. London: Farrer, Strauss and Giroux, 1965.
Elmhirst, Leonard. Rabindranath Tagore and Sriniketan. *The Visva Bharati Quarterly* 24, no. 2 (Autumn 1958): 122–144.
Emerson, 'Education' (1864), Accessed 24.11. 2015, http://aboq.org/emerson/essays/education.htm.
Emerson, Edward Waldo (ed.). *The Complete Works of Ralph Waldo Emerson*. Vol. X. Boston: Houghton, Mifflin and Company, 1903–04.
Erasmus. On Education for Children. In *The Erasmus Reader* (ed.) E. Rummel, 65–102. Toronto: University of Toronto Press, 1990.
Evernden, Neil. *The Social Creation of Nature*. Baltimore: The Johns Hopkins University Press, 1992.
Eyken, W van der, and B. Turner. *Adventures in Education*. Harmondsworth: Penguin Press Ltd., 1969.

Faverty, Frederic E. *Matthew Arnold, the Ethnologist.* Evanston: Northwestern University Press, 1951.

Fearn, Margaret. William Godwin and the Wilds of Literature. *British Journal of Educational Studies* 29, no. 3 (1981): 247–257.

Follet, Mary Parker. *The New State: Group Organization and the Solution of Popular Government.* New York: Longmans, Green and Co., 1918.

Forst, Rainer. Toleration, justice and reason. In *The Culture of Toleration in Diverse Societies,* (eds.), C. McKinnon and D. Castiglion, 71–85. Manchester: Manchester University Press, 2003.

Foucault, Michel. *Discipline and Punish: The Birth of the Prison.* New York: Vintage, 1979.

Fox, Warwick. *Toward a Transpersonal Ecology: Developing New Foundations for Environmentalism.* Boston: Shambhala, 1990.

Fraser, Bashabi (ed.). *The Tagore-Geddes Correspondence.* Kolkata: Visva Bharati, 2004.

Freire, Paulo. *Pedagogy of the City.* New York: Continuum, 1993.

Freire, Paulo. *Pedagogy of the Oppressed.* New York: Continuum, 1997.

Freire, Paulo. *Pedagogy of Freedom: Ethics, Democracy, and Civic Courage.* Lanham: Rowman & Littlefield, 1998.

Freire, Paulo. *Education for Critical Consciousness.* London: Continuum, 2005.

Friedlander, Eli. *Walter Benjamin: A Philosophical Portrait.* Cambridge, MA: Harvard University Press, 2012.

Froebel, Friedrich. *The Education of Man.* New York: D. Appleton and Company, 1887, 73, 75–6.

Froebel, Friedrich. *The Education of Man.* New York: Dover Publications Inc., 2009.

Fusco, Coco. *English Is Broken Here: Notes on Cultural Fusion in the Americas.* New York: New Press, 1995.

Gadamer, Hans Georg. *Truth and Method.* London: Sheed & Ward Ltd., 1989.

Gadamer, Hans Georg. Education is Self-Education. *Journal of Philosophy of Education* 35, no. 4 (November, 2001): 529–538.

Gane, Nicholas. *Max Weber and Postmodernism: Rationalization vs Disenchantment.* Basingstoke: Palgrave, 2002.

Gaponov-Grekov, A. V., and M. I. Rabinovich. *Nonlinearities in Action: Oscillations, Chaos Order, Fractals.* Berlin: Springer-Verlag, 1992.

Garrison, Jim. Dewey, Eros and Education. *Education and Culture* xi, no. 2 (Fall. 1994): 1–5.

Gaudig. *Schools and School Life.* Leipzig: Quelle & Meyer, 1923.

Ghosh, Aurobindo. *The Human Cycle.* Pondicherry: Sri Aurobindo Ashram Publication Department, 1998.

Ghosh, Ranjan. A Poet's School: Rabindranath Tagore and the politics of Aesthetic Education. *South Asia: Journal of South Asian Studies* 35 Issue (2012): 13–32.

Ghosh, Ranjan. Intra-active Transculturality. *Modern Language Notes* 130 (December 2015): 1998–1220.

Ghosh, Ranjan. Caught in the Cross Traffic: Rabindranath Tagore and the Trials of Child Education. *Comparative Education Review* 59, no. 3 (August 2015): 399–419.

Ghosh, Ranjan. *Transcultural Poetics and the Concept of the Poet.* London: Routledge, 2016.

Ghosh, Ranjan. Rabindranath and Rabindranath Tagore: Home, History, World. *History and Theory*, Vol. 54, No. 4, (December, 2015): 125–148.

Ghosh, Ranjan. Reading and Experiencing a Play Transculturally. *Comparative Drama* 46.3 (Fall 2012): 259–281.

Ghosh, Ranjan, and J. Hillis Miller. *Thinking Literature Across Continents.* Durham & London: Duke University Press, 2016.

Ghosh, Suresh Chandra. *The History of Education in Modern India (1757–2007).* Hyderabad: Orient Blackswan, 2010.

Godfrey, J. J. *A Philosophy of Human Hope.* Dordrecht: Martinus Nijhoff, 1987.

Godwin, William. *The Enquirer: Reflections on Education, Manners, and Literature: In a Series of Essays.* London: G.G. & J. Robinson, 1797.

Godwin, William. *Enquiry Concerning Political Justice*, 3rd edn. (1798). facsimile ed. in. Vol. 3. (ed.) F. E. L. Priestley. Toronto: University of Toronto Press, 1946.

Goethe, Johann Wolfgang von. *The Sorrows of Young Werther and Selected Writings.* (trans.) Catherine Hutter. New York: New American Library, Inc., 1962.

Goldman, Robert P. Historicising the Ramakatha: Valmiki's Ramayana and its medieval commentators. *India International Centre Quarterly* 31, no. 4 (Spring 2005): 83–97.

Gomez-Pena, Guillermo. *The New World Border.* San Francisco: City Lights Books, 1996.

Green, J. A. (ed.). *Pestalozzi's Educational Writings.* London: Edward Arnold, 1912.

Guha, Ranajit. *History at the Limit of World-History.* New York: Columbia University Press, 2002.

Gumbrecht, Hans Ulrich. *Production of Presence: What Meaning Cannot Convey.* Stanford: Stanford University Press, 2004.

Gumbrecht, Hans Ulrich. *Our Broad Present: Time and Contemporary Culture.* New York: Columbia University Press, 2014.

Gupta, Amita. *Early Childhood Education, Postcolonial Theory, And Teaching Practices in India.* New York: Palgrave Macmillan, 2006.

Haapala, A. (ed.). *The City as Cultural Metaphor.* Lahti: International Institute of Applied Aesthetics, 1998.

Hamacher, Werner. Now: Walter Benjamin on Historical Time. In *Walter Benjamin and History*, (ed.) Andrew Benjamin, 38–68. London: Continuum, 2005.

Hamilton, E., and H. Cairns (eds.). *The Collected Dialogues of Plato.* Princeton: Princeton University Press, 1961.

Hans, N. English Pioneers of Comparative Education. *British Journal of Educational Studies* 1, no. 1 (Nov., 1952): 56–59.

Hardy, Thomas. *Jude the Obscure* (ed.) Norman Page. New York: Norton, 1978.

Harrold, C. F. (ed.). *The Idea of a University Defined and Illustrated.* New York: Longmans, Green and Co, 1947.

Hegel, G. W. F. *Phenomenology of Spirit.* (trans.) A. V. Miller. Oxford: Oxford University Press, 1977.

Hegel, G. W. F. *Hegel: The Letters.* (trans.) C. Butler and C. Seiler. Bloomington: Indiana University Press, 1984.

Hegel's Logic. *Part One of the Encyclopaedia of The Philosophical Sciences.* (trans.) W. Wallace. Oxford: Oxford University Press, 1975.

Heidegger, Martin. *Being and Time.* (trans.) J. Macquarrier, & E. Robinson. New York: Harper & Row, 1962.

Heidegger, Martin. *Discourse on Thinking.* (trans.) John M. Anderson and E. Hans Freund. New York: Harper & Row, 1966.

Heidegger, Martin. Homeland. (trans. Thomas F. O'Meara), *Listening* 6 (1971): 231–38.

Heine, Steven. History, Transhistory, and Narrative History: A Postmodern View of Nishitani's Philosophy of Zen. *Philosophy East and West* 44, no. 2 (Apr., 1994): 251–278.

Helm, Bert P. Emerson Agonistes: Education as Struggle and Process. *Educational Theory* 42.2 (1992): 165–180.

Hicks, Judith. The Educational Theories of John Ruskin: A Reappraisal. *British Journal of Educational Studies* 22, no. 1 (1974): 56–77.

Hillis, Miller, J. *Black Holes.* Stanford: Stanford University Press, 1999.

Horkheimer, M. *Eclipse of Reason.* New York: Oxford University Press, 1946.

Hoy, Terry. *The Political Philosophy of John Dewey: Towards a Constructive Renewal.* Westport: Praeger Publishers, 1998.

Inada, Kenneth K. Time and Temporality: A Buddhist Approach. *Philosophy East and West* 24, no. 2 (April, 1974): 171–179.

James, William. *The Principles of Psychology.* New York: Dover, 1950.

James, William. *Talks to Teachers.* New York: Norton, 1958.

James, William. *Pragmatism.* Cambridge, MA: Harvard University Press, 1975.

Jaspers, Karl. *The Perennial Scope of Philosophy.* New York: Philosophical Library, 1949.

Johnson, Barbara. *A World of Difference.* Baltimore: Johns Hopkins University Press, 1988.

Kaiser, Birgit Mara. Worlding ComLit: Diffractive Reading with Barad, Glissant and Nancy. *Parallax* 20, no. 3 (2014): 274–287.

Kant, Immanuel. *Critique of Pure Reason.* London: Macmillan, 1978.

Kant, Immanuel. *Anthropology, History and Education*. (ed. & trans.) Robert B. Louden. Cambridge: Cambridge University Press, 2007.

Kennedy, David. *The Well of Being*. Albany: State University of New York Press, 2006.

Ker, Ian. *The Achievement of John Henry Newman*. London: University of Nortre Dame Press, 1991.

Kerschensteiner, Georg. *Theorie der Bildung*. Leipzig: B. G. Teubner, 1926.

Kim, Duk-Yung. *Georg Simmel und Max Weber: Über zwei Entwicklungswege der Soziologie*. VS Verlag für Sozialwissenschaften, 2002.

Kleingeld, Pauline (ed.). *Toward Perpetual Peace and Other Writings on Politics, Peace and History*. New Haven: Yale University Press, 2006.

Kohan, Walter. *Childhood, Education and Philosophy*. London: Routledge, 2015.

Kumar, Nita. The Educational Efforts of Rabindranath Tagore. *Journal of Contemporary Thought* 34 (Winter 2011): 119–133.

Kunzman, Robert. *Grappling with the Good: Talking About Religion and Morality in Public Schools*. Albany: SUNY, 2006.

Kymlicka, W. (ed.). *The Rights of Minority Cultures*. Oxford: Oxford University Press, 1995.

LaChapelle, Doris. *Earth Wisdom*. San Diego: Guild of Tudors Press, 1978.

Lago, Mary. *Imperfect Encounter: Letters of William Rothenstein and Rabindranath Tagore*. Cambridge, MA: Harvard University Press, 1972.

Lawrence, D. H. *Phoenix: The Posthumous Papers of D. H. Lawrence*, (ed.). Edward D. Macdonald. New York: Viking Press, 1972.

Lawrence, D. H. *Fantasia of the Unconscious*. Rockville: Serenity Publishers, 2008.

Lefebvre, Henri. *The Production of Space*. Oxford: Basil Blackwell, 1991.

Leistyna, P. *Presence of Mind*. Boulder: Westview, 1999.

Leopold, Aldo. *A Sand County Almanac, with Essays on Conservation from Round River*. New York: Ballantine Books, 1966.

Levinas, Emmanuel. *Otherwise Than Being or Beyond Essence*. (trans.) Alphonso Lingis. Pittsburgh: Duquesne University Press, 1998.

Lewis, C. S. *The Abolition of Man*. New York: Macmillan, 1947.

Leyden, W. von. History and the Concept of Relative Time. *History and Theory* 2, no. 3 (1963): 263–285.

Lipman, Matthew. *Philosophy Goes to School*. Philadelphia: Temple University Press, 1988.

Lyotard, Jean Francois. Foreword: 'Spaceship'. (trans.) Rosemary Arnoux. In *Education and the Postmodern Condition*, (ed.) Michael Peters. Westport: Bergin & Garvey, 1995.

Mabille, Pierre. *Egregores ou la vie des civilisations*. Paris: Sagittaire, 1977.

Maddock, Lawrence H. Emerson on Education. *Educational Theory* 7, no. 1 (1957): 56–58.

Mahalanobis, P. C. *Rabindranath Tagore's Visit to Canada*. New York: Haskell House Publishers Ltd., 1977.

Manju, Jain (ed.). *T. S. Eliot: Selected Poems.* Delhi: Oxford University Press, 1992.

Marcel, Gabriel. *The Mystery of Being.* London: Regnery Publishing Inc, 1950.

Marcuse, Herbert. *Counterrevolution and Revolt.* London: Allen Lane, 1972.

Masschelein, Jan. Éxperimentum Scholae: The World Once More . . . But Not (Yet) Finished'. In *Making Sense of Education,* (ed.) G. J. J. Biesta, 101–108. Dordrecht: Springer, 2012.

Masschelein, Jan, and Norbert Ricken. Do We (Still) Need the Concept of Bildung?. *Educational Philosophy and Theory* 35, no. 2 (2003): 139–154.

Matoré, G. *L'Espace humain.* Paris: La Columbe, 1962, 22–3.

Maude, A. *The Life of Tolstoy.* Vol. 1. First fifty years. London: Constable & Co., 1908.

McEwen, Indra Kagis. *Socrates' Ancestor: An Essay on Architectural Beginnings.* Cambridge, MA: MIT Press, 1993.

McLaren, Peter. *Multiculturalism: Pedagogies of Dissent for the New Millennium.* Boulder: Westview Press, 1997a.

McLaren, Peter. *Revolutionary Multiculturalism.* Boulder: Westview Press, 1997b.

McLaren, Peter. Paulo Freire's Pedagogy of Possibility. In *Freirean Pedagogy, Praxis, and Possibilities: Projects for the New Millennium,* (ed.) H. Mark Krank, Peter Mclaren, and E.Bahruth Robert. New York: Falmer Press, 2000.

McMillan, M. *Education Through the Imagination.* London: Sonnenschein, 1923 [1904].

McMillan, M. *The Nursery School.* London: Dent, 1930.

Merleau-Ponty, M. *Sense and Nonsense.* Evanston: Northwestern University Press, 1964a.

Merleau-Ponty, M. 1964b. *The Primacy of Perception.* (ed.) James M. Edie. Evanston: Northwestern University Press.

Merleau-Ponty, M. *The Visible and the Invisible.* Evanston: Northwestern University Press, 1968.

Merleau-Ponty, M. *Phenomenology of Perception.* London: Routledge & Kegan Paul, 2003.

Mertins, Louis. *Robert Frost: Life and Talks-Walking.* Norman: University of Oklahoma Press, 1965.

Michel, Alhadeff Jones. Three Generations of Complexity Theories: Nuances and ambiguities. *Educational Philosophy and Theory* 40, no. 1 (2008): 66–82.

Millar, S. *The Psychology of Play.* Harmondsworth: Penguin Books, 1968.

Mitra, Madhu. *Shikor-er Udaan Swabhimaan o Rabindranath.* Kolkata: Udaar Aashash, 2014.

Mohanty, Jitendra Nath. *Reason and Tradition in Indian Thought.* New Delhi: Oxford University Press, 1992.

Moltmann, J. *Hope and Planning.* London: SCM Press, 1971.

Montessori, Maria. *Dr. Montessori's Own Handbook.* New York: F. A. Stokes, 1914.

Montessori, Maria. *The Absorbent Mind.* New York: Holt, Rinehart and Winston, 1967.

Moraru, Christian. Fringes, Margins, Diaphragms: The University and Textual Reason after Derrida. *Crossings* 3 (1999): 79–100.

Mouffe, Chantal. *Politics and Passion: The Stakes of Democracy.* London: Centre for the Study of Democracy, 2002.

Moulin, Dan. *Leo Tolstoy.* London: Continuum, 2011.

Moulin, Dan. Leo Tolstoy the Spiritual Educator. *International Journal of Children's Spirituality* 13, no. 4 (November 2008): 345–353.

Mukherjee, Himanshu. *Education for Fullness.* London: Asia Publishing House, 1962.

Mukherjee, K. C. Tagore-Pioneer in Education. *British Journal of Educational Studies* 18, no. 1 (Feb., 1970): 69–81.

Mulcahy, D. G. Newman's Theory of a Liberal Education: A Reassessment and its Implications. *Journal of the Philosophy of Education* 42, no. 2 (2008): 219–231.

Mulcahy, D. G. *The Educated Person: Toward a New Paradigm for Liberal Education.* Lanham: Rowman and Littlefield, 2008.

Mumford, L. *The Myth of the Machine: The Pentagon of Power.* New York: Harcourt Brace Jovanovich, 1970.

Murdoch, I. *Metaphysics as a Guide to Morals.* New York: Penguin, 1992.

Newman, Jay. *The Idea of a University.* Oxford: Clarendon Press, 1976.

Newman, Jay. *The Mental Philosophy of John Henry Newman.* Waterloo: Wilfrid Laurier University Press, 1986.

Niblett, W.R. On Existentialism and Education. *British Journal of Educational Studies* 2 no. 2 (May 1954): 101–111.

Nicholls, David, and Fergus Kerr. *John Henry Newman: Reason, Rhetoric, and Romanticism.* Carbondale: Southern Illinois University Press, 1991.

Nietzsche, Friedrich. *Ecce Homo.* (trans.) Walter Kaufmann. New York: Random House, 1967.

Nietzsche, Friedrich. Schopenhauer as Educator. In *Untimely Meditations,* (ed.) Daniel Breazeale. trans. R.J. Hollingdale. Cambridge: Cambridge University Press, 1983.

Novak, Bruce. "National Standards" vs the Free Standards of Culture: Matthew Arnold's Culture and Anarchy and Contemporary Educational Philistinism. *Philosophy of Education,* 2003. http://ojs.ed.uiuc.edu/index.php/pes/article/view/1763/480.

Nussbaum, Martha. *Cultivating Humanity.* Cambridge, MA: Harvard University Press, 1997.

O'Connell, Kathleen M. *Rabindranath Tagore: The Poet as Educator.* Visva Bharati, 2002.

O'Hagan, Timothy. *Rousseau.* London: Routledge, 1999.

Oakeshott, Michael. *On Human Conduct.* Oxford: Clarendon, 1975.

Oakeshott, Michael. The Idea of a University. *Academic Questions* 17, no. 1 (Winter 2003–2004): 37–53.

Oelkers, Jürgen. Some Historical Notes on George Herbert Mead's Theory of Education, www.ife.uzh.ch/dam/jcr:ffffffff-bb47-55f9 . . . /Meadtranslation first.pdf

Owen, H., and I. Bell. *Wilfred Owen: Collected Letters.* London: Oxford University Press, 1967.

Paine, M. M, and J. Schad (eds.). *Life.After.Theory.* London/New York: Continuum, 2003.

Palmer, P. J. *The courage to teach: Exploring the inner landscape of a teacher's life.* San Francisco: Jossey-Bass, 1998.

Papastephanou, Marianna. *Thinking Differently about Cosmopolitanism: Theory, Eccentricity and the Globalised World.* London: Routledge, 2015.

Parekh, B. *Rethinking Multiculturalism: Cultural diversity and Political Theory.* Basingstoke: Palgrave, 2000.

Pennycook, Alistair. English, Universities and Struggles over Culture and Knowledge. In *East-West Dialogue in Knowledge and Higher Education* (eds.) Ruth Hayhoe and Julia Pan, 64–82. New York: M.E. Sharpe, 1996.

Perkinson, Henry J. *Learning from Our Mistakes: A Reinterpretation of Twentieth-Century Educational Theory.* Westport: Greenwood Press, 1984.

Peters, Michael (ed.). *Education and the Postmodern Condition.* Westport: Bergin & Garvey, 1995.

Philips, Mark Salber. *On Historical Distance.* New Haven: Yale University Press, 2013.

Phillips, David. Beyond Travellers' Tales: Some Nineteenth-Century British Commentators on Education in Germany. *Oxford Review of Education* 26 no. 1 (Mar., 2000): 49–62.

Piaget, J. *The Moral Judgement of the Child.* New York: Free Press, 1965.

Plato. *The Collected Dialogues of Plato.* (ed.) E. Hamilton and H. Cairns. Princeton: Princeton University Press, 1963.

Quint, David. "Alexander the Pig": Shakespeare on History and Poetry. *boundary* 2, no. 10.3 (Spring, 1982): 49–67.

Radhakrishnan, R. *History, the Human, and the World Between.* Durham: Duke University Press, 2008.

Radhakrishnan, S. (ed.). *The Principal Upanishads, Taittriya Upanishad.* London: George Allen & Unwin Ltd, 1953.

Radhakrishnan, S. *The Philosophy of Rabindranath Tagore.* Baroda: Good Companions Publishers, 1961.

Rancière, J. *The Philosopher and His Poor.* (trans.) J. Drury, C. Ostert & A. Parker. Durham: Duke University Press, 2003.

Rancière, J. From Politics to Aesthetics?. *Paragraph* 28, no. 2 (2005): 12–25.

Rapple, Brendan. Matthew Arnold's Views on Modernity and a State System of Middle–Class Education in England: Some Continental Influences. *The Journal of General Education* 39, no. 4 (1988): 206–221.

Rapple, Brendan. Matthew Arnold and Comparative Education. *British Journal of Educational Studies* 37, no. 1 (Feb., 1989): 54–71.

Reiss, Hans (ed.). *Political Writings*. Cambridge: Cambridge University Press, 1970.

Relph, E. *Place and Placelessness*. London: Pion, 1976.

Richard, Poirier (ed.). *Ralph Waldo Emerson*. Oxford: Oxford University Press, 1990.

Rilke, Rainer Maria. *Letters to a Young Poet*. (trans.) Stephen Mitchell. New York: Random House, 1984.

Rinaldi, Carlina. *In Dialogue with Reggio Emilia Listening, Researching and Learning*. London/New York: Routledge, 2006.

Rodríguez, S. *Obra Completa Tomos*. Vols. I-II. Caracas: Presidencia de la República, 2001.

Rorty, Richard. *Philosophy and the Mirror of Nature*. Princeton: Princeton University Press, 1979.

Rorty, Richard. *Contingency, Irony, Solidarity*. Cambridge: Cambridge University Press, 1989.

Rosenberger, Nancy Ross Rosenberger (ed.). *Japanese Sense of Self*. New York: Cambridge University Press, 1992.

Rousseau, J. J. *Emile*. (trans.) B. Foxley. London: Dent, 1911.

Rousseau, J. J. *Emile*. (trans.) Barbara Foxley. London/New York: Everyman's Library, 1966.

Rousseau, J. J. *The Social Contract*. New York: Washington Square Press Pocket Books, 1971.

Rousseau, J. J. *Reveries of the Solitary Walker*. (translated with an introduction) P. France. London: Penguin, 1979.

Rousseau, J. J. *Confessions*. Vol. I. New York: Random House, 1992.

Ruskin, John. *The Crown of Wild Olive: Three lectures on work, traffic and war*. London: Smith, Elder & co., 1866.

Russell, Bertrand 1903. A Free Man's Worship, http://www3.nd.edu/afreddos/courses/264/fmw.htm.

Russon, John Edward. Erôs and Education: Plato's Transformative Epistemology. *Laval Théologique Et Philosophique* 56, no. 1 (2000): 113–125.

Ryle, Gilbert. *The Concept of Mind*. London: Hutchinson, 1949.

Saha, Gourchandra (ed.). *Chitipatreh Vidyalaya Prosongoh, The context of the school in letters of Tagore,Rabindranath*. Rabindrabhavan: Visva Bharati, 2001.

Saha, Poulomi. Singing Bengal into a Nation: Tagore the Colonial Cosmopolitan?. *Journal of Modern Literature* 36, no. 2 (Winter 2013): 1–24.

Samuel, Francis A. Educational Visions from Two Continents: What Tagore adds to the Deweyan Perspective. *Educational Philosophy and Theory* 43, no. 10 (2011): 1161–1174.

Sathyamurthy, T.V. Relationship between Teacher and Pupil in Ancient India: An Upanishadic View. *Educational Theory* 15, no. 1 (1965): 26–34.

Scaff, Lawrence. *Fleeing the Iron Cage: Culture, Politics and Modernity in the Thought of Max Weber*. Berkeley: University of California Press, 1989.

Schaeder, Grete. *The Hebrew Humanism of Martin Buber*. (trans.) Noah Jacobs. Detroit: Wayne State University Press, 1973.

Schama, Simon. *Citizens: A Chronicle of the French Revolution*. London: Viking, 1989.

Scharfe, Hartmut. *Education in Ancient India*. Leiden: Brill, 2002.

Schiller, Friedrich von. *Naive and Sentimental Poetry and On the Sublime*. New York: Frederick Unger, 1966.

Schiller, Friedrich von. *On the Aesthetic Education of Man*. (translation with an introduction) Reginald Snell. New York: Dover Publications, 2004.

Schumacher, E. F. *Small is Beautiful*. London: Abacus, 1974.

Schweitzer, Albert. 'The Ethic of Reverence for Life' [1923]. In *Animal Rights and Human Obligations* (eds.) Tom Regan and Peter Singer, 133–138. Englewood Cliffs: Prentice Hall, 1976.

Seal, Bhupendranath. Santiniketan: The Innisfree of C. F. Andrews, Visva-Bharati News, (February-March 1971): 218–221.

Sen, Amartya. Indian Traditions & the Western Imagination. *Daedalus* 134, no. 4 (Fall, 2005): 168–185.

Serres, Michel. *The Troubadour of Knowledge*. (trans.) S. F. Glaser with W. Paulson. Ann Arbor: The University of Michigan Press, 1997.

Serres, Michel, and Bruno Latour. *Hermes: Literature, Science, Philosophy*. Baltimore: John Hopkins University, 1982.

Serres, Michel, and Bruno Latour. *Conversations on Science, Culture and Time*. (trans.) R. Lapidus. Ann Arbor: The University of Michigan Press, 1995.

Seth, Sanjay. *Subject Lessons*. Durham: Duke University Press, 2007.

Shapiro, Sherry B. *Pedagogy and the Politics of the Body*. New York: Garland Publishing, 1999.

Shor, I., and P. Freire. *A Pedagogy for Liberation*. Washington, D.C.: Bergin & Garvey, 1987.

Shusterman, Richard. *Performing Live: Aesthetic Alternatives for the Ends of Art*. New York: Cornell University Press, 2000.

Siegel, D. J. *The Mindful Brain: Reflection and Attunement in the Cultivation of Well-Being*. New York: W.W. North., 2007.

Sinha, Dikshit. *Rabindranather Pallypunargathan Prayas*. Kolkata: Paschimbanga Bangla Academy, 2010.

Sisirkumar, Ghose (ed.). *Angel of Surplus*. Visva Bharati, 1978.

Sisk, John P. The Literary Imagination and the Sense of the Past, *Salmagundi*, No. 68/69 (Fall 1985– Winter 1986), 76.

Spencer, Thomas E. Emerson on Education. *Educational Theory* 18, no. 1 (1968): 77–86.

Stone, Donald D. Matthew Arnold and the Pragmatics of Hebraism and Hellenism. *Poetics Today* 19, no. 2 (Summer, 1998): 179–198.

Strand, Torill. The Cosmopolitan Turn: Recasting 'Dialogue' and 'Difference. *Paideusis* 19, no. 1 (2010): 49–58.

Super, R. H. (ed.). *The Complete Prose Works of Matthew Arnold*. Ann Arbor: University of Michigan, 1960–1977.

Suzi, Adams (ed.). *Cornelius Castoriadis: Key Concepts*. London: Bloomsbury, 2014.

Synder, A. D. *Coleridge on Logic and Learning*. New Haven: Yale University Press, 1929.

Tagore. City and Village. *Visva-Bharati Bulletin*, no. 10 (1928): 24–5.

Tagore, The History and Ideals of Sriniketan, *The Modern Review*, November 1941, 433.

Tagore, Rabindranath. *Shantiniketan*. London: Macmillan, 1916.

Tagore, Rabindranath. *The Centre of Indian Culture*. Calcutta: Visva-Bharati, 1921.

Tagore, Rabindranath. *A Vision of India's History*. Calcutta: Visva Bharati Bookshop, 1951.

Tagore, Rabindranath. *Towards Universal Man*. London: Asia Publishing House, 1961a.

Tagore, Rabindranath. The Place for Discipline. *The Visva Bharati Quarterly* 27, no. 2 (1961b): 89–96.

Tagore, Rabindranath. *Creative Unity*. London: Macmillan, 1962.

Tagore, Rabindranath. *The Co-operative Principle (translated from Bengali)*. Calcutta: A.K. Chanda & Others, 1963.

Tagore, Rabindranath. Schooling. *The Visva Bharati Quarterly* 29, no. 4 (1963–64): 273–279.

Tagore, Rabindranath. *Rabindra Rachanabali*. Vol. 13. Kolkata: Government of West Bengal, 1990.

Tagore, Rabindranath. *Rabindra Rachanabali*. Vol. 14. Kolkata: Govt. of West Bengal, 1992.

Tagore, Rabindranath. *Rabindra Rachanabali*. Vol. 15. Kolkata: Government of West Bengal, 1994.

Tagore, Rabindranath. *Letters to a Friend. Rabindranath Tagore's Letters to C.F. Andrews*. New Delhi: Rupa, 2002a.

Tagore, Rabindranath. *Personality*. Calcutta: Rupa, 2002b.

Tagore, Rabindranath. The Schoolmaster, *Visva Bharati News*, (May-June, 1980): 252–259.

Tagore, Rabindranath. Thoughts on Education. *The Visva Bharati Quarterly* XIII (Parts (May-Oct 1947): 1–7.

Tagore, Rathindranath. *On the Edges of Time*. Kolkata: Visva-Bharati, 1958.

Tagore, Saranindranath. Tagore's Conception of Cosmopolitanism: A Reconstruction. *University of Toronto Quarterly* 77, no. 4 (2008): 1071–1084.

Taguchi, H. L. *Going beyond Theory/Practice Divide in Early Childhood Education*. London: Routledge, 2010.

Taylor, Charles. *Sources of the Self*. Cambridge: Harvard University Press, 1989.

Taylor, Charles. *Multiculturalism and the Politics of Recognition*. Princeton: Princeton University Press, 1992.

Taylor, Paul W. *Respect for Nature: A Theory of Environmental Ethics*. Princeton: Princeton University Press, 1986.

Thakur, Supriyo. *Chelebelar Santiniketan (Santiniketan of My Boyhood Years)*. Kolkata: Ananda Publishers, 2012.

Thompson, J., and D. Held (eds.) *Habermas: Critical Debates*. London: Macmillan, 1982.

Timothy, Fuller (ed.). *The Voice of Liberal Learning: Michael Oakeshott on Education*. New Haven: Yale, 1989.

Tolstoy, Leo. Wisdom of Children (1910). *Recollections and Essays*, (trans. & ed.) A. Maude, 446–493. Oxford: Oxford University Press, 1937.

Tolstoy, Leo. *A Calendar of Wisdom*. (trans.) P. Sekirin. London: Hodder and Stoughton, 1998.

Tovar-Restrepo, Marcela. *Castoriadis, Foucault and Autonomy: New Approaches to Subjectivity, Society and Social Change*. London: Continuum, 2012, 33–64.

Trainer, F. *Abandon Affluence*. London: Zed Books, 1985.

Trautmann, Thomas R. Does India Have History? Does History Have India?. *Comparative Studies in Society and History* 54, no. 1 (January 2012): 174–205.

Tuan, Yi-Fu. *Space and Place: The Perspective of Experience*. Minneapolis: University of Minnesota Press, 1977.

Tuan, Yi-Fu. *Cosmos and Hearth: A Cosmopolite's Viewpoint*. Minneapolis: University of Minnesota Press, 1996.

Tubbs, Nigel. Return of the Teacher. *Educational Philosophy and Theory* 35, no. 1 (2003): 71–88.

Tubbs, Nigel. Hegel's. Educational Theory and Practice. *British Journal of Educational Studies* 44, no. 2 (Jun., 1996): 181–199.

Untermeyer, Louis. *Robert Frost: A Backward Look*. Washington, D.C.: Reference Department, The Library of Congress, 1964.

Vajpayi, Ananya. *Righteous Republic: The Political Foundations of Modern India*. Cambridge, MA: Harvard University Press, 2012.

Vico, Giambattista. *The New Science*. (trans.) Max H. Fisch and Thomas G. Bergin. Ithaca: Cornell University Press, 1944.

Vico, Giambattista. *On the Study Methods of Our Time.* (trans.) Elio Gianturco. Indianapolis: Bobbs Merrill Co., 1965.

Weber, Max. 1994. *Political Writings.* (ed.) Peter Lassman and Ronald Speirs. Cambridge: Cambridge University Press.

Wegenstein, Bernadette. *Getting Under the Skin, The Body and Media Theory.* Cambridge, MA: MIT Press, 2006.

Wei-ming, Tu. *Confucian Thought: Selfhood as Creative Transformation.* Albany: State University of New York Press, 1985.

Weiner, L. (trans.) and (ed.). *The Complete Works of Count Tolstoy.* London: J.M. Dent & Co., 1904.

Weiner, L. (trans.). *Tolstoy on Education.* Chicago/London: University of Chicago Press, 1967.

White, Jessie. *The Educational Ideas of Froebel.* New Delhi: Cosmo Publications, 2007.

Whitehead, Alfred North. *The Aims of Education and Other Essays.* New York: Mentor Books, 1929.

Whitehead, A. N. *The Aims of Education and Other Essays.* New York: The Free Press, 1967.

Whitehead, Clive. *Colonial Educators: The British Indian and Colonial Education Service 1858–1983.* London: I.B.Tauris, 2003.

Wijesinghe, Gita. Indian Philosophy as a Means for Understanding Modern Ashram Schools. *Comparative Education* 23, no. 2 (1987): 237–243.

Williams, Louise Blakeney. *Modernism and the Ideology of History.* Cambridge: Cambridge University Press, 2002.

Williams, Louise Blakeney. Overcoming the "Contagion of Mimicry": The Cosmopolitan Nationalism and Modernist History of Rabindranath Tagore and W. B. Yeats. *The American Historical Review* 112, no. 1 (Feb., 2007): 69–100.

Wolff, Kurt H. (ed. & trans.). *The Sociology of Georg Simmel.* New York: Free Press, 1950.

Yelland, Nicola (ed.). *Contemporary Practices in Early Childhood Education.* Maidenhead: Open University Press, 2012.

Yuasa, Yasuo. *The Body: Toward an Eastern Mind-Body Theory.* (ed.) Thomas P. Kasulis & (trans.) Nagatomo Shigenori. Albany: State University of New York Press, 1987.

Zakin, Emily. Crisscrossing Cosmopolitanism: State-Phobia, World Alienation, and the Global Soul. *Journal of Speculative Philosophy* 29, no. 1 (2015): 58–72.

Index

R. Ghosh, *Aesthetics, Politics, Pedagogy and Tagore*, Palgrave Studies in Education and Transculturalism, DOI 10.1057/978-1-137-48026-2